SMALL ARMS

1914–45

THE ESSENTIAL
WEAPONS IDENTIFICATION GUIDE

SMALL ARMS

1914–45

MICHAEL E. HASKEW

amber
BOOKS

This edition published in 2012 by
Amber Books Ltd
Bradley's Close
74–77 White Lion Street
London N1 9PF
United Kingdom
www.amberbooks.co.uk

A catalogue record for this book is available from the British Library.

ISBN: 978-1-908273-75-8

Project Editor: Michael Spilling
Design: Hawes Design
Picture Research: Terry Forshaw

Printed in China

Contents

Introduction

The two world wars prosecuted during the first half of the twentieth century and the interwar years of the 1920s and 1930s were heavily influenced by advancing small-arms technology.

A S THE GREAT POWERS fought for preeminence in Europe and Asia and indeed around the globe from 1914 to 1918 and again from 1939 to 1945, the rifle or the submachine gun in the hands of the individual soldier often meant the difference between victory and defeat. The great plans of military strategists were regularly reduced to the outcome of single combat between soldiers loading and firing their weapons to the best of their ability.

From the turn of the century forward, modern military men were becoming increasingly aware of the advancing technology that confronted them on land and sea and in the air. Nowhere was the profound effect of man's ingenuity more dramatically proved than on the battlefield. The repeating rifle had given way to the improved bolt-action shoulder arms

of Mauser, Lee-Enfield, Springfield and others, and in turn the semiautomatic rifle had emerged in the mid-1930s with the introduction of the M1 Garand. By 1944, US general George S. Patton Jr. (1885–1945) had commented that the Garand was the 'greatest battle implement ever devised'.

Without doubt, the generation of firearms designers that altered, improved and generally revised the rifles of the years prior to World War I were influenced by a legion of innovators and designers who had gone before them. The Mauser line can claim descendants around the world, for example, and many of the rifles that were fielded by armies of World War II trace their components to the Mauser Gewehr 98, the forerunner of the Karabiner 98k standard issue rifle of the *Wehrmacht* from the 1930s until the end of World War II. More than 14 million examples of the K98k were manufactured in the decade from 1935 to 1945.

Accuracy, endurance and firepower were the three pillars on which a successful rifle was built, and the crucible of war provided a proving ground for design innovation. The US M1 Garand, a semiautomatic weapon, was followed by Germany's Sturmgewehr 44, an awesome innovation that could truly be called the first assault rifle to see major

◀ **Prisoner round-up**
This rare colour photograph shows French infantry rounding up German prisoners. The sky blue tunic, conspicuous red trousers and black leather gaiters indicate that this was early in World War I, before the French Army adopted the more practical 'horizon blue' uniform in 1915.

deployment in the history of warfare. Thus between 1939 and 1945, the bolt-action rifle of a half-century earlier was fighting alongside the semiautomatic and fully automatic rifles that would dominate the battlefield into the twenty-first century. From the Sturmgewehr 44 rose the iconic Kalashnikov AK-47 assault rifle, the US-made M16 and other such weapons that shaped the future of warfare.

Machine-gun menace

Perhaps no other infantry-level weapon has illustrated the tragic failure of military tactics to keep pace with advancing technology more than the machine gun, which proliferated during World War I. Reaping a harvest of death like no other small arms in history, machine guns fired from entrenched positions killed infantrymen with reckless abandon during the war of attrition in the trenches. The British Vickers and German Maschinengewehr designs were both influenced heavily by the work of Hiram Maxim (1840–1916), an American-born inventor who

emigrated to Britain and revolutionized modern warfare with an automatic weapon that produced an incredibly high sustained rate of fire.

In the summer of 1916, British sergeant Charles Quinnell faced German machine guns on the Western Front and lived to tell of his horrifying ordeal. 'The first wave were down,' he remembered. 'Two machine guns played on them and they were completely wiped out. Everybody was either killed or wounded. We went through. We got halfway across [no-man's-land] and then the machine guns found us and they played on us like spraying with a hose. At the finish I was the only one standing.'

During the interwar years, the battlefield prowess of the machine gun was further refined as capacity and calibre were increased. The landmark German machine gun of the 1930s, the MG 34, was a precision-built weapon with a substantial rate of fire. It was a primary support weapon of World War II and respected by all who opposed it; however, the need for increased production and the scarcity of raw materials

▼ **Ottoman Maxim Gun**
Turkish infantry undergo training with tripod-mounted Maxim Maschinengewehr 08 heavy machine guns, supplied by their German allies.

▲ **Bayonet charge**
Bayonets fixed to Lee-Enfield No. 1 Mk III SMLE rifles, Commonwealth infantry advance across open ground during the Battle of El Alamein, October 1942.

began to take precedence over the precise tolerances and machining process that went into the manufacture of the individual weapon. With the MG 42, an outstanding machine gun in its own right, some of the fit and finish of the MG 34 was lost, although the lethal weapon was respected as the 'Buzzsaw' by Allied troops and its rate of fire was astonishing.

From the Vickers to the Bren, British machine guns were either reliable, updated versions of World War I-era weapons or the product of research and development undertaken during the 1930s. The Vickers Mk I and its successors served the British Army from 1912 through to the late 1960s, and the weapon gained a tremendous reputation for reliability and ruggedness in prolonged combat. The story of the famous Bren began in 1931 with the British military establishment in search of a light machine gun. A Czechoslovakian design was chosen and modified to British specifications, resulting in one of the best known automatic weapons of World War II.

In the United States, the influence of John Browning (1855–1926) was widespread. His Model 1911 11.4mm (.45in) pistol remains an icon of form and function to this day, while the Browning Automatic Rifle (BAR), primarily a 7.62mm (.3in) weapon, resonates with veterans from all theatres of World War II. The Model 1919 7.62mm (.3in) infantry machine gun and the M2 12.7mm (.5in) heavy machine gun have earned distinctive places in the history of modern firearms.

Soviet automatic weapons such as the PPSh-41 7.62mm (.3in) submachine gun were produced in huge quantities during World War II and gave rise to a reconsideration of infantry firepower. A squad of Red Army soldiers, each of them armed with an automatic weapon, was a formidable adversary indeed. When the *Wehrmacht* tide began to recede on the Eastern Front, it was the Red Army that showed the world the awesome potential of the submachine gun issued to large formations of foot soldiers.

Along with the rifle, machine gun and assault rifle, the anti-tank weapon developed during the interwar years and rapidly matured in World War II. As the anti-tank rifle was generally discarded in favour of rocket- or spring-propelled bombs or hollow-charge projectiles, the tank-killer team armed with the Bazooka, Panzerfaust or PIAT foreshadowed a generation of smart, fire-and-forget weapons designed to thwart the advantage of armour today.

Terrible technology

Although small-arms technology steadily advanced prior to World War I, its pace quickened substantially with the onset of global conflict, subsiding only slightly during the years between the wars due primarily to budget constraints from the high cost of the war of 1914–18. The coming of World War II brought innovation and even deadlier small arms to the battlefield as mass production churned out semiautomatic and automatic weapons at tremendous rates to augment the efficiency of the click-and-fire bolt-action rifles still in use.

Building on proven systems and working with innovations of their own, small-arms designers of the twentieth century further validated that the more some weapons change the more they do indeed remain the same. The refinement of one man's ability to dispatch another efficiently and economically is the continuing key to victory on the battlefield. But then, of course, the weapon itself is only as productive in its understood mission as the soldier who carries it.

▲ **Island battle**
A US Marine cradles his Browning Model 1919 7.62mm (.3in) machine gun, while he and his buddy take time out for a cigarette during mopping-up operations on Peleliu Island, September 1944.

Chapter 1

World War I: Western Front and Dardanelles

The global conflagration of World War I brought about destruction and loss of life on an unprecedented scale as the war of attrition in the trenches of the Western Front and the abortive Allied campaign in the Dardanelles demonstrated the devastating firepower of modern small arms. During the latter half of the nineteenth century, improvements in weapons technology, including the deadly accuracy of shoulder arms and the enhanced operational effectiveness of the machine gun, reaped a ghastly harvest of dead and wounded. Unfortunately, battlefield tactics often did not take into account the newly realized lethality of such weapons. Soldiers of both the Allied and Central Powers were sacrificed before the muzzles of modern weapons, the victims of outmoded tactics.

◀ Dardanelles stalemate

ANZAC infantrymen wait in their trenches during one of the many lulls in the fighting on the Gallipoli peninsula, 1915. All are armed with the Lee-Enfield SMLE bolt-action rifle.

Introduction

Rapid movement soon gave way to the stalemate of the trenches on the Western Front, as both sides experienced heavy losses before fortified positions.

NEITHER THE ALLIES nor the Central Powers had real reason to expect a costly, protracted war on the Western Front as World War I began. However, the continuing modernization of armies was to accelerate appreciably during the four long years of the Great War. Fuelled by the French obsession with regaining the provinces of Alsace and Lorraine lost in the humiliating defeat of the Franco-Prussian War of 1870–71, the German desire for eminence among the nations of Europe through achieving its 'place in the sun', a complex tangle of treaties and alliances, and the burgeoning arms race that had continued unabated for decades, world war broke out in August 1914, sparked by the assassination of Archduke Franz Ferdinand of Austria-Hungary at the end of June.

Terrifying technology

At war's outbreak, the armies of the belligerent nations were undergoing substantial reorganization while such innovations as the aeroplane, the submarine and the armoured fighting vehicle were evaluated as to their roles in modern warfare. Artillery had been divided into field and heavy categories, with the famed French 75mm (2.9in) M1897 setting the standard for mobile, sustained fire support. Heavy siege guns were the order of the day as well, with mammoth mortars and howitzers such as the improvised British Mark I, initially fashioned from rebored naval weapons, reaching calibres of 200–400mm (7.9-15.7in) and heavier. The Mark I fired a 91kg (200lb) shell a distance of 9600m (10,500 yards).

The role of the anachronistic cavalry was changing as well. Unlike during its glory days, cavalry was recognized as a reconnaissance, screening or pursuit arm with very limited capabilities to exploit a breakthrough in enemy lines, rather than as a weapon of lightning quick 'shock and awe'. Further, even the scouting role of the cavalry was coming into question as visionary military thinkers such as British

▲ **Moving up**
French infantry rest on their way to the front in the Verdun sector, 1916. The French Army sustained over 300,000 casualties at Verdun – roughly the same number as the German forces.

▲ **Bayonet charge**
Australian infantry charge across no-man's-land towards Turkish trenches, Gallipoli, Dardanelles 1915. In this case, the Turkish positions had been evacuated and the trench was uncontested.

Major-General J.F.C. Fuller (1878–1966) and Sir Basil Liddell Hart (1895–1970) pondered the role of the tank and armoured vehicle in modern warfare and the aeroplane assumed a more prominent role in reconnaissance and, later, in aerial combat.

Despite the pronounced evolution of weapons and, though lagging behind substantially, the development of tactical doctrine to employ them effectively, the infantry remained the backbone of the armies of 1914. Although its size varied from nation to nation, the combat infantry division might well reach a strength of more than 16,000 riflemen. The primary shoulder arm of the infantryman was the bolt-action, magazine-fed rifle. Depending upon the design of his weapon and the degree of training he had undergone, the skilled rifleman could deliver a devastating rate of fire upon the advancing enemy. Improved ammunition was employed as well, particularly the aerodynamic jacketed bullet. The ubiquitous bayonet remained a standard issue item among infantrymen.

In terms of small arms, the most devastating innovation of the late nineteenth century was the machine gun. French use of the Reffye *mitrailleuse* during the Franco-Prussian War had proved disappointing; however, recent improvements, particularly those of American-born inventor Hiram Maxim (1840–1916), were to prove deadly. Along with the substantial killing capacity of the artillery, the proliferation of the machine gun on the Western Front was responsible for soaring casualty rates in World War I. Beyond the obvious consequences of these modern weapons, the experience of combat often took on a more impersonal nature.

While the rifle had been intended as the principal infantry weapon in the twentieth century and its role was not appreciably diminished, the machine gun added a new and horrifying dimension to the battlefield. Troops going over the top and into no-man's-land often instinctively turned their shoulders to the enemy as if walking into a strong wind. In reality, there was little defence against a hail of bullets.

Belgian Army
1914–15

Severely outnumbered and under-equipped, the Belgian Army of King Albert I (1875–1934) disrupted the German timetable and held its ground at Liège and Namur.

WHEN THE GERMAN ARMY crossed into Belgium on its trek to attack its arch-enemy, France, it did so with little regard for the tiny nation's field army of fewer than 120,000 soldiers. The Belgians had already initiated a reorganization plan which was intended to be completed over the course of several years; however, this effort was barely a year old when war came.

Only 102 machine guns were available to equip the six field army divisions, each of which consisted of up to four mixed brigades, including single regiments of infantry, cavalry and artillery, an engineer battalion, transport unit and telegraph section. The relatively few machine guns available were primarily variants of the Maxim Gun, and these were often mounted on sleds that were hauled by teams of dogs.

To their own detriment, the Germans underestimated the Belgian will to fight and had completely discounted the stubborn fortress defences of Liège and Namur. At both locations, Belgian forces disrupted German progress and delayed the advance against the French Army and the British Expeditionary Force for up to two weeks. Near the Channel coast, the Belgians refused to yield a defensive salient along the Yser River and held out during four years of trench fighting.

The Belgian soldier was typically equipped with a variant of the German Mauser rifle designated the Fusil FN-Mauser Mle 1889. This weapon had been

▲ **In retreat**
Belgian infantry retreat along a road, 1914. The Belgian Army used dogs to tow machine guns and light guns. Many European armies used dogs to pull small carts carrying ammunition, supplies and provisions.

manufactured by the Fabrique Nationale d'Armes de Guerre, a company formed in 1889 to produce the rifle for the Belgian government. The first rifles produced by Mauser had been the 1871 series, and the development of the Model 1889 was begun in the early 1880s. It was introduced with a five-round vertical magazine, heavier wooden stock and a barrel shroud.

Although it had initially been hoped that the rifle would be sold to the German government, Mauser was not completely successful in competing with another excellent design produced by Mannlicher. Nevertheless, the Belgian attaché had seen the rifle in action during the Bavarian Arms Trials of 1884, and subsequently the Fabrique Nationale was formed to produce the Model 1889 in Belgium. When FN's production capacity at Herstal, near Liège, was deemed inadequate, a contract was concluded with a British firm to manufacture the Model 1889

and combined production figures reached approximately 250,000.

An officer variant of the Chamelot Delvigne Mle 1873 revolver, the Mle 1874, was widely used by both the Belgian and French Armies in the early years of World War I, and more than 35,000 were manufactured. Although it was eventually replaced by the Mle 1892, it remained in service for more than half a century and was issued to Belgian officers and soldiers as late as 1940. The Mle 1874 differed from the standard issue 1873 in having a darker finish and lighter weight. Both revolvers fired a light 10.4mm (.41in) round, which at times provided insufficient knockdown power at even close range. Among other sidearms issued to Belgian troops in 1914 were a variant of the Browning Model 1899 pistol designated the Model 1900 and the Colt Model 1903 pistol. These fired an interchangeable 8.1mm (.32in) Colt round.

◀ **Chamelot Delvigne Mle 1874**
Belgian Army / 11 Régiment de Ligne, 1914
Firing an understrength 10.4mm (.41in) bullet, the Chamelot Delvigne revolver was nevertheless considered a heavy and solidly built sidearm. The Modèle 1874 was the officer variant and essentially the same weapon as the Modèle 1873.

Specifications

Country of Origin: Belgium	Overall Length: 284mm (11.18in)
Date: 1874	Barrel Length: 159mm (6.25in)
Calibre: 10.4mm (.41in)	Muzzle Velocity: 190m/sec (625ft/sec)
Operation: Revolver	Feed/Magazine: 6-round cylinder
Weight: 1.13kg (2.5lb)	Range: 6m (20ft)

▲ **Fusil FN-Mauser Mle 1889**
Belgian Army / 31 Régiment de Ligne, 1914
Manufactured under licence from the German Mauser firm, the Modèle 1889 incorporated a robust wooden stock and a barrel shroud. It was produced both in Belgium and Great Britain.

Specifications

Country of Origin: Belgium	Overall Length: 1295mm (51in)
Date: 1889	Barrel Length: 780mm (30.6in)
Calibre: 7.65mm (.301in)	Muzzle Velocity: 610m/sec (2000ft/sec)
Operation: Bolt action	Feed/Magazine: 5-round box magazine
Weight: 4.1kg (8.8lb)	Range: 1000m (3280ft)

French Army
1914–15

Although it had suffered a tremendous blow to its prestige during the Franco-Prussian War, the French Army was still regarded as the most formidable land force in Western Europe.

IN THE SUMMER OF 1914, the French Army stood 750,000 strong and could be mobilized with reserves up to a strength of more than 1.1 million men. In theory, the French high command stressed a doctrine of the offensive, maintaining the initiative in combat wherever and whenever possible; however, in practice such tactics proved costly in the face of improved weaponry fielded by the German Army. A typical French division consisted of two brigades formed of 12 battalions and populated by approximately 12,000 riflemen.

The standard issue French rifle of 1914–15 was the 8mm (.314in) Lebel design of 1886 which had been subsequently modified a decade later. The Lebel entered service in the spring of 1887 and quickly became noticeable for a shortcoming with its magazine. Although the magazine held a generous eight rounds, the reloading process was time consuming and accomplished by feeding the bullets end to end through a tube bored into the forward end of the weapon. The rifle faced the criticism that it became increasingly inaccurate as the magazine was emptied, due to a changing centre of gravity.

Although it was the first rifle to use smokeless powder, the Model 1886 was functionally obsolescent by 1915 and was replaced by the lighter

Models 1902 and 1907 Lebel Berthier rifles, which were never produced in large numbers but offered a three-round clip and wider sights. However, the Model 1886 rifle remained the primary infantry shoulder arm for French forces throughout World War I. Following the introduction of the Berthier models, the Lebel remained in service not only as a primary weapon but also as a sniper rifle when equipped with high-powered sights. From 1887 to 1920, a total of 2,880,000 examples of the Model 1886 and variants were produced, and it was issued to French troops as late as 1940. A relative few examples were known to have been used by the Germans. Although it was considered a highly serviceable weapon, the Lebel Berthier rifle was deemed less than adequate by some simply because of its paltry three-round clip. During heated combat, such a short supply of ammunition and the necessity to reload often proved problematic. By the summer of 1918, the Fusil Mle 1907/15-M16 with a five-round clip had reached the front in limited numbers.

Colonial carbine

The 1907 Berthier carbine was originally introduced as a replacement for the ageing Mle 1874 Gras single-shot carbine but also proved superior to the Model

▲ **Lebel Berthier Mle 1907/15 carbine**

French Army / 43rd Territorial Infantry Regiment, 1914

Although it proved unpopular with some troops and equipped primarily the colonial troops of the French Army, the Berthier 1907/15 carbine provided some improvement over the slow-loading Lebel rifle.

Specifications

Country of Origin: France	Overall Length: 945mm (37.2in)
Date: 1907	Barrel Length: 455mm (17.9in)
Calibre: 8mm (.314in)	Muzzle Velocity: 725m/sec (2379ft/sec)
Operation: Bolt action	Feed/Magazine: 5-round box magazine
Weight: 3.2kg (7.056lb)	(from 1915)
	Range: 500m (1640ft)

1886 in that it incorporated a single-piece stock and a three- or five-round clip rather than the cumbersome tubular magazine. By 1916, a shortage of Model 1886 rifles had resulted in the issue of the Mle 1907/15 Berthier rifle to French regular army troops, while colonial soldiers and those of the Foreign Legion had been issued the weapon somewhat earlier. During World War I, nearly 440,000 examples of the Fusil Mle 1907/15 were produced. This weapon employed a three-round clip.

Used as late as the 1960s by French police officers, the Lebel Mle 1892 revolver was the standard sidearm of French Army officers during World War I. Firing an 8mm (.314in) cartridge from a six-chambered cylinder, the Modèle 1892 was a popular weapon but lacked power in comparison with other revolvers of the day. It was manufactured by the state-owned and state-operated Manufacture d'armes de Saint-Etienne from 1892 to 1924, and more than 350,000 examples were produced.

Another well-known French sidearm of World War I was the Pistolet Automatique de 7 millim.65 genre, popularly known as the Ruby pistol and similar in construction to the Browning M1903. Noted for its ease of operation, even among those with little experience of handling firearms, the Ruby pistol was manufactured in Spain and Belgium and fired a 7.65mm (.301in) bullet from a detachable nine-round magazine. More than 750,000 were produced in over 50 variants.

▲ **Lebel Mle 1892**

French Army / 50th Line Infantry Regiment, 1914

The standard issue French sidearm of World War I, the Modèle 1892 revolver was produced by the state-run Manufacture d'armes de Saint-Etienne and remained a popular weapon among the military and civilian law enforcement agencies for decades.

Specifications

Country of Origin: France	Overall Length: 240mm (9.44in)
Date: 1892	Barrel Length: 117mm (4.60in)
Calibre: 8mm (.314in)	Muzzle Velocity: 213m/sec (698ft/sec)
Operation: Revolver	Feed/Magazine: 6-round cylinder
Weight: .94kg (2.1lb)	Range: 20m (66ft)

FRENCH INFANTRY COMPANY, 1914		
Unit	**Officers**	**Men**
Company HQ	5	15
1st Section	2	
1st Half-section	1	
1st Squad (riflemen)	1	14
2nd Squad (riflemen)	1	13
2nd Half-section	1	
3rd Squad (riflemen)	1	14
4th Squad (riflemen)	1	13
2nd Section	2	
1st Half-section	1	
1st Squad (riflemen)	1	14
2nd Squad (riflemen)	1	13
2nd Half-section	1	
3rd Squad (riflemen)	1	14
4th Squad (riflemen)	1	13
3rd Section	2	
1st Half-section	1	
1st Squad (riflemen)	1	14
2nd Squad (riflemen)	1	13
2nd Half-section	1	
3rd Squad (riflemen)	1	14
4th Squad (riflemen)	1	13
4th Section	2	
1st Half-section	1	
1st Squad (riflemen)	1	14
2nd Squad (riflemen)	1	13
2nd Half-section	1	
3rd Squad (riflemen)	1	14
4th Squad (riflemen)	1	13
Total Strength	37	231

2nd Ypres: British II and V Corps
APRIL–MAY 1915

Canadian troops gained a measure of national identity as a machine-gun crew stemmed the enemy tide, while German forces deployed poison gas on a grand scale.

IN THE SPRING OF 1915, the Allied defensive positions in the northern sector of the Western Front included a definitive bulge or salient around the Belgian town of Ypres. A tenacious enclave of Belgian troops clung to the line north of the salient, while French and colonial Algerian soldiers along with the men of the British II and V Corps defended the perimeter of the salient to the north and east. As German forces attempted to reduce the salient, which threatened their positions on its flanks, four separate engagements erupted in April and May. By the time the fighting ended, the Allied lines had held, but the size of the salient had been reduced.

During the opening phase of what came to be collectively known as the Second Battle of Ypres, the Germans released chlorine gas from thousands of cylinders into the positions manned by French and colonial troops. Within minutes, the defenders were withdrawing in disarray as thousands were killed or incapacitated by the gas. As the Germans advanced, troops of the Canadian 1st Division counterattacked to stabilize the situation, culminating their assault in the area of Kitchener's Wood with a bayonet charge.

Meanwhile, near the village of St. Julien, Lance-Corporal Frederick Fisher of the Canadian 13th Battalion machine-gun detachment led a small group of soldiers in an attempt to prevent the Germans from outflanking the Canadian line. Manning a Colt machine gun, Fisher demonstrated the battlefield capabilities of the weapon, thwarting the German advance and preventing the collapse of the Canadian forward positions. For his heroism, Lance-Corporal Fisher was awarded the Victoria Cross. Unfortunately, he was killed the following day during a similar defensive action.

The 7.7mm (.303in) Colt machine gun fired by Fisher was among the first successful gas-operated machine guns to see action. Designated the Colt-Browning M1895 and nicknamed the Potato Digger because of its mechanics, the weapon was patented in 1892. Canadian troops took it into battle in 1914; however, it was replaced by the Vickers machine gun in a relatively short period of time.

Nevertheless, the Colt-Browning M1895 proved remarkably adept on the battlefield, with a cyclic rate of fire of 450 rounds per minute. Although this was slightly lower than other guns of the period, its air-cooled feature kept the barrel in action for a longer period of time without overheating. Further, it was of simpler design than its water-cooled contemporaries, much lighter in weight and therefore more portable. The weapon itself weighed about 16kg (35.25lb), while its tripod and gunner's seat added another 25.4kg (56lb).

◀ **Webley Bulldog**

British Expeditionary Force / 2nd Battalion East Yorkshire Regiment, 1915

The Webley Bulldog was shorter and lighter than other Webley revolvers of the period. Although it was cheap to produce, it proved a robust weapon.

Specifications

Country of Origin: United Kingdom	Overall Length: 140mm (5.5in)
Date: 1878	Barrel Length: 53mm (2.1in)
Calibre: 8.1mm (.32in)	Muzzle Velocity: 190m/sec (625ft/sec)
Operation: Revolver	Feed/Magazine: 5-round cylinder
Weight: .31kg (.7lb)	Range: 15m (49ft)

Specifications

Country of Origin: United Kingdom

Date: 1912

Calibre: 7.7mm (.303in)

Operation: Recoil, water cooled

Weight: 18kg (40lb)

Overall Length: 1155mm (40.5in)

Barrel Length: 725mm (28.5in)

Muzzle Velocity: 600m/sec (1970ft/sec)

Feed/Magazine: Belt fed

Cyclic Rate: 600rpm

Range: 2000m (6560ft) + ; later 3000m (9842ft)

Vickers volume

The most famous British machine gun of World War I, the Vickers Mk I was based upon the design popularized by American-born inventor Hiram Maxim, who lived in Great Britain for many years. Maxim was credited with producing the earliest self-powered machine gun during the mid-1880s. The Maxim Gun was first demonstrated in the autumn of 1884 and later was deployed with British troops in Central Africa. A larger model saw action during the Boer War at the turn of the twentieth century. The British Army officially adopted the Vickers machine gun in the autumn of 1912, and updated variants of the weapon remained in service with the British armed forces until the late 1960s.

The Vickers Mk I differed from the Maxim Gun in that it was considerably lighter due to an inverted

▲ **Vickers Mk I**

British Expeditionary Force / 2nd Battalion Seaforth Highlanders, 1915

An improvement of the Maxim Gun, the Vicker Mk I machine gun entered service with the British Army in 1912 and was later designated a heavy weapon following the introduction of the light Lewis Gun. Its durability and versatility extended its service life into the 1960s.

BATTALION MACHINE-GUN SECTION (VICKERS HMG), 1915	
Unit	Strength
Lieutenant	1
Sergeant	1
Corporal	1
Driver	2
Batman	1
Privates	24

▼ British Battalion Machine-Gun Section, 1915

The British battalion machine-gun section was capable of producing a combined cyclic rate of fire of 2400 rounds per minute with each of its four Vickers heavy machine guns. Originally, the machine-gun section contained only two guns, but this was increased in February 1915. Such formations were transferred to the Machine Gun Corps in October of that year in an effort to improve the efficiency of machine guns deployed on the Western Front.

Section (4 x Vickers HMG)

toggle lock that moved upwards rather than downwards and allowed the receiver to be considerably smaller. Additionally, the Vickers machine gun was noted for its durability. The gun had a cyclic rate of fire of about 450 rounds per minute and the water-cooled barrel was routinely changed every 10,000 rounds. However, it has been recorded that during periods of intense combat the Vickers gun fired as many as 100,000 rounds before the barrel was changed. In one remarkable engagement, the 100th Company of the British Machine Gun Corps was reported to have fired its 10 Vickers guns for 12 hours continuously, each gun changing barrels 10 times. A total of one million rounds of 7.7mm (.303in) ammunition were fired without any of the guns failing.

Following the introduction of the light Lewis Gun, the Vickers was redesignated as a heavy machine gun.

Numerous variants were introduced in succeeding decades, and during World War I the weapon was also used aboard aircraft.

Other weapons in action at Second Ypres included the Webley Bulldog and Fosbury revolvers. These sidearms were from a family of break-top or self-extracting handguns that were produced from 1887 to 1963. The best known of the Webley revolvers is probably the Mark VI, introduced in 1915 and in service during World War I. The smaller Bulldog fired an 8.1mm (.32in) bullet and was effective to about 15m (49ft), while the Fosbury is easily recognized due to the distinctive zig-zag pattern on the cylinder. It fired an 11.55mm (.455in) round.

▶ **Webley Fosbury**

British Expeditionary Force / 3rd Battalion King's Royal Rifle Corps, 1915

The operation of the Webley Fosbury revolver utilized recoil energy rather than a standard mechanism and was responsible for the term 'automatic revolver'. Production of the weapon was discontinued in 1915 after repeated breakdowns.

Specifications

Country of Origin: United Kingdom	Overall Length: 292mm (11.5in)
Date: 1915	Barrel Length: 190mm (7.5in)
Calibre: 11.55mm (.455in)	Muzzle Velocity: 198m/sec (650ft/sec)
Operation: Automatic revolver	Feed/Magazine: 6-round cylinder
Weight: 1.08kg (2.4lb)	Range: 20m (66ft)

▲ **Pattern 1914 Enfield**

British Expeditionary Force / 5th Battalion Durham Light Infantry, 1915

Although it was originally configured to fire a high-powered round, the Pattern 1914 Enfield was eventually adapted to the 7.7mm (.303in) ammunition generally in use. It never reached the front in great numbers.

Specifications

Country of Origin: United Kingdom/United States	Overall Length: 1175mm (46.2in)
Date: 1914	Barrel Length: 660mm (26in)
Calibre: 7.7mm (.303in)	Muzzle Velocity: 762m/sec (2500ft/sec)
Operation: Bolt action	Feed/Magazine: 5-round box magazine
Weight: 4.35kg (9.6lb)	Range: 500m (1640ft)

▶ **Webley & Scott Mk IV**

British Expeditionary Force / 5th (Royal Irish) Lancers Regiment, 1915

The Webley & Scott Mk IV was introduced in 1899 and soon became known as the Boer War Model. Like other Webley & Scott designs, it was a break-top revolver. At the outbreak of World War I, it was in the possession of many British officers.

Specifications

Country of Origin: United Kingdom	Overall Length: 279mm (11in)
Date: 1899	Barrel Length: 152mm (6in)
Calibre: 11.55mm (.455in)	Muzzle Velocity: 198m/sec (650ft/sec)
Operation: Revolver	Feed/Magazine: 6-round cylinder
Weight: 1.5kg (3.3lb)	Range: 20m (66ft)

2nd Ypres: German Fourth Army
APRIL–MAY 1915

Carrying out the assault against the Ypres salient, the German Fourth Army had been in the vanguard of the early 1914 advance, defeating Belgian and French troops in the attempt to capture Paris. Eventually, it settled into the trenches of Flanders.

O N THE AFTERNOON OF 22 APRIL 1915, German forces launched a massive poison gas attack against French positions in the Ypres salient. The troops who followed this curtain of lethal vapour into action were veterans of the Fourth Army, which had rushed towards Paris the previous year and raced the Allies to the Channel coast.

These soldiers were armed with one of the iconic shoulder arms in military history, the Mauser Gewehr 98 rifle. Designed by the Mauser brothers and manufactured by the arsenals of Imperial Germany and numerous private contractors, the weapon replaced the Gewehr 1888 and was the standard German shoulder arm of World War I. During a 20-year period from 1898 to 1918, an estimated five million were produced. The weapon was withdrawn in 1935 in favor of the Karabiner 98k but reintroduced with home defence forces during the later years of World War II.

At the Belgian village of Bleid in August 1914, with the 6th Württemberg Infantry Regiment, young Lieutenant Erwin Rommel, who would rise to the rank of field marshal and earn the nickname of the Desert Fox during World War II, carried a Mauser into combat. 'I quickly informed my men of my intention to open fire. We quietly released the safety catches; jumped out from behind the building; and standing erect, opened fire on the enemy nearby. Some were killed or wounded on the spot; but the majority took cover behind steps, garden walls, and woodpiles and returned our fire. Thus, at very close range, a very hot fire fight developed. I stood taking aim alongside a pile of wood. My adversary was twenty yards ahead of me, well covered, behind the steps of a house. Only part of his head was showing. We both aimed and fired almost at the same time and missed. His shot just missed my ear. I had to load fast, aim calmly and quickly, and hold my aim. That was not easy at twenty yards with the sights set for 400 meters, especially since we had not practised this type of fighting in peacetime. My rifle cracked; the enemy's head fell forward on the step.'

The might of Mauser

The Mauser Gewehr 98 fired a 7.92mm (.312in) cartridge from a five-round internal box magazine that was fed by a brass stripper clip. Loading was accomplished with relative ease as the stock was cut

◀ Mannlicher M1903

Imperial German Army / Landwehr Regiment 77, 1915

The Mannlicher M1901/M1903 utilized a spring and cam system to manage the action of the slide during rearward traverse, thus operating on a delayed blowback principle. Originally chambered for 8mm (.314in) ammunition, it was later modified to 7.65mm (.3in). The M1903 used a six-round magazine, while the M1901 magazine held eight rounds.

Specifications

Country of Origin: Austria	Overall Length: 239mm (9.4in)
Date: 1903	Barrel Length: 165mm (6.5in)
Calibre: 7.65mm (.3in)	Muzzle Velocity: 312m/sec (1025ft/sec)
Operation: Blowback	Feed/Magazine: 6-round magazine
Weight: .94kg (2.1lb)	Range: 30m (98ft)

▶ Bergmann 1896

Imperial German Army / Reserve Infantry Regiment 242, 1915

The Bergmann 1896 corrected a dangerous element in the operation of its predecessor. Rather than impacting the next unfired round while extracting the spent case, the new closed design ejected it safely. This design was active for a number of years.

Specifications

Country of Origin: Germany	Overall Length: 254mm (10in)
Date: 1896	Barrel Length: 102mm (4in)
Calibre: 7.63mm (.3in)	Muzzle Velocity: 380m/sec (1250ft/sec)
Operation: Blowback	Feed/Magazine: 5-round magazine
Weight: 1.13kg (2.5lb)	Range: 30m (98ft)

▶ Parabellum M1908

Imperial German Army / Infantry Regiment 132, 1915

Commonly known as the Luger, the Parabellum M1908 utilized a toggle-locking system rather than a slide as in most semiautomatic pistols. More than two million were made during the world wars.

Specifications

Country of Origin: Germany	Barrel Length: 127mm (5in)
Date: 1908	Muzzle Velocity: 351m/sec (1150ft/sec)
Calibre: 9mm (.35in)	Feed/Magazine: 8-round detachable box
Operation: Toggle locked, short recoil	magazine
Weight: .96kg (2.125lb)	Range: 30m (98ft)
Overall Length: 222mm (8.8in)	

down on the right side to allow the rifleman to insert the cartridge more rapidly and safely than with the downward motion of the thumb which was required with the British Lee-Enfield. The bolt-action weapon served well although it was prone to jamming if exposed to excessive amounts of debris or dust.

The action of the heavy bolt required a steady hand in combat, as the soldier often was tasked with realigning his vision through the sights after operating the mechanism. The Mauser Gewehr 98 was ideally suited for mobile warfare as conducted in the early months of the Great War; however, when relegated to the trenches it was a somewhat ponderous weapon with an unloaded weight of four kilograms (nine pounds) and a length of 1250mm (49.2in). Its five-round magazine held fewer cartridges than the British Lee-Enfield; however, a skilled and well-trained user could manage a rate of fire up to 12 rounds per minute.

Sniper variant

In the spring of 1915, the order was given to equip more than 15,000 of the Mauser Gewehr 98 with telescopic sights to employ them as highly accurate sniper rifles. By the end of the war, adaptations had been completed for the sights and more than 18,000 of the sniper variants had actually been issued. Prior to World War I, a shortened version, the Karabiner 98a, was produced as a cavalry weapon. However, this experiment was disappointing and production discontinued. The Belgian Army fielded a modified version of the Mauser Gewehr 98, while the armies of Serbia and Turkey were equipped with it as well.

One of the most popular weapons to emerge from World War I was the Pistole Parabellum M1908, commonly known as the Luger in reference to its designer, Georg J. Luger, who patented the weapon in 1898. Perhaps due to its distinctive profile, the Luger has been highly sought after by collectors for decades, while its reputation is one of reliability, accuracy and ease of operation. It was commonly carried by officers of the German Army during World War I, including those of the Fourth Army during the four separate engagements that constituted the Second Battle of Ypres. Not until the late 1930s was the weapon scheduled for replacement with the Walther P38. Even then, though, its popularity did not wane.

The Pistole Parabellum M1908 utilizes a toggle-locking system rather than the slide that is more often found on semiautomatic pistols, while locating its magazine in the handgrip made the weapon shorter overall and more compact than placing it in front of the trigger. The chamber was spring fed, and as the weapon was fired the backward action advanced the next round upwards through the detachable eight-round box magazine. Reloading was accomplished with relative ease.

Production of the Luger was begun in 1900 by Imperial German arsenals and various private manufacturers, particularly the Deutsche Waffen und Munitionsfabriken, and continued until 1945 with wartime production exceeding two million. The pistol was originally designed to fire the 7.65mm (.301in) Parabellum round but later was reconfigured and came to be recognized as the pistol that popularized the 9mm (.35in) Parabellum cartridge.

Specifications

Country of Origin: Germany	Overall Length: 1250mm (49.2in)
Date: 1898	Barrel Length: 740mm (29.1in)
Calibre: 7.92mm (.312in)	Muzzle Velocity: 640m/sec (2100ft/sec)
Operation: Bolt action	Feed/Magazine: 5-round box magazine
Weight: 4.2kg (9.25lb)	Range: 500m (1640ft)

▲ **Mauser Gewehr 98**

Imperial German Army / Infantry Regiment 136, 1915

Although it is respected as one of the finest infantry shoulder arms ever made, the Mauser Gewehr 98 was not well suited for trench warfare. An estimated five million were manufactured, and the weapon is prized by sporting riflemen today.

French Army at Verdun
1916–17

Remembered as one of the costliest battles in human history, the 10-month struggle at Verdun resulted in the deaths of more than 300,000 soldiers with a half million wounded.

CONTROVERSY SURROUNDS the actual motive of the German high command for its offensive against the fortified city of Verdun in northeastern France. While some historians assert that the motivation was to reduce a troublesome French salient in the stalemated trenchlines, achieve a decisive breakthrough and then march on Paris, others contend that the intention was purely to bleed the French Army white.

Actually, it was German chief of staff Erich von Falkenhayn (1861–1922) who asserted that a decisive breakthrough was not achievable after both the Allies and the Central Powers had repeatedly failed to accomplish one. Therefore, in his personal memoirs he related that the purpose of the bloodbath at Verdun was to inflict such high casualties on the French that they would be compelled to ask for surrender terms. In the end, both French and German losses at Verdun were catastrophic during the protracted ordeal that lasted from February 1916 through to the end of the year.

While artillery played a major role in delivering death and destruction at Verdun, small arms were responsible for a good deal of the carnage as well. Hand-to-hand combat occurred on numerous occasions, and pistols, knives and bayonets were regularly employed. While serving as an infantry officer at Verdun, Charles de Gaulle, future leader of the Free French in World War II and architect of the nation's Fifth Republic, was seriously wounded by shrapnel from a hand grenade and a bayonet thrust to the hip and taken prisoner.

When the fighting at Verdun had finally ebbed, the longest battle of the Great War was assessed as a tactical victory for the French, who prevented a German breakthrough but suffered horrendous casualties. From a strategic perspective, the battle must be considered a draw, emphasizing the terrible waste and apparent futility of war.

By 1915, the shortcomings of the Lebel rifle were well known to the French high command, and the decision was made to replace it with the Fusil Berthier Mle 1907/15; however, the Lebel was never completely phased out of service and the Berthier was limited in heavy combat due to its woefully inadequate three-round magazine. The following year, a modified Berthier, the Fusil Mle 1907/15-M16 (Mle 1916), with a five-round magazine, was authorized. The improved model did not reach frontline units of the French Army until the summer of 1918, generally too late to have a positive impact on the prosecution of the war. In the meantime, a number of French officers insisted on equipping their troops with the older Lebel. Thus, the French Army

▲ **Fusil Berthier Mle 1907/15**

French Army / 87th Infantry Regiment, 1916

By 1915, it had become apparent that an upgrade to the old Lebel rifle was needed; almost 440,000 examples of the Berthier Mle 1907/15 were produced during World War I.

Specifications

Country of Origin: France	Overall Length: 1306mm (51.4in)
Date: 1915	Barrel Length: 797mm (31in)
Calibre: 8mm (.314in)	Muzzle Velocity: 640m/sec (2100ft/sec)
Operation: Bolt action	Feed/Magazine: 3-round box magazine
Weight: 3.8kg (6.4lb)	Range: 500m (1640ft)

struggled with the development and deployment of an adequate shoulder arm for the duration of the war. At Verdun, the Lebel was present in great numbers.

The development of French machine guns lagged following the perceived poor performance of the Reffye *mitrailleuse* during the Franco-Prussian War. In 1914, the air-cooled 8mm (.314in) St. Etienne Mle 1907 was the standard machine gun of the French Army. The adjustable rate of fire of the St. Etienne was from eight to 650 rounds per minute, and it was a considerable improvement over its predecessor, the Puteaux M1905.

By the summer of 1917, the reliable Hotchkiss Mle 1914 (M1914) was being deployed and the St. Etienne was shuttled to reserve units. The M1914 was the last in a series of machine guns developed by the French arms manufacturer Hotchkiss et Cie, which had been founded by American inventor Benjamin B. Hotchkiss (1826–85). The weapon ejected spent cartridges with a gas system rather than through recoil. It was fed by strips of 24 rounds which could be linked together, and was operated by a crew of three. Its weight of 23.6kg (52lb) was cumbersome for an infantry weapon. Production of the hefty Hotchkiss steadily increased, and nearly 50,000 were delivered to the French Army by 1918. It remained in service until 1945.

FRENCH INFANTRY COMPANY, 1916		
Unit	Officers	Men
Company HQ	1	
Four Sections each	2	
1st Half-section	1	
1st Squad (grenadiers)	1	
throwers		2
ammo suppliers		2
assistants		2
floater		1
2nd Squad (automatic riflemen)	1	
gunners		2
ammo suppliers		2
assistants		2
2nd Half-section	1	
3rd Squad (troopers)	1	
VB rifle-grenadiers		2
ammo suppliers		1
riflemen		8
4th Squad (troopers)	1	
VB rifle-grenadiers		2
ammo suppliers		1
riflemen		9
Total Strength	32	144

▲ **Hotchkiss Mle 1914**

French Army / 151st Infantry Regiment, 1916

The Hotchkiss Mle 1914 entered service as the standard machine gun of the French Army in 1917 and was deployed in significant numbers until the 1940s. When production ceased in 1920 more than 65,000 had been manufactured.

Specifications

Country of Origin: France
Date: 1914
Calibre: 8mm (.314in)
Operation: Gas operated, air cooled
Weight: 23.6kg (52lb)

Overall Length: 1270mm (50in)
Barrel Length: 775mm (30.5in)
Muzzle Velocity: 725m/sec (2380ft/sec)
Feed/Magazine: Strip fed
Cyclic Rate: 600rpm
Range: 2000m (6580ft)

The Somme
1916–17

Concentrated fire from machine guns and other small arms took a fearful toll in British and Commonwealth lives on the Somme, calling into question the judgment of senior Allied commanders who had ordered the units into action.

THE BRITISH ARMY lost nearly 60,000 dead and wounded on the first day of the Battle of the Somme. Such carnage was unprecedented, and the fighting was to last five months, from July to November 1916. The offensive against the German trenches in northern France was initially undertaken in an effort to coordinate with the Russian armies on the Eastern Front. Allied war planners reasoned that German forces would be stretched to the breaking point as British and French troops launched simultaneous attacks in the West while the Russians assumed the offensive in the East.

The German offensive at Verdun, begun in February 1916, altered Allied planning to a degree and required the British rather than the French to assume the primary role along the Somme River as French troops battled the emerging threat at Verdun. Therefore, the Somme offensive developed a twofold

▲ **Infantry support**
A British or Commonwealth infantryman aims a Lewis Gun somewhere on the Western Front. The American-designed Lewis Gun was one of the first infantry support weapons to be widely deployed.

▲ Lee-Enfield Rifle No. 1 Mk III SMLE

British Army / 1st Tyneside Irish Brigade, 1916

The Lee-Enfield No. 1 Mk III SMLE, the best known version of the 10-round rifle, began production in 1904 and entered service with Commonwealth forces three years later. The Mk III* was initially a wartime expedient version but continued in production into the 1950s.

Specifications

Country of Origin: United Kingdom	Overall Length: 1133mm (44.6in)
Date: 1907	Barrel Length: 640mm (25.2in)
Calibre: 7.7mm (.303in)	Muzzle Velocity: 634m/sec (2080ft/sec)
Operation: Bolt action	Feed/Magazine: 10-round box, loaded with
Weight: 3.93kg (8.625lb)	5-round charger clips
	Range: 500m (1640ft)

▲ Ross

Canadian Corps / 24th Battalion Victoria Rifles, 1916

Prone to jamming due to a susceptibility to dirt and debris and inherent mechanical problems, the Canadian Ross rifle proved a disappointment in the field after performing well on the firing range.

Specifications

Country of Origin: Canada	Overall Length: 1285mm (50.6in)
Date: 1903	Barrel Length: 765mm (30.1in)
Calibre: 7.7mm (.303in)	Muzzle Velocity: 792m/sec (2600ft/sec)
Operation: Bolt action	Feed/Magazine: 5-round magazine
Weight: 4.48kg (9.875lb)	Range: 500m (1640ft)

▲ Lewis Gun Mk I

60(R) Squadron Royal Air Force, 1917

The American-designed Lewis Gun was modified by British manufacturers and widely used from 1916 until the end of the Great War. It was a familiar weapon among Allied air forces as well.

Specifications

Country of Origin: United States	Barrel Length: 665mm (26.25in)
Date: 1914	Muzzle Velocity: 600m/sec (1970ft/sec)
Calibre: 7.7mm (.303in)	Feed/Magazine: Magazine fed
Operation: Gas operated, air cooled	Cyclic Rate: 550rpm
Weight: 11.8kg (26lb)	Range: 1000m (3280ft)
Overall Length: 965mm (38in)	

BRITISH INFANTRY PLATOON, 1917	
Unit	Strength
Rifle section	9
scout	1
sniper	1
Bombing (grenade) section	5
expert bombers	2
ammunition carriers	3
Rifle grenade section	9
rifle grenadiers	4
riflemen	5
Lewis Gun section	9

purpose – to stretch the Germans thin both East and West and to relieve mounting pressure against the French defenders of Verdun. As the Somme offensive began, 24 Allied divisions, 13 from the British Fourth Army and 11 of the French Sixth Army, confronted slightly more than 10 divisions of the German Second Army. Eventually, German strength committed on the Somme was to swell to more than 50 divisions.

The ordeal of the Tyneside Irish Brigade is indicative of the horrific losses endured on that fateful first day on the Somme front. The brigade was assigned to a support role as its sister brigades, the 101st and 102nd of the 34th Division, attacked. Crossing no-man's-land, the Tyneside Irish were caught in the open when the initial attack failed to progress satisfactorily. With the brigade brought to a halt, elements of two battalions (the 1st and the 4th) were able to reach positions on the German side, but these were killed or captured to a man. When the slaughter abated, the 1st and 4th Tyneside Irish battalions had lost nearly 1200 dead.

Canadian divisions

Of the 780 Newfoundlanders who moved forward on the morning of 1 July 1916, only 68 were fit for duty the following day. The Newfoundland Regiment was decimated in less than 20 minutes and without advancing beyond the British trenchline. From July to September, three Canadian divisions were heavily engaged in the vicinity of the Somme. On 15 September, the Canadian Second Division attacked at Courcelette, supported by tanks for the first time.

When the fighting ended on the Somme, Allied forces had gained only a few kilometres of territory.

In total, the British had lost 420,000 casualties. On the first day alone, more than 20 per cent of the effective British fighting force had been killed or wounded. The Battle of the Somme raised questions concerning the proper commitment of troops before enemy positions defended with modern small arms. Its shadow continues to loom across the British psyche to this day.

The British and Commonwealth soldiers at the Somme carried the standard issue Lee-Enfield Rifle No. 1 Mk III, the famous 7.7mm (.303in) Short Magazine Lee-Enfield (SMLE). This bolt-action rifle entered service with the British Army in 1907, and along with its predecessor the MLE (Magazine Lee-Enfield) was the primary shoulder arm of the British soldier from 1895 to 1957. Named for designer James Paris Lee and the Royal Small Arms Factory at Enfield, the Mk III incorporated a 10-round box magazine loaded from the top with five-round chargers. Unlike that of its Mauser counterpart, the Mk III's bolt action was smooth to the point that the rifleman could maintain his sight picture while operating it, thus providing a more stable and accurate shooting perspective.

The British Army placed a high priority on the concentrated, efficient rifle fire of its infantry, and the Mk III was ideally suited for this purpose. Well-trained soldiers often achieved a sustained rate of fire of 15 rounds per minute. At the height of combat, British troops sometimes referred to the 'mad minute' during which up to 30 rounds were discharged. In fact, on more than one occasion during the Great War German infantrymen taken under fire by British

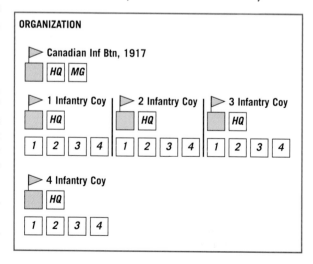

◀ Colt New Service

Canadian Corps / 4th Battalion (Central Ontario) Canadian Infantry,
Hill 145, 1917

The Colt New Service revolver fired an 11.43mm (.45in) cartridge and was adopted by the US armed forces as the Model 1909. It was later developed into the M1917 for the US military. Actually, the revolver had been in production since 1898. A large number were purchased by the Canadian Army prior to World War I and by the British during the war.

Specifications

Country of Origin: United States	Overall Length: 273mm (10.75in)
Date: 1909	Barrel Length: 140mm (5.51in)
Calibre: 11.43mm (.45in)	Muzzle Velocity: 198m/sec (650ft/sec)
Operation: Revolver	Feed/Magazine: 6-round cylinder
Weight: 1.3kg (2.9lb)	Range: 20m (66ft)

▶ Smith & Wesson Triple Lock

Canadian Corps / 27th Battalion (City of Winnipeg) Canadian Infantry,
Battle of Courcelette, 1916

The triple lock designation for this revolver arose from the third locking lug on the cylinder crane enabling the weapon to handle its cartridge. It is also known as the Smith & Wesson .44 Hand Ejector.

Specifications

Country of Origin: United States	Overall Length: 298mm (11.75in)
Date: 1908	Barrel Length: 185mm (7.3in)
Calibre: 11.2mm (.44in)	Muzzle Velocity: 198m/sec (650ft/sec)
Operation: Revolver	Feed/Magazine: 6-round cylinder
Weight: 1.08kg (2.4lb)	Range: 30m (98ft)

▲ M1895 Colt-Browning

2nd Canadian Division / 13th Canadian Machine Gun Company,
Vimy Ridge, April 1917

This gas-operated machine gun saw extensive service with Allied forces. It was produced in a number of calibres, including 7.7mm (.303in) and led to improvements with the development of the water-cooled M1917, one of the most famous families of machine guns in military history.

Specifications

Country of Origin: United States
Date: 1895
Calibre: 7.62mm (.3in), 6mm (.23in)
Operation: Gas operated
Weight: 16kg (35.25lb)
Overall Length: 1040mm (40.94in)
Barrel Length: 711mm (28in)
Muzzle Velocity: 732m/sec (2400ft/sec)
Feed/Magazine: Belt fed
Cyclic Rate: 400rpm
Range: 2740m (8990ft)

troops equipped with the Mk III actually believed they were confronted by machine guns.

The basic Mk III rifle was modified several times through the years, and a sniper variant served with Commonwealth forces into the 1990s. An estimated 17 million examples of the MLE, SMLE and variants have been manufactured.

The emergent Lewis Gun

By late 1915, the British Army had adopted the light Lewis Gun as an infantry support alternative to the heavier Vickers weapon in conjunction with the reorganization of the infantry machine-gun battalions into the Machine Gun Corps. The Lewis and the Vickers were designated as light and heavy machine guns respectively. By the end of World War I, the Lewis outnumbered the Vickers in service with the British Army by approximately three to one.

The Lewis Gun was of American design, and it was widely used by British and Commonwealth forces through World War I and into the Korean Conflict. British manufacturers modified the weapon to fire the 7.7mm (.303in) cartridge rather than the original 7.62mm (.3in) in use by the Americans, who never

▲ **Machine-gun team**
A German machine-gun squad operate a Maxim '08 from wooded cover during the latter stages of the war. The Maxim was the most widely used heavy machine gun of World War I.

officially adopted the Lewis Gun. It was produced from 1913 to 1942, and over 100,000 were sold by the British to Imperial Russia. British production of the Lewis Gun far exceeded that in the United States, and by the end of World War I more than 145,000 were in service with Commonwealth forces. In contrast to the heavier Vickers, the gas-operated, air-cooled Lewis Gun weighed only 11.8kg (26lb). It was easily identified with its drum-pan magazine that held up to 97 rounds and its long cooling sleeve. The Lewis Gun gained equal notoriety with Allied air forces during World War I, often mounted aboard fighter and reconnaissance aircraft with its cooling sleeve removed.

▶ **Mauser M1912**

Imperial German Army / Infantry Regiment 23 (Upper Silesian), 1916

The military version of the Mauser C96, nicknamed the Broomhandle, the M1912 semiautomatic pistol was originally chambered for 7.63mm (.3in) ammunition but retooled for 9mm (.35in).

Specifications

Country of Origin: Germany
Date: 1912
Calibre: 7.63mm (.3in)
Operation: Short recoil
Weight: 1.25kg (2.75lb)
Overall Length: 295mm (11.6in)
Barrel Length: 140mm (5.51in)
Muzzle Velocity: 427m/sec (1400ft/sec)
Feed/Magazine: 6-, 10- or 20-round integral or detachable magazine
Range: 100m (328ft)

Specifications

Country of Origin: Germany
Date: 1908
Calibre: 7.92mm (.312in)
Operation: Short recoil, water cooled
Weight: 26.44kg (58.25lb)
Overall Length: 1175mm (46.25in)
Barrel Length: 719mm (28.33in)
Muzzle Velocity: 829m/sec (2925ft/sec)
Feed/Magazine: Belt fed (250-round fabric belt)
Cyclic Rate: 300–450rpm
Range: 1500m (4921ft)

▲ **Maxim Maschinengewehr 08**

Imperial German Army / Infantry Regiment 180 (Württemberg), 1917

A variant of the British Maxim Gun originally built under licence, the Maschinengewehr 08 served as the primary machine gun of the German Army during World War I. Its service life was extended into the 1940s due to shortages of newer types.

The Michael Offensive
1918

With Russia out of World War I, the Germans planned a decisive offensive for the spring of 1918. The main thrust of four separate attacks was codenamed Michael, and intended to crush the British Army from the Somme to the Channel.

A S THE GREAT WAR STRETCHED into its fourth year, Imperial Germany had reason for optimism with the Treaty of Brest-Litovsk, which ended Russian participation in the fighting. At long last, the German Army was able to transfer as many as 50 fresh divisions to the Western Front, amassing enough strength on the ground for what General Erich Ludendorff (1865–1937), Chief Quarter Master of the Army and joint senior commander with Field Marshal Paul von Hindenburg (1847–1934), hoped would be the decisive campaign against the British and French.

War fatigue was beginning to plague Germany. The strangulation of a blockade by the Royal Navy created shortages of foodstuffs and war materiel. The casualty rolls were lengthy, and manpower shortages were becoming an issue. Perhaps the most daunting prospect for the continuation of the war was the mobilization of the United States, which had entered the conflict on the Allied side in April 1917. Ludendorff knew that the immense military and industrial potential of the United States could doom Germany to defeat, and some American troops were already fighting in France. The window of opportunity was closing when the Michael Offensive commenced on 21 March 1918.

Although the British sustained more than 20,000 casualties on the first day of the offensive and components of both the Fifth and Third Armies were compelled to retreat to avoid being outflanked, isolated pockets of resistance held out. German penetrations utilizing new 'stormtrooper tactics' were significant in some areas; however, these were of little strategic importance. At key positions the British held their ground, repulsing German attacks and buying precious time.

Eventually, the Michael Offensive slowed and lost momentum. Supply lines were stretched thinly, and artillery could not maintain the pace of advance necessary. The Germans failed to capture the vital rail and road links through the town of Amiens in northern France, and by the first week of April Ludendorff ordered a halt to the attacks. Although Allied and German losses were comparable at about 250,000, the Allied losses were replaceable – particularly with the pending arrival of more

▲ **Parabellum M1908 Artillery Model**

Imperial German Army / Infantry Regiment 121 (Württemberg), 1918

The artillery version of the legendary Parabellum M1908 pistol, popularly known as the Luger after its designer, Georg Luger, featured a lengthened barrel and a wooden stock which allowed it to function as a carbine.

Specifications

Country of Origin: Germany

Date: 1913

Calibre: 9mm (.35in)

Operation: Toggle locked, short recoil

Weight: .96kg (2.125lb)

Overall Length: 324mm (12.75in)

Barrel Length: 190mm (7.5in)

Muzzle Velocity: 351m/sec (1150ft/sec)

Feed/Magazine: 8- or 32-round magazine

Range: 80m (260ft)

American troops – while the German dead and wounded were not. Elsewhere during the spring offensive, the outcome was predictably similar. The last, best opportunity for German victory was extinguished.

The Spandau spectre

In addition to the employment of stormtrooper tactics, which involved rapid movement and the isolation of strongpoints to be mopped up by slower-moving units, the potential for success in the Michael Offensive relied on the capabilities of the Maxim Maschinengewehr 08 (MG 08), the heavy machine gun that had become the stalwart defender of the German trenches for most of World War I. The MG 08 had proved its worth in a defensive capacity on numerous occasions, most notably at the Somme where the butcher's bill exacted from the British was catastrophic.

The greatest issue with the MG 08, however, was its heavy weight at 26.44kg (58.25lb). The weapon was so heavy that it was either transported on sleds or carried by several soldiers who hoisted it to their shoulders or bore it like a stretcher. The solution was the introduction of the Maxim Maschinengewehr 08/15, a bipod version of the same weapon that was somewhat lighter at 18kg (39.75lb). With added firepower and mobility, the German offensive in the spring of 1918 suffered primarily from unrefined tactics to exploit the initial gains won by the stormtroopers and ill-defined objectives once significant progress was made.

Nevertheless, the performance of the MG 08 during World War I was outstanding. The workhorse remained in service with the German Army of the Weimar Republic and into World War II to bridge shortages in newer models such as the Maschinengewehr 34 (MG 34). The reputation of

▶ **Langenham pistol**

Imperial German Army / 2nd Grenadier Regiment 'King Friedrich Wilhelm IV'
(1st Pomeranian), 1918

More than 50,000 Langenham pistols were made during the Great War for the German Army. The weapon was fed by an eight-round box magazine. A pocket version was also made for the civilian market.

Specifications

Country of Origin: Germany	Overall Length: 165mm (6.5in)
Date: 1914	Barrel Length: 101.5mm (4in)
Calibre: 7.65mm (.301in)	Muzzle Velocity: 282m/sec (925ft/sec)
Operation: Blowback	Feed/Magazine: 8-round box magazine
Weight: .77kg (1.7lb)	Range: 30m (98ft)

◀ **Dreyse M1907**

Imperial German Army / Reserve Infantry Regiment 40, 1918

Heavily influenced by the early Browning pistol designs, the Dreyse was issued to German and Austrian officers and later used by the German *Volkssturm* units in World War II.

Specifications

Country of Origin: Germany	Barrel Length: 92mm (3.6in)
Date: 1907	Muzzle Velocity: 300m/sec (984ft/sec)
Calibre: 7.65mm (.301in)	Feed/Magazine: 7-round detachable single stack
Operation: Blowback	magazine
Weight: .71kg (1.6lb)	Range: 50m (164ft)
Overall Length: 160mm (6.3in)	

the MG 08 was so fearsome that every German automatic weapon came to be known as a Spandau, for the arsenal where many of the machine guns were manufactured.

The Maxim Maschinengewehr 08 was a variant of an original German licence-produced copy of the British Maxim Gun, designed by American-born inventor Hiram Maxim. It fired the 7.92mm (.312in) Mauser round and was capable of a cyclic rate of fire of up to 450 rounds per minute. Using the short-recoil and toggle-lock mechanism, the weapon continued to fire as long as the trigger was depressed or until the 250-round fabric belt of ammunition was exhausted. Truly the most outstanding defensive weapon of World War I, the gun was produced in large quantities from 1916 forward, achieving a peak of 14,400 examples per month.

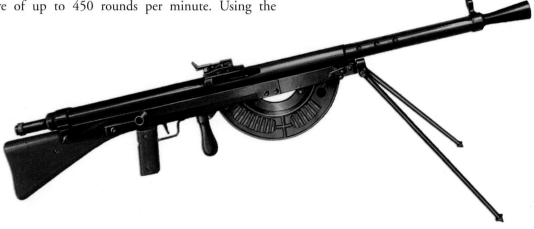

Specifications

Country of Origin: France	Barrel Length: 470mm (18.5in)
Date: 1915	Muzzle Velocity: 700m/sec (2300ft/sec)
Calibre: 8mm (.314in) Lebel	Feed/Magazine: Magazine fed
Operation: Recoil, air cooled	Cyclic Rate: 250rpm
Weight: 9kg (20lb)	Range: 1000m (3280ft)
Overall Length: 1145mm (45in)	

▲ Fusil Mitrailleur M'15

French Army / 118th Chasseurs, 1918

Deployed in large numbers by both the French and US Armies, the Fusil Mitrailleur M'15 weighed 9kg (20lb) but proved unfit for heavy combat. The weapon was produced in both French and US versions, firing the 8mm (.314in) and 7.62mm (.3in) cartridge respectively.

▲ Mousqueton Berthier Mle 1892/M16 carbine

French Army / 87th Infantry Regiment, 1918

The crowning achievement of the Berthier system was this carbine variant of the five-shot Mle 1916 Berthier rifle. Light troops, cavalry and reconnaissance units favoured the weapon.

Specifications

Country of Origin: France	Barrel Length: 453mm (17.8in)
Date: 1916	Muzzle Velocity: 640m/sec (3000ft/sec)
Calibre: 8mm (.314in)	Feed/Magazine: 5-round charger-loaded
Operation: Bolt action	magazine
Weight: 3.1kg (6.8lb)	Range: 500m (1640ft)
Overall Length: 945mm (37.2in)	

Specifications

Country of Origin: Germany	Barrel Length: 195mm (7.75in)
Date: 1918	Muzzle Velocity: 395m/sec (1300ft/sec)
Calibre: 9mm (.35in) Parabellum	Feed/Magazine: 32-round detachable drum
Operation: Blowback	magazine
Weight: 4.2kg (9.25lb)	Range: 70m (230ft)
Overall Length: 815mm (32in)	

▲ **Bergmann MP 18**

Imperial German Army / 73rd Fusilier Regiment, 1918

The world's first operational submachine gun for ground troops, the Bergmann MP 18 fired up to 500 rounds per minute and served as a basis for the design of automatic infantry weapons into the 1960s.

The Maschinengewehr 08/15 reached the army in great numbers in the spring of 1917 and rapidly became a success on the battlefield, although it remained somewhat cumbersome and required a crew of four to operate. By the time of the Michael Offensive approximately six MG 08/15s were fielded by each infantry company and up to 72 by each regiment, eclipsing the number of heavy Maschinengewehr 08 weapons in service.

Approximately 130,000 MG 08/15s were manufactured during World War I, primarily at the arsenals of Spandau and Erfurt and the works of civilian arms manufacturer Deutsche Waffen und Munitionsfabriken. Other variants of the MG 08 were used aboard aircraft, while the Chinese Army and some Southeast Asian forces deployed versions of the weapon until the 1960s.

First submachine gun

One of the most innovative weapons utilized by German troops during the Michael Offensive was the Bergmann MP 18, the first blowback-operated submachine gun in the world. Development of the Bergmann MP 18 was undertaken by Hugo Schmeisser (1884–1953) in 1916, and production was initiated by Theodor Bergmann Waffenbau Abteilung. Within a few months the weapon was issued on the Western Front and proved effective in providing suppressive fire against fixed objectives and in clearing trenches of massed enemy troops.

Although exact figures are unknown and full-scale production did not begin until early 1918, it is believed that between 5000 and 10,000 MP 18s were manufactured by the end of World War I. The spring offensive of 1918 saw the most prolific deployment of the MP 18, and its presence on the battlefield was noted by the Allied troops who encountered its distinctive report, high degree of mobility and rate of fire of up to 500 rounds per minute. The relatively few MP 18s available in the spring of 1918 were placed in the hands of the newly formed stormtrooper units, whose primary task was to rapidly penetrate enemy lines and clear the way for larger numbers of troops to advance.

The Treaty of Versailles outlawed the manufacture of the Bergmann MP 18; however, production continued on a clandestine basis into the 1920s. Although technically the MP 18 was not the world's first submachine gun, preceded by the Italian Villar-Perosa in 1915, it is considered the first serviceable weapon of its kind for ground troops. The Villar-Perosa was initially intended for use in aircraft and was later adapted for infantry.

The technology of the MP 18 was advanced for its time; however, limited production prevented it from effecting the course of World War I and potentially breaking the stalemate of trench warfare. Still, the battle-tested weapon formed the basis for the development of submachine guns and individual automatic weapons for the next half-century.

MACHINE GUN COMPARISON

Equipment	Crew	Calibre	Cyclic Rate
German MG 08/15	4	7.92mm	300–450 rpm
British Vickers Mk I	3	7.7mm	600 rpm
French Hotchkiss M1914	3	8mm	600 rpm
U.S. Browning M1917	4	7.62mm	450 rpm

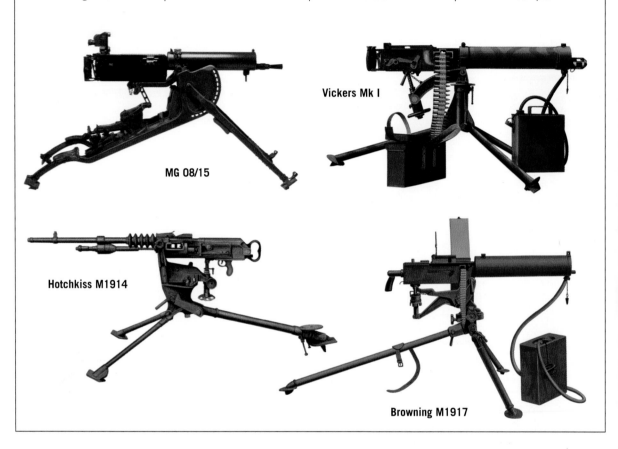

Vickers Mk I

MG 08/15

Hotchkiss M1914

Browning M1917

▶ Webley & Scott 1912

British Army / 5th Battalion West Yorkshire Regiment, Le Havre, 1917

Issued to airmen of the Royal Flying Corps and personnel of the Horse Artillery, the Webley & Scott 1912 fired a heavy 11.55mm (.455in) cartridge and was fed by a six-round magazine.

Specifications

Country of Origin: United Kingdom	Overall Length: 216mm (8.5in)
Date: 1912	Barrel Length: 127mm (5in)
Calibre: 11.55mm (.455in)	Muzzle Velocity: 220m/sec (720ft/sec)
Operation: Self-loading	Feed/Magazine: 6-round magazine
Weight: .66kg (1.5lb)	Range: 20m (66ft)

▲ **Lee-Enfield Rifle No. 1 Mk III SMLE with Grenade Launcher**
British Expeditionary Force / 4th Battalion Duke of Wellington's Brigade (West Riding Regiment), 1917
The body and upper barrel of the Mk III SMLE were wrapped in brass wire and soldered together to prevent the rifle from bursting when converted as a grenade launcher. The grenade is a No. 5 Mk I 1916.

American Expeditionary Force
1917–18

When the United States entered World War I in April 1917, it was far from prepared to provide troops and war materiel in great quantities. However, the first soldiers of the American Expeditionary Force reached France within 90 days.

WHEN THE FIRST AMERICAN SOLDIERS arrived in France a contingent marched through Paris, and its commander, General John J. Pershing (1860–1948), was reported to have commented, 'LaFayette, we are here!' American troops were eventually deployed in large numbers, and by May 1918 more than a million had reached the Western Front. Half of these were in the trenches and forward Allied positions. The American troops were welcomed by the war-weary French and British Armies; however, friction developed when some Allied commanders wanted the Americans to fight under foreign leadership. Pershing sought to maintain independent command for US forces. While some American units gained combat experience with British and French troops, Pershing trained his soldiers tirelessly.

Under French command, the US 1st Division engaged in the initial American offensive action at Cantigny on 18 May 1918. Later during the Second Battle of the Marne at Belleau Wood and Chateau Thierry, US Army troops and Marines defeated opposing German forces. Subsequently, American troops fought major actions in the autumn of 1918 during the reduction of the St. Mihiel salient and the Meuse-Argonne Offensive. At St. Mihiel, Pershing led the American First Army, which consisted of seven infantry divisions and 500,000 men. It was the largest US military operation in history up to that time. During their participation in the Great War, the Americans suffered casualties amounting to nearly 117,000 dead and 204,000 wounded. At the peak of his command tenure, Pershing led more than a million American and French combat troops.

Springfield special

Although the American Expeditionary Force arrived in France within weeks of the declaration of war in 1917, the rapid movement required that most of its heavy equipment be left behind. Therefore, many of the aircraft and artillery pieces fielded by the Americans were of British or French manufacture. When it came to shoulder arms, however, the primary rifle of the US Army was the Springfield Model 1903, a descendant of the prolific German

Mauser G98 design which was put into production at the Springfield Arsenal in Massachusetts.

While there were some minor alterations to the original Mauser design, which the Americans had fought against during the Spanish-American War, the basic weapon varied little from its German configuration. In fact, Mauser eventually filed a suit against the US government and received royalty payments. US military leaders had struggled for years to find an appropriate rifle, purchasing both the German Mauser G98 and the Norwegian Krag-Jørgensen. The Springfield 1903 entered service in

▶ Colt M1911

American Expeditionary Force / 2nd Division / 9th Regiment, 1917

For more than 70 years, the Colt Model 1911 remained in service with the US Army and was later known as the M1911A1. Designed by John Browning, it used a swinging-link, short-recoil system.

Specifications

Country of Origin: United States	Overall Length: 216mm (8.5in)
Date: 1911	Barrel Length: 127mm (5in)
Calibre: 11.43mm (.45in)	Muzzle Velocity: 262m/sec (860ft/sec)
Operation: Short recoil	Feed/Magazine: 7-round magazine
Weight: 1.1kg (2.425lb)	Range: 30m (98ft)

▶ Smith & Wesson M1917

American Expeditionary Force / 26th Division / 102nd Regiment, 1917

Loaded using two three-round half-moon clips, the Smith & Wesson M1917 was called into service to ease a shortage of handguns in the US Army. The clips were required for the ejector to grip the rimless 11.43mm (.45in) round.

Specifications

Country of Origin: United States	Overall Length: 208mm (11.75in)
Date: 1917	Barrel Length: 185mm (7.3in)
Calibre: 11.43mm (.45in)	Muzzle Velocity: 198m/sec (650ft/sec)
Operation: Revolver	Feed/Magazine: 6-round cylinder
Weight: 1.08kg (2.4lb)	Range: 20m (66ft)

▶ Colt .45 Army 1917

American Expeditionary Force / 42nd Division / 165th Infantry Regiment, 1918

The last standard issue US military revolver, the Colt .45 Army 1917 was pressed into service during World War I until enough of the semiautomatic M1911 were available.

Specifications

Country of Origin: United States	Overall Length: 273mm (10.75in)
Date: 1917	Barrel Length: 140mm (5.5in)
Calibre: 11.43mm (.45in)	Muzzle Velocity: 198m/sec (650ft/sec)
Operation: Revolver	Feed/Magazine: 6-round cylinder
Weight: 1.13kg (2.5lb)	Range: 20m (66ft)

COLT M1911 MILITARY PRODUCTION FIGURES	
Period	**Total**
1912	20,000
Jan 1913 – Jan 1915	90,000
Feb 1915 – Oct 1918	440,000
Nov 1918 – April 1919	180,000

1905 and was not officially replaced until the M1 Garand was adopted in 1937. Its sniper version is still in use to this day. The M1903A4, which appeared in 1942, was the first attempt by the US military to standardize a sniper rifle.

The Springfield 1903 fired the 7.62mm (.3in) .30-03 and subsequently .30-06 cartridges. Although smaller than other contemporary rifles, it was accurate and sturdy and remained popular with the troops. The experienced soldier was capable of firing an average of 15 rounds per minute with ammunition fed from a five-round stripper clip to an internal box magazine. Production numbers topped 800,000 prior to World War I and eventually several million were manufactured.

Browning brawler

Despite the fact that only about 1200 Browning M1917 heavy machine guns reached the front prior to the end of World War I, the gun managed to acquire a reputation as a first-rate defensive weapon. Weighing 47kg (103lb) including gun, tripod, water for cooling the barrel and a standard supply of ammunition, it compared favourably in weight with the German MG 08 and the British Vickers Mk I, while its rate of fire was

comparable at 450 rounds per minute. The gun itself was actually considerably lighter than the MG 08 or the Vickers Mk I.

Due to the shortage of Browning weapons, most American troops in France were equipped with British Vickers machine guns built by Colt or French Hotchkiss models. The service life of the Browning M1917 extended for more than half a century as it was improved and later designated the Model 1917A1. The development of the M1917 began around the turn of the twentieth century as John Browning sought to produce a serviceable recoil-operated, water-cooled machine gun. Its sliding-block mechanism was a significant departure from the toggle lock favoured by Hiram Maxim, the father of the prominent European models. When the US government requested designs from several potential manufacturers in the spring of 1917, Browning's entry fired 20,000 rounds without jamming or overheating.

A scant one-third of the US divisions sent to France received the Browning M1917, and its combat use during the Great War was only about 10 weeks in duration. The M1917A1 refined the successful design with an improved bottom plate; however, the basic original design proved more than adequate for defensive purposes until supplanted by the M60.

▶ **Expeditionary troops**
The first contingent of US servicemen to arrive in England in 1917 for deployment to the Western Front stand at ease, their Springfield 1903 rifles arranged in front of them.

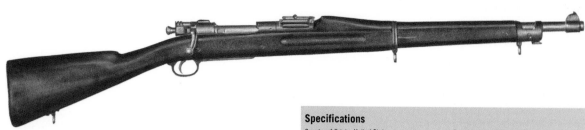

▲ Springfield Model 1903

American Expeditionary Force / 42nd Division / 168th Infantry Regiment, 1917

Based on a Mauser design, the Springfield 1903 entered service with the US Army in 1905 and remained the standard issue rifle until replaced by the M1 Garand in 1937. Its service life, however, was extended for decades.

Specifications

Country of Origin: United States

Date: 1903

Calibre: 7.62mm (.3in)

Operation: Bolt action

Weight: 3.9kg (8.625lb)

Overall Length: 1115mm (43.9in)

Barrel Length: 610mm (24in)

Muzzle Velocity: 823m/sec (2700ft/sec)

Feed/Magazine: 5-round stripper clip, box magazine

Range: 750m (2460ft)

▲ M1917 Enfield Rifle

American Expeditionary Force / 41st Division / 161st Infantry Regiment, 1918

An adaptation of the earlier P14, the M1917 was the product of a joint effort by British and American designers. It fired the US 7.62mm (.3in) .30-06 cartridge.

Specifications

Country of Origin: United Kingdom/United States

Date: 1917

Calibre: 7.62mm (.3in)

Operation: Bolt action

Weight: 4.17kg (9.2lb)

Overall Length: 1175mm (46.25in)

Barrel Length: 660mm (26in)

Muzzle Velocity: 823m/sec (2700ft/sec)

Feed/Magazine: 6-round magazine, 5-round clip-fed reloading

Range: 500m (1640ft)

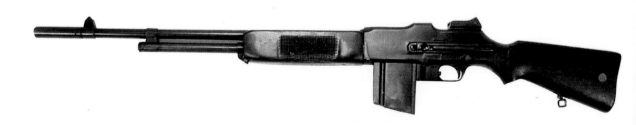

Specifications

Country of Origin: United States

Date: 1917

Calibre: 7.62mm (.3in)

Operation: Gas operated

Weight: 7.26kg (16lb)

Overall Length: 1194mm (47in)

Barrel Length: 610mm (24in)

Muzzle Velocity: 853m/sec (2800ft/sec)

Feed/Magazine: 20-round straight box

Range: 1000–1500m (3280–4921ft)

▲ Browning BAR

American Expeditionary Force / 1st Division / 16th Infantry Regiment, 1918

The Browning Automatic Rifle (BAR) provided automatic fire support for advancing infantry of the US Army. The weapon was heavy and limited by an ammunition supply of only 20 rounds.

Specifications

Country of Origin: United States

Date: 1917

Calibre: 7.62mm (.3in)

Operation: Recoil, water cooled

Weight: 15kg (32.75lb)

Overall Length: 980mm (38.5in)

Barrel Length: 610mm (24in)

Muzzle Velocity: 850m/sec (2800ft/sec)

Feed/Magazine: Belt fed

Cyclic Rate: 450rpm

Range: 2000m (6560ft)

▶ Browning M1917

**American Expeditionary Force / 1st Division /
1st Machine Gun Battalion, 1918**

An excellent defensive weapon, the Browning M1917 machine gun was capable of firing at 450 rounds per minute, while an improved version, the M1917A1, could reach 600rpm. The M1917 served with US and other forces for more than half a century.

Dardanelles Campaign
1915

The Dardanelles campaign, conceived as a blow against Ottoman Turkey with the possible capture of Constantinople, ended in a bloody debacle for Commonwealth troops who landed under heavy enemy fire at Gallipoli.

IN THE FIRST MAJOR CAMPAIGN undertaken during World War I by the Australian and New Zealand Army Corps (ANZAC), these Commonwealth troops suffered tremendous losses but gained a measure of national identity for their countries in the process. Although they failed to advance on Constantinople, the capital of Ottoman Turkey, or to open a supply route to Russia, they fought heroically although being at times poorly led.

In early 1915, the Royal Navy and the French Navy mounted a series of abortive naval attacks against Turkish fortifications in the Dardanelles, a strait running between the Aegean Sea and the Sea of Marmara. These resulted in embarrassing losses, and it was determined that a land campaign was necessary to secure passage through the strait and on towards the Bosporus and the Black Sea. On 25 April British and French forces landed at Helles on the tip of the Gallipoli peninsula, while ANZAC troops went ashore at Gaba Tepe on the coast of the Aegean Sea. In memory of their sacrifice there, the small inlet at Gaba Tepe has since been known as ANZAC Cove.

▲ **FN-Mauser Infantry Rifle Model 1889**

Turkish Army / 57th Infantry Regiment, 1915

Delivered to the Turks to complete a contract for the earlier Model 1887, the FN-Mauser Model 1889 was a standard rifle of the Belgian Army as well. The Turkish version was known as the M90, and a small number were produced as shorter-barrelled carbine versions.

Specifications

Country of Origin: Belgium	Overall Length: 1295mm (51in)
Date: 1889	Barrel Length: 780mm (30.6in)
Calibre: 7.65mm (.301in)	Muzzle Velocity: 610m/sec (2000ft/sec)
Operation: Bolt action	Feed/Magazine: 5-round box magazine
Weight: 4.1kg (8.8lb)	Range: 1000m (3280ft)

▶ **Mauser C96**

Turkish Army / 35th Regiment, 1915

The semiautomatic Mauser C96 pistol was front-loading and chambered for the high-powered 7.63mm (.3in) cartridge. At least 1000 C96s were delivered to the Turkish Army and designated the 1897 Turkish Army Mauser.

Specifications

Country of Origin: Germany	Barrel Length: 140mm (5.51in)
Date: 1896	Muzzle Velocity: 305m/sec (1000ft/sec)
Calibre: 7.63mm (.3in)	Feed/Magazine: 6- or 10-round integral or
Operation: Short recoil	detachable magazine
Weight: 1.045kg (2.3lb)	Range: 100m (328ft)
Overall Length: 295mm (11.6in)	

The landings in both locations were bitterly contested. At Helles, senior commanders failed to exploit advances in poorly defended sectors. Instead, their soldiers suffered heavy casualties on and near the beaches. The transport ship *River Clyde* was intentionally run aground, and those unfortunate troops who were required to vacate the ship through sally ports found themselves under withering Turkish machine-gun fire. Only 21 of the initial 200 soldiers of the Royal Hampshires and Royal Munster Fusiliers managed to reach the beach.

Although Turkish troops were hard pressed at both Helles and ANZAC Cove, they held off the Commonwealth and French forces, which were supported by naval gunfire. At Helles, Turkish Lieutenant-Colonel Mustafa Kemal realized that his situation was desperate and issued an order to his 57th Infantry Regiment which read: 'I do not expect you to attack. I order you to die. In the time which passes until we die, other troops and commanders can come forward and take our places.'

Kemal survived the fighting around Gallipoli and went on the become the 'Father of Modern Turkey'. As the first president of the Turkish Republic, he earned the name Atatürk.

Deadly stalemate

Rather than being a rapidly successful campaign, the Dardanelles adventure lapsed into a deadly stalemate. Commonwealth troops were withdrawn in late 1915 and early 1916. The affair at Gallipoli had been the brainchild of First Lord of the Admiralty Winston Churchill, who suffered a severe political setback as a result of its failure. However, Churchill emerged as a hero a generation later, leading Great Britain as prime minister during the dark days of World War II. During the Dardanelles campaign, Commonwealth casualties amounted to 44,000 dead and 97,000

▶ Webley & Scott Mk VI

British Commonwealth Army / 5th Australian Brigade / 20th Battalion, 1915

One of several sturdy revolvers produced by Webley & Scott, the Mark VI entered service in 1915 and fired a large 11.55mm (.455in) cartridge. A bayonet was produced but found little practical usage.

Specifications

Country of Origin: United Kingdom	Overall Length: 279mm (11in)
Date: 1915	Barrel Length: 152mm (6in)
Calibre: 11.55mm (.455in)	Muzzle Velocity: 198m/sec (650ft/sec)
Operation: Revolver	Feed/Magazine: 6-round cylinder
Weight: 1.1kg (2.425lb)	Range: 20m (66ft)

▲ Lee-Enfield Rifle No. 1 Mk III SMLE

British Commonwealth Army / 5th Australian Brigade / 20th Battalion, 1915

The Lee-Enfield No. 1 Mk III SMLE equipped many regiments of the Commonwealth troops that fought alongside British units. The definitive version of the SMLE entered service with the British military in 1907 and fired a high-velocity 7.7mm (.303in) cartridge.

Specifications

Country of Origin: United Kingdom	Barrel Length: 640mm (25.2in)
Date: 1907	Muzzle Velocity: 634m/sec (2080ft/sec)
Calibre: 7.7mm (.303in)	Feed/Magazine: 10-round box, loaded with
Operation: Bolt action	5-round charger clips
Weight: 3.93kg (8.625lb)	Range: 500m (1640ft)
Overall Length: 1133mm (44.6in)	

wounded. A total of 87,000 Turkish troops were killed and 165,000 wounded.

Among the shoulder arms carried by the Turkish Army during the Dardanelles campaign and throughout World War I was a weapon similar to the FN-Mauser Model 1889 and known as the Mauser M90, which was delivered to the Turks in completion of an order that had been originally filled with the earlier Mauser Model 1887. A clause in the Turkish contract with the German arms manufacturer stated that if any other nation purchased an improved version of the Model 1887 the Turks would be entitled to an upgrade to complete their deliveries. When Belgium purchased the Model 1889, Mauser made up the Turkish order with the M90, which was based on the Model 1889.

Like the Model 1889, the bolt-action Mauser M90 fired the 7.65mm (.301in) cartridge and was fed by a five-round vertical box magazine, a considerable improvement over tubular magazines in older weapons. With the rifle's open action, the magazine was loaded using a charger.

The Mauser C96 front-loading semiautomatic pistol was another import from Germany that equipped Turkish soldiers during the Dardanelles campaign. Known as the Mauser Broomhandle, the weapon was chambered for a high-velocity 7.63mm (.3in) cartridge and fed by a six- or 10-round integral or detachable magazine. Many of the C96 pistols in service with the Turks had been delivered under the first arms contract between Mauser and the Turkish government which was placed in 1897 for 1000 weapons. These pistols were designated the 1897 Turkish Army Mauser and bore distinctive markings such as the year stamp 1314 to correspond with the Muslim calendar.

Chapter 2

World War I: Eastern Front, Italy and the Balkans

The Great War had begun in the Balkans with the assassination of Archduke Franz Ferdinand at Sarajevo. Subsequently, the web of alliances and treaties negotiated for mutual protection, military support and potential territorial expansion triggered a trail of mobilizations and declarations of war. The global nature of World War I became readily apparent as nations fought on three major fronts – in the east, west, and south of Europe – as well as in the Middle East, equatorial Africa and across the oceans of the world. The vastness of Russia and its seemingly endless supply of manpower loomed in the East, compelling the Central Powers to weaken their troop strength elsewhere as the prospects for a war of attrition taxed German resources beyond capacity.

◀ Trench warfare
Russian troops eat during a respite in the fighting, sometime during a spring thaw. Their Mosin-Nagant rifles are left resting on the trench lip, ready to be fired if their position is attacked.

Introduction

Military, political and ideological confrontation fuelled World War I in the East as the Central Powers, particularly Germany, found themselves fighting a costly war on multiple battlefields from the wide expanse of the steppes to the rugged Carpathian mountains.

THE GREAT WAR on the Eastern Front was played out in territory stretching from the Baltic Sea in the north to the Black Sea in the south, roughly 1600km (1000 miles). Because the forces of the various belligerents were thinly stretched at times, the stagnation of trench warfare did not develop as in the West. Although large numbers of soldiers were deployed by the warring nations, concentrations of troop strength were often difficult or impossible to accomplish from a logistical standpoint; therefore, successful offensive actions resulting in a breakthrough of enemy lines might be accomplished, and subsequently halted not by enemy action but by severe strains on supply lines.

With the outbreak of hostilities, the German high command anticipated that its primary adversary would be France and accordingly deployed the majority of its military assets in the West. At the same time, the army of Imperial Russia was twice the size of the 10 divisions arrayed in the East by the Germans. The capacity of the Russians to conscript and mobilize additional forces was considerably greater than that of the Germans or their Austro-Hungarian allies. However, the discipline, military structure and relative availability of weapons and equipment equalized this imbalance in manpower to some degree.

Given the political climate throughout Europe and the burgeoning potential for hostilities, the German high command fully expected a war on at least two fronts, as France and Great Britain took up arms in the West and the Russians went to war in the East. In

▲ **Tannenberg campaign**

Carrying full packs and wearing their distinctive boiled-leather *Pickelhaube* helmets, German infantry climb a slope during the Tannenberg campaign.

▲ Power of the Revolution
Dressed in imperial uniforms, early Russian revolutionaries point their Mosin-Nagant rifles at some imagined enemy.

late 1905, German Army chief of staff General Alfred von Schlieffen (1833–1913) had introduced a war contingency plan that envisioned a rapid, sweeping attack against France while a defensive deployment on the Eastern Front was intended to hold the Russians at bay. Schlieffen reasoned that the swift defeat of France would make Britain and Russia reluctant to continue the war, resulting in an advantageous round of peace negotiations.

The Russians also considered the likelihood of war with Germany and neighbouring Austria-Hungary. The response was Plan 19 developed in 1910 by General Yuri Danilov (1866–1937), correctly anticipating that German attention would focus on France and advocating a Russian offensive into East Prussia with a strength of 19 corps grouped in four field armies. By 1912, Plan 19 was altered to deal more directly with the perceived threat from Austria-Hungary. The subsequent shuffle of troops effectively halved the number of Russian soldiers intended to fight in East Prussia and redirected

substantial forces to the front opposite the Austro-Hungarian Army.

The high standards of German firearms and equipment production were well known to the Russians, as was the strict regimen of military training and the efficiency of the conscription system that generated nearly 300,000 new recruits to the German Army annually. However, the armies of Austria-Hungary and Ottoman Turkey were forces with which to be reckoned. In 1914, the standing Turkish Army amounted to only 250,000; however, that number increased by more than half a million within months. For some time, German advisors had assisted the Turks with training, provided some arms, and helped to instil a measure of military order.

As in the West, the armies in the East relied on the bolt-action rifle and the availability of the machine gun. Weapons were developed within the national arsenals and private manufacturers of Germany, Austria-Hungary and Russia, while Italian-made weapons went into action on Italy's northern border.

Balkan Prelude
1914–15

Shots from a single pistol assassinated Austro-Hungarian royalty and plunged the world into the most costly military conflict in history to that time.

WHEN BOSNIAN SERB and Serbian nationalist Gavrilo Princip (1894–1918) assassinated Austro-Hungarian Archduke Franz Ferdinand (1863–1914) and his wife Sophie, Duchess of Hohenberg (1868–1914), in Sarajevo on 28 June 1914, the shots from his pistol literally changed the course of history and set in motion the horrific conflagration of World War I. Princip had chosen as his weapon the Browning FN Model 1910 blowback-operated semiautomatic pistol. By that time, Browning had already produced several successful designs for Colt and for the Belgian manufacturer Fabrique Nationale. However, when Colt decided to forego production of the Model 1910, Browning gravitated towards Europe and patented the weapon there. The pistol used by Princip held a seven-round detachable box magazine of 7.65mm (.301in) ammunition. A number of these weapons found their way into the hands of ultra-nationalists and terrorist elements in the Balkans, including the shadowy group known as the Black Hand, to which Princip had been reported sympathetic.

With the Austro-Hungarian declaration of war on Serbia, the major powers followed suit. Germany honoured its obligation to support Austria-Hungary, while Russia had guaranteed the sovereignty of Serbia. And so the dominoes fell into conflict. In 1914, the Serbian Army consisted of five divisions. This was rapidly doubled, and the strength of Serbian men under arms rose to 180,000. Many of these were armed with Russian weapons that had flowed to the Serbian state for more than 20 years.

Prominent among the shoulder arms used by the Serbian Army was the Berdan series of rifles developed by American inventor Hiram Berdan (1824–93) and produced in Russia from the late 1860s until 1891. The trapdoor-breechblock Berdan I and the single-shot bolt-action Berdan II were used extensively by the Russian military even after the arrival of the Mosin-Nagant rifle in the early twentieth century. The Berdan series was also in service with the armies of Finland and Bulgaria, and by 1914 more than 75,000 had been exported to Serbia. The early Berdan rifle fired a heavy 10.75mm (.42in) cartridge, and an accomplished soldier was capable of a rate of fire of six to eight rounds per minute.

Among the sidearms in service in the Balkans was the Montenegro revolver produced by the Austrian firm Gasser. Firing an 11.2mm (.44in) cartridge, the Montenegro was originally developed for the Austro-Hungarian cavalry around 1870, while the Smith & Wesson No. 2 was popularized as a private purchase handgun during the American Civil War. It fired an 8.1mm (.32in) cartridge.

▶ **Gasser Montenegro**

Austro-Hungarian Army / 41st Infantry Brigade, 1914

The star-shaped automatic ejector of the Montenegro assisted the ejection of spent cartridges by pushing them outwards when the barrel was tipped down for reloading.

Specifications

Country of Origin: Austria-Hungary	Overall Length: 185mm (7.28in)
Date: 1870	Barrel Length: 135mm (5.3in)
Calibre: 11.2mm (.44in)	Muzzle Velocity: 168m/sec (550ft/sec)
Operation: Revolver	Feed/Magazine: 5-round cylinder
Weight: 1.3kg (2.9lb)	Range: 20m (66ft)

▲ Berdan Rifle

Serbian Army / 2nd Timok Infantry Division, 1914

Large numbers of the extremely accurate Berdan rifle were produced in two variants for the Russian military prior to World War I and exported to friendly neighbouring countries.

Specifications

Country of Origin: United States/Russia	Overall Length: 1300mm (51.18in)
Date: 1869	Barrel Length: 830mm (32.67in)
Calibre: 10.75mm (.42in)	Muzzle Velocity: Not known
Operation: Berdan I: 'Trapdoor'; Berdan II: 'Bolt'	Feed/Magazine: Single shot, breech-loader
Weight: 4.2kg (9.25lb)	Range: 280m (919ft)

▶ Browning FN Model 1910

Gavrilo Princip, assassination of Archduke Ferdinand, June 1914

The Model 1910 was notable for an innovative spring location around the barrel and its triple safety feature, with an external safety flipper plus safeties at the grip and magazine. The spring design served as a basis for future famous pistols such as the German Walther PPK.

Specifications

Country of Origin: Belgium	Overall Length: 154mm (6in)
Date: 1910	Barrel Length: 88.5mm (3.5in)
Calibre: 7.65mm (.301in), 9mm (.35in)	Muzzle Velocity: 299m/sec (981ft/sec)
Operation: Blowback	Feed/Magazine: 7-round magazine
Weight: .57kg (1.25lb)	Range: 30m (98ft)

▼ Road march

Bayonets fixed, Serbian troops march to their camp near Mikra, April 1916. Following the Austro-Hungarian-led invasion of 1914, Britain and France set about re-equipping the Serbian Army from 1915.

War in Russia
1914–17

War with the Central Powers and civil unrest within combined to doom the Czarist regime in Russia after the nation had suffered nearly seven million killed, wounded or taken prisoner.

THE WIDENING CLASS DISTINCTION among the people of Imperial Russia had sparked violence in the streets of major cities from time to time since the turn of the century, while ethnic diversity and latent nationalism simmered beneath the surface of the mammoth Eastern European nation, destabilizing the monarchy of Czar Nicholas II (1868–1918). As the Czar and his ministers sought to maintain strong ties with Serbia in the restive Balkans and solidify their relations with France in the event of hostilities with Germany, Russia also was intent on expanding its influence with the smaller nations of Eastern Europe, particularly the Baltic states of Lithuania, Estonia and Latvia and the Scandinavian territory of Finland.

To the south, the Russians had long nurtured designs on a warm-water port. Victory over the Central Powers, including Ottoman Turkey, might pave the way for control of the Bosporus and the Dardanelles, which controlled marine transport from the Black Sea to the Mediterranean.

The Great Bear

With the outbreak of World War I, Grand Duke Nicholas (1856–1929), cousin of the Czar, was named initial commander of all Russian forces in the field. Russian troop strength was estimated at slightly more than 1.4 million soldiers; however, with mobilization the ranks were expected to swell to near five million. In reality, a series of legal modifications, exemptions and administrative missteps resulted in the pace of conscription and mobilization slowing appreciably. Although its population greatly outnumbered that of Germany, Russia's effort to augment its armed forces was only slightly more productive in raw numbers.

A diversity of ethnic backgrounds, harbouring centuries-old rivalries and hatreds among certain groups, posed a challenge to forming a cohesive Russian Army, while the majority of Russian soldiers were of peasant stock and had little, if any, formal education. Literate soldiers were often sent to the artillery or to occupy staff positions, while the officer corps was seriously deficient in junior and senior level commanders.

Although senior Russian military officers were familiar with the advancing technology of the day and Russian weapons manufacturers had demonstrated the capabilities of producing modern small arms, the country's industrial establishment had not successfully implemented a programme of

▲ **Mosin-Nagant Model 1891**

Imperial Russian Army / 5th Rifle Brigade, 1915

Both Belgian and Russian designers contributed to the Mosin-Nagant, and this sturdy rifle equipped Russian infantry units for many years. An estimated 37 million were eventually produced.

Specifications

Country of Origin: Russia	Overall Length: 1305mm (51.4in)
Date: 1891	Barrel Length: 802mm (31.6in)
Calibre: 7.62mm (.3in)	Muzzle Velocity: 810m/sec (2657ft/sec)
Operation: Bolt action	Feed/Magazine: 5-round box magazine
Weight: 4.37kg (9.625lb)	Range: 500m (1640ft)

production to keep pace with that of its potential adversaries. Further, the military had allowed the implementation of advanced weapons to drift to a great extent.

As a result, in 1914 the Russian Army could field only a single machine gun per infantry battalion, and the total number of such weapons deployed with Russian troops was just over 4000. Artillery production and maintenance were woefully deficient, with only one factory manufacturing field guns and only a handful of others capable of keeping them battleworthy. Only two-thirds of the estimated rifles needed to equip the mobilized army could be procured, leaving the fighting forces short at least 400,000 shoulder arms. During the war, the production of rifles rose from about 70,000 per month in 1915 to more than 110,000 per month the

following year. However, the estimated need of 200,000 per month was never realized.

Plan 19 and disaster at Tannenberg

In August 1914, General Alexander Samsonov (1859–1914) set the Russian Second Army in motion, implementing the altered Plan 19 for the invasion of East Prussia that had been adopted two years earlier. Samsonov advanced eastwards at a snail's pace, and the initial plan of linking up with another Russian army coming from the north under General Paul von Rennenkampf (1854–1918) was thwarted by rapid German movement. By the end of the month, Samsonov had been surrounded at Tannenberg.

Attempts to relieve the Second Army were bungled or intentionally undermined by Samsonov's rivals in the Russian command structure. Nearly 100,000

▶ **Nagant M1895**

Imperial Russian Army / 3rd Cavalry Division, 1914

A formidable sidearm, the Nagant M1895 revolver featured a cylinder that moved forward when the weapon was cocked, creating a tighter gas seal and higher muzzle velocity.

Specifications

Country of Origin: Russia	Overall Length: 229mm (9in)
Date: 1895	Barrel Length: 110mm (4.33in)
Calibre: 7.62mm (.3in)	Muzzle Velocity: 178m/sec (584ft/sec)
Operation: Revolver	Feed/Magazine: 7-round cylinder
Weight: .79kg (1.75lb)	Range: 20m (66ft)

▲ **Madsen Let Maschingevaer**

Imperial Russian Army / 3rd Guards Infantry Division, 1915

The Danish Madsen was the world's first true light machine gun. It was infantry-portable, adopted by the Danish Army in 1902, and deployed by Russian forces during World War I.

Specifications

Country of Origin: Denmark	Barrel Length: 585mm (23in)
Date: 1897	Muzzle Velocity: 715m/sec (2350ft/sec)
Calibre: 8mm (.314in) M89	Feed/Magazine: 25-, 30- or 40-round box
Operation: Recoil, air cooled	magazine
Weight: 9kg (20lb)	Cyclic Rate: 450rpm
Overall Length: 1145mm (45in)	Range: 1000m (3280ft)

Russian troops were captured and 30,000 killed. Samsonov committed suicide, and the Battle of Tannenberg is remembered as one of the greatest victories in German military history. German commanders Paul von Hindenburg (1847–1934) and Erich Ludendorff (1865–1937) were hailed as national heroes.

Soon, a German thrust towards Warsaw in the winter of 1914 was stopped at Lodz by the Russians, who suffered 120,000 casualties in the process and were forced to abandon an offensive action in Silesia. Russian losses continued to mount, compounding the difficulties of conscription and replenishing their rapidly depleting ranks. By the end of 1915, it was estimated that the Russian Army had lost two million men killed, wounded or captured within the previous six months.

On the Austro-Hungarian front, Russian troops made early gains during an offensive into Galicia. An Austro-Hungarian counterattack threw the Russians back, but the Autro-Hungarian forces were, in turn, compelled to retreat to the foothills of the Carpathian mountains. By the autumn of 1915, the Russians had been completely ejected from Galicia.

Red regime rising

The Germans considered the potential for the success of future offensive actions in the East to be limited, and for much of 1916 the fighting on the Eastern Front was inconclusive. The Russian Kerenski Offensive launched in the summer of 1917 ended in failure. Even though the Russians had absorbed horrendous losses and conscription riots had erupted in major cities, their vast manpower resource presented an obstacle that senior German commanders believed insurmountable in terms of achieving absolute and total victory. Therefore, greater numbers of German troops were concentrated in the West, while a campaign to foment continuing civil unrest in Russia was emphasized.

The German government facilitated the return of Bolshevik leader Vladimir Lenin (1870–1924) to Russia from exile, and by the autumn of 1917 the October Revolution had brought the Communists to power in Russia. The Treaty of Brest-Litovsk was concluded in the spring of 1918 and effectively ended Russian participation in World War I. Although they had won a victory in the East, the Central Powers sustained a high number of casualties in more than

▲ **Pulemot Maksima Obrazets 1910**

Imperial Russian Army / 4th Infantry Division, 1916

Licensed and built as a copy of the Maxim Gun, the PM M1910 was of simpler overall design. It was mounted on a cumbersome carriage rather than a tripod.

Specifications

Country of Origin: Russia	Barrel Length: 720mm (28.35in)
Date: 1910	Muzzle Velocity: 863m/sec (2831ft/sec)
Calibre: 7.62mm (.3in)	Feed/Magazine: Belt fed
Operation: Recoil, water cooled	Cyclic Rate: 520–600rpm
Weight: 23.8kg (52.47lb)	Range: Not known
Overall Length: 1107mm (43.6in)	

three years of fighting. German losses alone are estimated at 1.4 million.

Eastern armaments

Those Russian-manufactured arms that reached their troops at the front were generally of good quality although never available in adequate numbers. Among the most prevalent rifles in the Russian ranks was the Mosin-Nagant bolt-action Model 1891, designed by Russian Army officer Sergei Mosin (1849–1902) and Belgian arms manufacturer Léon Nagant (1833–1900). The weapon was initially produced in Belgium and later adopted by the Russian military and built at locations in Russia as well as the United States.

▲ **Red columns**

A unit of revolutionary soldiers marches, Mosin-Nagant rifles shouldered and bayonets fixed. Most are wearing Russian Army uniform, and many of the combatants of the revolution and ensuing civil war were former Imperial soldiers.

The 7.62mm (.3in) bolt-action Mosin-Nagant rifle was fed by a five-round box magazine, and the weapon proved to be robust under the harsh conditions often encountered on the Eastern Front. Improvements to the rifle were made during the 1930s, including the introduction of a feed mechanism, greatly decreasing incidences of failure in combat. As production reached sufficient levels, the Mosin-Nagant was widely distributed to Russian Army units, and by the Russo-Japanese War of

▶ **Mauser Zig-Zag**

German Army / 43rd Infantry Regiment, 1915

The innovative series of external grooves that moved the cylinder of the Mauser Zig-Zag was a departure from the more traditional pawl-and-ratchet system.

Specifications

Country of Origin: Germany	Overall Length: 298mm (11.75in)
Date: 1878	Barrel Length: 165mm (6.5in)
Calibre: 10.9mm (.42in)	Muzzle Velocity: 198m/sec (650ft/sec)
Operation: Revolver	Feed/Magazine: 6-round cylinder
Weight: 1.19kg (2.625lb)	Range: 20m (66ft)

1904–05 nearly four million had been delivered. During World War I, the Russian government ordered an additional 3.2 million rifles from the American firms of Remington and Westinghouse. The Bolshevik Revolution, however, halted these deliveries. Variants of the Mosin-Nagant were in service with the Russian and Soviet armies for decades, and when production ceased in 1965 an estimated 37 million had been made.

The Russian variant of the often-imitated Maxim Gun was the Pulemot Maksima Obrazets 1910, more often referred to as the PM M1910. Adapted by the Russians to fire their 7.62mm (.3in) cartridge, this heavy machine gun was fed by a 250-round belt. Unlike the versions deployed by other nations, the Russian PM M1910 was mounted on a two-wheeled Sokolov carriage rather than a tripod, adding to its 23.8kg (52.47lb) weight and making the gun difficult to transport in some conditions. The Russians also added a gun shield which increased the weapon's unwieldy character. Regardless of its shortcomings, the PM M1910 proved durable and served with the Imperial Russian Army and later the Red Army through to the end of World War II.

▲ Maxim Maschinengewehr 08/15 'light'
German Air Force / Jagdstaffel 11, 1917

The MG 08/15 'light' was an air-cooled version of the original MG 08 intended for use aboard aircraft. About 23,000 were manufactured during World War I.

Specifications

Country of Origin: Germany	Barrel Length: 719mm (28.33in)
Date: 1915	Muzzle Velocity: 900m/sec (2953ft/sec)
Calibre: 7.92mm (.312in) Mauser	Feed/Magazine: 50-, 100- or 250-round fabric
Operation: Short recoil	belt
Weight: 18kg (39.75lb)	Cyclic Rate: 450rpm
Overall Length: 1398mm (55in)	Range: 1500m (4921ft)

▲ Parabellum Maschinengewehr Model 14
German Air Force / Jagdstaffel 16, 1917

The Parabellum Model 14 was specially adapted for use with aircraft. An air-cooled version was mounted to fixed-wing planes, while a water-cooled version was placed aboard Zeppelins. In 1918 a ground-mounted variant was introduced.

Specifications

Country of Origin: Germany	Barrel Length: 705mm (27.75in)
Date: 1914	Muzzle Velocity: 890m/sec (2925ft/sec)
Calibre: 7.92mm (.312in) Mauser	Feed/Magazine: Belt fed (belt contained in drum)
Operation: Recoil, water or air cooled	Cyclic Rate: 650–750rpm
Weight: 9.8kg (21.5lb)	Range: 2000m (6560ft) +
Overall Length: 1225mm (48.25in)	

Specifications

Country of Origin: Germany

Date: 1915

Calibre: 7.92mm (.312in) Mauser

Operation: Short recoil, water cooled

Weight: 18kg (40lb)

Overall Length: 1398mm (55in)

Barrel Length: 719mm (28.33in)

Muzzle Velocity: 900m/sec (2953ft/sec)

Feed/Magazine: 250-round box

Cyclic Rate: 450rpm

Range: 3500m (11,483ft)

▲ **Maxim Maschinengewehr 08/15**

German Army / 4th Infantry Brigade, 1916

As the need for mobile fire support for infantry was realized, it became apparent that heavy machine guns were better suited to defensive roles. In response, the lighter MG 08/15 was adapted from the original MG 08 design and proved effective as a portable automatic weapon.

Austro-Hungarian Army
1914–18

The monarchy of Austria-Hungary had long considered Slavic Serbia a threat to its hold on the population within its borders, and the assassination of the heir to the nation's throne presented an immediate *casus belli*.

THE STANDING PEACETIME ARMY of Austria-Hungary numbered about 500,000 men, and by the summer of 1914 it had expanded to about one million. Plans to rapidly increase its numbers to 1.5 million and eventually to more than 3.3 million were formulated. Although the average number of conscripts prior to the war had numbered a respectable 160,000, the troops who wore the uniform were potentially problematic in themselves. The ethnic diversity within Austria-Hungary had long been an issue for the government, and fully 60 per cent of its people were of varied Slavic ancestry. Ardent nationalism among these ethnic peoples within the borders of Austria-Hungary was fuelled by the Slavic Serbs; therefore, the reliability of some troops was always suspect.

The Austro-Hungarian military establishment considered neighbouring Serbia a nuisance and anticipated a campaign that would be easily won despite a lack of military spending and relatively little modernization of weaponry in the years preceding World War I. Confident that their German allies would provide the needed support to win a decisive victory over the Serbs, the Austro-Hungarians embarked on a belligerent course for which they were significantly underprepared.

With the outbreak of hostilities, the Austro-Hungarian Army fielded more than 100 infantry regiments. Each infantry company included four platoons and a complement of 267 soldiers, five of them officers. As was the case with their Russian enemies, machine guns were relatively scarce. Therefore, machine-gun detachments were organized at the battalion level and fielded only a pair of the adequately serviceable Schwarzelose M07.

The shortcomings within the Austro-Hungarian Army became starkly apparent in 1914 with the decisive defeat at the Battle of Cer Mountain only weeks after the assassination of Archduke Franz Ferdinand. During three days of fighting, well-placed

◀ Frommer Model 1910

Austro-Hungarian Army / 11th Infantry Regiment, 1914

The Frommer Model 1910 pistol was characterized by a long recoil that extended beyond the length of the cartridge it fired. An improved model, the Frommer Stop, was introduced in 1912.

Specifications

Country of Origin: Austria-Hungary	Overall Length: 184mm (7.25in)
Date: 1910	Barrel Length: 108mm (4.25in)
Calibre: 7.65mm (.301in)	Muzzle Velocity: 335m/sec (1100ft/sec)
Operation: Blowback	Feed/Magazine: 7-round magazine
Weight: .59kg (1.3lb)	Range: 20m (66ft)

◀ Schönberger

Austro-Hungarian Army / 24th Infantry Regiment, 1915

The Schönberger was the first semiautomatic sidearm to enter commercial production. Based on its predecessor, the Laumann 1892, it was a failure with the civilian market.

Specifications

Country of Origin: Germany	Overall Length: Not known
Date: 1892	Barrel Length: Not known
Calibre: 8mm (.314in)	Muzzle Velocity: 300m/sec (1200ft/sec)
Operation: Recoil	Feed/Magazine: 5-round fixed magazine
Weight: Not known	Range: 30m (98ft)

▲ Steyr-Mannlicher M1895

Austro-Hungarian Army / 90th Infantry Brigade, 1916

The standard issue rifle of the Austro-Hungarian Army during World War I, the Steyr-Mannlicher M1895 featured a straight-pull bolt action. It remained in service for decades after the war ended.

Specifications

Country of Origin: Austria-Hungary	Overall Length: 1272mm (50.12in)
Date: 1895	Barrel Length: 765mm (30.14in)
Calibre: 8mm (.314in)	Muzzel Velocity: Not known
Operation: Straight-pull bolt action	Feed/Magazine: 5-round en-bloc clip, internal
Weight: 3.8kg (8.36lb)	box magazine
	Range: 500m (1640ft)

Serbian artillery and infantry units rained shells and small-arms fire on the Austro-Hungarian forces inflicting 23,000 casualties, including 18,500 killed and wounded.

Nevertheless, the Austro-Hungarian Army was instrumental in maintaining a counterbalance to the overwhelming manpower of the Russians on the Eastern Front, although on repeated occasions its commanders were compelled to call upon the Germans for military assistance. Although they were initially pushed back by the Russian offensive in Galicia in 1914, the Austro-Hungarians rallied to drive the enemy back and held the line at the Carpathians.

The primary shoulder arm of the Austro-Hungarian Army in World War I was the Steyr-Mannlicher M1895 straight-pull bolt-action rifle. The Steyr-Mannlicher performed admirably during the war and facilitated a higher rate of fire (up to an astonishing 35 rounds per minute) than other contemporary rifles due to the fact that the rifleman was not required to turn the bolt during the reloading process. However, the bolt was a challenge to pull back and offered more resistance to its basic manipulation than other models.

Fed via an internal box magazine by a five-round en-bloc clip which was updated to a stripper clip in subsequent variants, the Steyr-Mannlicher fired an 8mm (.314in) cartridge. The rifle was produced from 1895 to 1918, and more than three million were manufactured. It remained in service with the armed forces of numerous countries through to the end of World War II and has since been discovered in the hands of paramilitary and guerrilla fighters around the globe.

Designed by Ferdinand Ritter von Mannlicher (1848–1904), the straight-pull bolt-action of the rifle

◀ Steyr M1911/1912

Austro-Hungarian Army / 1st Tyrolean Kaiserjäger Regiment, 1915

The M1911 and M1912 Steyr pistols were of Austrian design and differed only in the enhanced front sight on the later model. The Austro-Hungarian Army issued the weapon at the outbreak of the war, and some were converted to automatic capability.

Specifications

Country of Origin: Austria-Hungary	Overall Length: 216mm (8.5in)
Date: 1911	Barrel Length: 128mm (5.1in)
Calibre: 9mm (.35in)	Muzzle Velocity: 340m/sec (1115ft/sec)
Operation: Short recoil	Feed/Magazine: 8-round magazine
Weight: 1.02kg (2.25lb)	Range: 30m (98ft)

◀ Roth-Steyr M1907

Austro-Hungarian Army / 2nd Cavalry Division, 1916

The first semiautomatic sidearm to be adopted by the military of a major power, the Roth-Steyr 1907 was initially issued to cavalry units. It fired a cartridge unique to the weapon.

Specifications

Country of Origin: Austria-Hungary	Overall Length: 233mm (9in)
Date: 1907	Barrel Length: 131mm (5in)
Calibre: 8mm (.314in)	Muzzle Velocity: 332m/sec (1089ft/sec)
Operation: Short recoil	Feed/Magazine: 10-round magazine
Weight: 1.03kg (2.25lb)	Range: 30m (98ft)

earned it the nickname Ruck-Zuck from the soldiers who carried it. Although the rate of fire achieved with the straight pull was an advantage, improving the overall sturdy performance of the weapon, it also created issues with maintenance and demanded regular cleaning since there was little to assist the bolt action itself in the ejection of the spent cartridge.

The Steyr-Mannlicher was purchased by the Bulgarian government in 1903 and equipped the majority of that nation's infantry units during World War I. The weapon's straight-pull bolt further served as a model for the Canadian Ross rifle, which proved to be a bitter disappointment.

The Roth-Steyr M1907 pistol holds the distinction of being the first semiautomatic pistol adopted for regular use by the army of a major world military power. Czech designer Karel Krnka (1858–1926) developed the pistol, which was manufactured from 1908 to 1914 and acquired by the Austro-Hungarian military. It entered service in 1909, and nearly 100,000 were produced at the Steyr-Mannlicher works in Steyr, Austria, and at the Fegyvergyar factory near Budapest, Hungary.

Issued primarily as a cavalry weapon prior to World War I, the Roth-Steyr M1907 fired an 8mm (.314in) cartridge that was unique to this weapon.

The pistol's distinctive locked breech and long bolt facilitate the recoil of the barrel and bolt together through the hollow receiver. The 10-round magazine is fixed and cannot be detached.

Following the break-up of Austria-Hungary after World War I, the Roth-Steyr M1907 remained in service with the armies of both Austria and Hungary, as well as Yugoslavia, Italy, Czechoslovakia and Poland. About 54,000 were originally issued to military units, while the remainder were purchased by civilians.

Another long-serving pistol that was adopted by the Austro-Hungarian Army was the Steyr M1917 blowback 9mm (.35in) pistol. The M1917 was developed from the earlier M1912, which, in turn, traced its roots to the M1907.

Also commonly known as the Steyr Hahn, or Steyr Hammer, the M1912 was produced for the Austro-Hungarian military and remained in service with various armies until the end of World War II. Its eight-round magazine was fixed and loaded from above with a stripper clip. The pistol proved a sturdy sidearm that stood up to harsh treatment with little maintenance. Its reputation for reliability was borne out in the varied and rugged conditions that were prevalent on the Eastern Front in World War I. In response to a shortage of sidearms in the Austro-Hungarian Army, production of the M1912 and later the M1917 were increased substantially during the

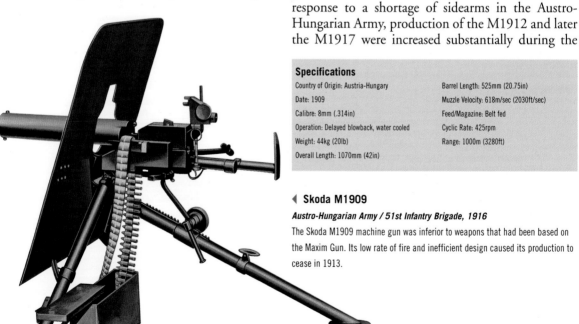

Specifications

Country of Origin: Austria-Hungary	Barrel Length: 525mm (20.75in)
Date: 1909	Muzzle Velocity: 618m/sec (2030ft/sec)
Calibre: 8mm (.314in)	Feed/Magazine: Belt fed
Operation: Delayed blowback, water cooled	Cyclic Rate: 425rpm
Weight: 44kg (20lb)	Range: 1000m (3280ft)
Overall Length: 1070mm (42in)	

◄ **Skoda M1909**

Austro-Hungarian Army / 51st Infantry Brigade, 1916

The Skoda M1909 machine gun was inferior to weapons that had been based on the Maxim Gun. Its low rate of fire and inefficient design caused its production to cease in 1913.

Great War, and more than 300,000 were manufactured before production ended in 1945.

The Frommer Model 1910 was a blowback, 7.65mm (.301in) semiautomatic pistol that utilized a long recoil of the barrel and bolt, exceeding the entire length of the cartridge. The cartridge itself was fashioned specifically for the Model 1910 with a crimp in the casing of the round. The pistol held a seven-round magazine and was effective to a range of

20m (66ft). Designer Rudolf Frommer (1868–1936) incorporated a short-recoil system into later models; however, in the years preceding World War I the long recoil was a hallmark of his handguns. In 1912, the Frommer Stop was introduced and offered a more traditional configuration in an updated version of the Model 1910. The Frommer Stop survived World War I as the standard issue sidearm of the Hungarian armed forces.

▶ **Steyr M1917**

Austro-Hungrian Army / 26th Infantry Brigade, 1917

Reloaded from the top using a charger, the Steyr M1917 semiautomatic pistol was an upgrade of the M1912 and remained in service with the Austrian and Hungarian armies through to the end of World War II.

Specifications

Country of Origin: Austria-Hungary	Overall Length: 216mm (8.5in)
Date: 1917	Barrel Length: 128mm (5.03in)
Calibre: 9mm (.35in)	Muzzle Velocity: 335m/sec (1100ft/sec)
Operation: Blowback	Feed/Magazine: 8-round fixed magazine
Weight: .99kg (2.18lb)	Range: 30m (98ft)

Specifications

Country of Origin: Austria-Hungary	Barrel Length: 525mm (20.75in)
Date: 1907	Muzzle Velocity: 618m/sec (2030ft/sec)
Calibre: 8mm (.314in)	Feed/Magazine: Belt fed
Operation: Blowback, water cooled	Cyclic Rate: 425rpm
Weight: 20kg (44lb)	Range: 1000m (3280ft) +
Overall Length: 1070mm (42in)	

▲ **Schwarzlose M07/12**

Austro-Hungarian Army / 88th Infantry Brigade, 1917

Though produced in four variants, the delayed-blowback operation of the Schwarzlose caused it to utilize a short barrel, which limited the range of the weapon and shortened its service life compared with other machine guns.

Austrian machine guns

The Austro-Hungarian Army deployed the water-cooled, 8mm (.314in) Schwarzlose M07/12 medium machine gun during World War I and exported the weapon to the armed forces of The Netherlands, Greece and Sweden as well. The Schwarzlose operated with a toggle-delayed blowback mechanism and was fed by a 250-round ammunition belt. Mounted on a tripod and served by a crew of three, it was initially capable of a cyclic rate of fire of 400 rounds per minute; however, this was later increased to 580 rounds with the addition of a more efficient spring. The weapon remained in service beyond the end of World War II, equipping the Czech Army during the early Cold War period.

Like its contemporaries, the Schwarzlose M07/12 had a design based on the Maxim Gun, but the weapon was of overall simpler construction. As an infantry weapon it may be deemed a success. However, in contrast to other medium machine guns, conversions to anti-aircraft or heavier support roles were disappointing.

Prior to Czech independence from Austria-Hungary in 1918, the famed arms works of Skoda in the city of Plzen produced weapons for the monarchy's armed forces. The M1909 machine gun was manufactured by Skoda from 1909 to 1913 and operated with a delayed blowback mechanism. The weapon was water-cooled and fired an 8mm (.314in) cartridge. It was fed by a 250-round belt, and later versions achieved an improved rate of fire above the initial 250 rounds per minute. Nevertheless, the M1909's overall performance was rated inferior to Maxim-inspired designs.

▲ **Defensive line**
Austrian troops set up a temporary defensive line with machine-gun pits and a shallow trench somewhere in the Caporetto area.

Italian Army
1915–18

Longstanding rivalry with Austria-Hungary pushed Italy towards the Allies and a protracted war of attrition along the nation's rugged mountainous border regions.

WHEN WAR BROKE OUT IN EUROPE IN 1914, Italy was not yet prepared to commit to either the Allies or the Central Powers. A relatively new nation in itself, a united Italy had emerged from the jumble of city states and minor monarchies a little over 50 years earlier. From a military standpoint, the Italian Army had embarked on an ill-fated venture into Ethiopia in 1896 and fought a costly war against Turkey for control of Libya in 1911–12.

Following the Italian declaration of war against the Central Powers, initially Austria-Hungary, in 1915, it was apparent to the country's military establishment that the army was not yet ready for combat. Its complement of just under a million men was raised considerably by spring 1915 when active operations began. However, the 35 divisions at the disposal of General Luigi Cadorna (1850–1928), the army chief of staff and overall commander, were woefully short

▲ **Moschetto 1891 per Cavalleria**

Italian Army / 8th Cavalry Regiment, 1915

A shortened stock facilitated use of this carbine by Italian cavalry units during World War I. The weapon was noted for its folding bayonet that was permanently fixed and could be deployed when the trooper dismounted.

Specifications

Country of Origin: Italy	Overall Length: 920mm (36.2in)
Date: 1891	Barrel Length: 610mm (24in)
Calibre: 6.5mm (.256in)	Muzzle Velocity: 700m/sec (2275ft/sec)
Operation: Bolt action	Feed/Magazine: 6-round integral box magazine
Weight: 3kg (6.6lb)	Range: 600m (1968ft)

Specifications

Country of Origin: Italy	Overall Length: 1291mm (50.79in)
Date: 1891	Barrel Length: 780mm (30.6in)
Calibre: 6.5mm (.256in)	Muzzle Velocity: 730m/sec (2400ft/sec)
Operation: Bolt action	Feed/Magazine: 6-round integral box magazine
Weight: 3.8kg (8.375lb)	Range: 1000m (3280ft)

▲ **Mannlicher Carcano Model 1891**

Italian Army / 37th Infantry Division, 1915

The primary rifle of the Italian infantry until it was modified in 1938, the Model 1891 fired a 6.5mm (.256in) cartridge. The Mannlicher Carcano name is somewhat misleading due to limited Austrian design influence.

of ammunition, machine guns and artillery as Italian arms manufacturers lacked the capacity to keep pace with demand.

Along a 644km (400-mile) line in the north of the country, Cadorna divided the front into three departments, the Isonzo, Alpine and Trentino. The bloodiest fighting was to take place along the Isonzo where some areas of hilly terrain provided space for troop manoeuvring but at length would expose an advancing army to killing fire from enemy-occupied higher ground.

Opposing the 35 Italian divisions across the frontier were 20 Austro-Hungarian divisions, and Cadorna assumed the offensive in the region in May 1915, nearly 10 months after the war had begun elsewhere. Throughout the summer and into 1916, the Italians repeatedly threw themselves against strong Austro-Hungarian defences along the Isonzo line, losing 60,000 soldiers in the first two weeks alone. Numerical superiority was of little advantage, and Italian casualties were horrific, often numbering more than 30,000 dead, wounded or taken prisoner in a single attack. Little ground was gained, and the landscape of trenches resembled that of the Western Front in France, although the hazardous terrain compounded the logistical difficulties faced by both sides on the Italian front.

Catastrophe at Caporetto

After 11 costly but indecisive battles on the Isonzo, the German high command at last responded to Austro-Hungarian appeals for reinforcements, allowing a combined army of the Central Powers to assume the offensive. On 24 October 1916, the 12th Battle of the Isonzo, perhaps better known as Caporetto, was launched with a tremendous German and Austro-Hungarian artillery bombardment followed by a devastating gas attack. The attackers realized early success, spurred by the rapid movement of their infiltrating stormtrooper formations.

The battle ended in disaster for the Italians, who were driven back great distances and finally made a stand a scant few kilometres from the great city of Venice. They had more than 10,000 dead and 300,000 wounded or captured, and losses in weapons and equipment were staggering as well. Britain, France and later the United States committed reinforcements to stabilize the front, and a wave of conscripts and recruits replenished the depleted Italian ranks. War-weary Austro-Hungarian troops essentially ceased offensive operations through 1917 while the Italians marshalled their forces.

Barely two weeks before the armistice of 11 November 1918, the Italians attacked, capturing the town of Vittorio Veneto as a demoralized Austro-Hungarian enemy fled or surrendered in large numbers and their government collapsed. From 1915 to 1918, Italy deployed just over five million troops and suffered 420,000 dead and more than 950,000 wounded.

Italian small arms

Italian infantry units in World War I were regularly armed with the Mannlicher Carcano Model 1891 bolt-action rifle, which incorporated elements of both the German Mauser and the Austrian

◀ **Glisenti Model 1910**

Italian Army / 54th Infantry Regiment, 1915

Although somewhat underpowered, the Glisenti Model 1910 was nevertheless adopted by the Italian Army. Its low muzzle velocity hampered performance during close combat; however, the handgun was common with Italian forces into World War II.

Specifications

Country of Origin: Italy	Overall Length: 210mm (8.25in)
Date: 1910	Barrel Length: 99mm (3.9in)
Calibre: 9mm (.35in)	Muzzle Velocity: 305m/sec (1000ft/sec)
Operation: Short recoil, locked breech	Feed/Magazine: 7-round magazine
Weight: .82kg (1.8lb)	Range: 20m (66ft)

Mannlicher shoulder arms. Engineer Salvatore Carcano (1827–1903) developed the rifle and chambered it for the 6.5mm (.256in) rimless cartridge fed by en-bloc charger clips into a six-round box magazine. The rifle is more properly identified as the Model 91, and the only real link to Mannlicher designs lies in the ammunition clip and feed system.

Production of the weapon in long rifle and carbine versions was undertaken at Turin, and it was adopted by the Italian Army in 1891. The carbine was issued primarily to cavalry and specialized units such as alpine troops. A half-stocked cavalry carbine known as the Moschetto 1891 per Cavalleria was produced by several manufacturers, including FNA Brescia,

Specifications

Country of Origin: Italy	Barrel Length: 320mm (12.6in)
Date: 1915	Muzzle Velocity: 320m/sec (1050ft/sec)
Calibre: 9mm (.35in)	Feed/Magazine: Box magazine
Operation: Blowback	Cyclic Rate: 350rpm
Weight: 6.5kg (14.33lb)	Range: 2000m (6560ft) +
Overall Length: 558.8mm (21in)	

▼ Villar-Perosa M1915

Italian Army / 8th Alpini Regiment, 1916

The world's first submachine gun, the Model 1915 provided a substantial rate of fire, but its use was inhibited by the need for a bipod or a platform slung across a soldier's shoulders.

▼ Villar-Perosa OVP M1918

Italian Army / 6th Alpini Regiment, 1917

Essentially a half-size version of the Model 1915 submachine gun, the Model 1918 was capable of automatic or single-shot modes, employed a rifle stock and was primarily issued to alpine troops to provide mobile fire support.

Specifications

Country of Origin: Italy	Barrel Length: Not known
Date: 1915	Muzzle Velocity: 301.82m/sec (990ft/sec)
Calibre: 9mm (.35in)	Feed/Magazine: 25-round detachable box
Operation: Blowback	magazine
Weight: 3.62kg (8lb)	Range: 70m (230ft)
Overall Length: 901.69mm (35.5in)	

and featured a folding bayonet permanently fixed to a muzzle mounting and hinged for storage backwards in a slot beneath the stock.

The Model 91 operated with a rotating bolt action and produced an adequate rate of fire, which was enhanced due to the fact that its clip was open and could be loaded from either end. The original rifle was standard issue with the Italian Army until 1938 when it was rechambered to fire the heavier 7.35mm (.29in) cartridge. It was produced until 1945, and thousands were sold as surplus, one of which gained infamy as the weapon used by assassin Lee Harvey Oswald (1939–1963) to kill US president John F. Kennedy (1917–1963).

The 9mm (.35in) Glisenti Model 1910 short-

▲ Hidden emplacement

Italian troops man a machine-gun emplacement protected by sandbags. They are firing through a small loophole and much care has been taken to conceal their position.

▼ Fiat-Revelli Modello 14

Italian Army / 3rd Bersaglieri Regiment, 1917

Prone to jamming, the Modello 14 was difficult to fire and proved unpopular with Italian troops. Its loading system was cumbersome and performed poorly in combat.

Specifications

Country of Origin: Italy

Date: 1914

Calibre: 6.5mm (.256in) M95

Operation: Delayed blowback, water cooled

Weight: 17kg (37.75lb)

Overall Length: 1180mm (46.5in)

Barrel Length: 655mm (25.75in)

Muzzle Velocity: 640m/sec (2100ft/sec)

Feed/Magazine: Magazine fed

Cyclic Rate: 400rpm

Range: 1500m (4921ft)

recoil pistol was common among Italian troops during World War I. The semiautomatic locked-breech handgun was fed by a seven-round detachable box magazine and was effective to a range of 20m (66ft). Produced by Real Factory D'arma Glisenti, the weapon was adopted in 1910 and served with Italian forces through World War II. Although it was intended to fire a unique cartridge, it could operate with the 9mm (.35in) Parabellum with substantial recoil that was difficult to manage and even dangerous.

Automatic weapons

Two Italian automatic weapons, the Villar-Perosa M1915 and OVP M1918 could be described as variants of the first deployed submachine gun. The M1915 was originally designed to provide mobile fire support for alpine troops. Its double barrel provided a substantial rate of fire, but the weapon was highly inaccurate. Although it was mobile, it was somewhat unwieldy and was fired from a bipod or a platform worn over the shoulders of the soldier in 'cigarette girl' fashion. The single-barrelled OVP M1918 utilized a rifle stock and was basically a 'half-version' of the M1915.

Italian machine-gun development lagged behind that of other belligerents prior to World War I, and two types, the Fiat-Revelli Modello 14 and the Perino M1913, were primarily used during the Great War. The Fiat-Revelli was indicative of an Italian penchant for overengineered loading mechanisms that required ammunition to be lubricated for firing and unsurprisingly this resulted in numerous incidents of jamming or failure in the field.

Fed from 10-round clips inserted in a revolving drum, the delayed-blowback-operating Modello 14 often split cartridges in the chamber. A later version, the Modello 35, eliminated some of the issues with loading and employed a belt-feed system. The Modello 14 was chambered for the 6.5mm (.256in) cartridge and was water-cooled, firing at a cyclic rate of 400 rounds per minute.

The Perino M1913, which worked on a combined recoil and gas-operated system, was both water- and air-cooled. It was a successor to at least two improvements to an original machine gun designed by engineer Giuseppe Perino in 1901. Perino is credited with developing the first Italian machine gun, and the M1913 fired a 6.5mm (.256in) cartridge at a cyclic rate of 500 rounds per minute.

Specifications

Country of Origin: Italy

Date: 1913

Calibre: 6.5mm (.256in) M95

Operation: Combined recoil/gas operated,
   water/air cooled

Weight: 13.65kg (30lb)

Overall Length: 1180mm (46.5in)

Barrel Length: 655mm (25.75in)

Muzzle Velocity: 640m/sec (2100ft/sec)

Feed/Magazine: Strip fed

Cyclic Rate: 500rpm

Range: 1500m (4921ft)

▶ **Perino M1913**

Italian Army / 151st Infantry Regiment, 1917

A descendant of the first operational Italian machine gun, the Model 1913 was a lighter version of the original, which was produced in 1901, and utilized a combined gas and recoil operating system.

Chapter 3

Interwar Years

During the turbulent twentieth century, the years between the world wars remained restive. Nascent nationalism, ideological awakenings and imperialistic ambitions steadily heightened tensions across the globe. In concert, the proliferation of rifles, machine guns and other small arms gave rise to military operations on both a grand and localized scale. While isolated battles were often fought between rival factions, larger conflicts served as proving grounds for new and innovative small arms, including a generation of machine guns and automatic weapons that increased the firepower of individual soldiers to unprecedented levels and raised casualty figures appreciably. Meanwhile, the war-proven shoulder arms from Mauser, Springfield, Lee-Enfield and other sources were refined, upgraded and supplemented as new rifles emerged to arm the legions of soldiers destined to prosecute the greatest military conflict the world has ever known.

◀ **House search**
Spanish troops loyal to General Franco search buildings somewhere in Spain during the Spanish Civil War. They are armed with Lebel Berthier 1915 bolt-action rifles.

Introduction

Ethnic and civil wars, the rise of totalitarian regimes and the reach for empire made the interwar years a turbulent period.

THE INTRODUCTION OF SMALL ARMS on a grand scale heightened an uneasy peace between the great powers and gave rise to guerrilla warfare and revolution. The Treaty of Versailles included 440 clauses. Of these, more than 400 were related to the guilt of Germany for fomenting World War I or the nation's responsibility to pay reparations and disarm. The terms of the treaty crippled Germany and exacerbated the impact of the Great Depression, which plunged the world into economic chaos in the autumn of 1929.

The treaty limited the *Reichswehr*, the German Army of the Weimar Republic, to 84,000 rifles, 18,000 carbines, 792 heavy machine guns and 1134 light machine guns. These were to be parcelled evenly throughout a standing army that numbered no more than 100,000 troops and consisted of seven infantry and three cavalry divisions. Therefore, a standard *Reichswehr* infantry division was to be allocated 12,000 rifles, while a cavalry division received 6000 carbines. Only 108 heavy and 162 light machine guns were theoretically available for each infantry division. The number of officers and non-commissioned officers was severely restricted to deprive the German armed forces of cohesive, experienced leadership.

In truth, however, Germany had never completely disarmed and a covert, shadow army remained active, with training in the use of small arms in effective offensive operations at its core. Even before the rise of the Nazi Party to power in 1933, the Germans were actively circumventing the harsh terms of the treaty. With General Hans von Seeckt (1866–1936) as its prime mover, the German military covertly exceeded the 100,000-man limitation on troop strength specified at Versailles, while clandestine arrangements were made with the Soviet Union to train soldiers and gain familiarity with infantry weapons and small-arms tactics. Major German arms manufacturers such as Krupp and Rheinmetall contracted with foreign companies or their own subsidiaries outside the borders of Germany to produce new weapons systems. With the outbreak of civil war in Spain, Nazi Germany took advantage of an opportunity to

◀ **Czechoslovakian manoeuvres**
Czechoslovakian soldiers armed with the Czechoslovakian version of the Mauser Kar 98 rifle, the vz. 24, and Maschinengewehr 08/15 Maxim-style machine guns carry out manoeuvres, mid-1930s. Many of the Czechoslovakians' impressive arsenal of weaponry fell into the hands of the *Wehrmacht* following the Nazi occupation of the Sudetenland in 1938.

▲ **Defence of the people**
Government troops fire on rebels from the shelter of a hastily erected barricade, Toledo, July 1936.

support the Nationalist forces of Generalissimo Francisco Franco (1892–1975), and along with Fascist Italy sent troops, planes (and pilots to fly them) and other war materiel to fight the Republican forces. Italy under Benito Mussolini (1883–1945) also invaded a virtually defenceless Ethiopia and occupied tiny Albania across the Adriatic Sea in the turbulent Balkans.

By the spring of 1935, German chancellor Adolf Hitler (1889–1945) had repudiated the Treaty of Versailles and told the world that Germany was rearming, albeit for peaceful and defensive purposes only. On 16 March, Hitler boldly declared Germany's initial compliance with the treaty and alleged that other nations had failed to take advantage of opportunities to disarm and promote peace. He claimed that Germany had actually destroyed more than six million rifles, 130,000 machine guns and 244,000 barrels, 340,000 tonnes (335,000 tons) of ammunition cartridges, more than 16.5 million hand and rifle grenades, 180 machine-gun sleds, and 174,000 gas masks among other weapons of war, large and small.

In the process of unveiling German rearmament to the world, Hitler further twisted the words of British prime minister Stanley Baldwin (1867–1947), who stated, 'A nation that is not willing to take the necessary precautionary measures for its own defence will never have any power in the world, neither of the moral nor of the material kind.'

As for Great Britain and France, post-war malaise persisted in the wake of a catastrophic global conflict that had nearly bankrupted their national treasuries, while various political factions sought to curb military preparedness and pointed to the tremendous casualty tolls of 1914–18 as the rationale for their protests. In the process, appeasement came to have heavy influence on British and French foreign policy. In the United States, a resurgence of isolationism emerged and the standing army dwindled towards 100,000 – not by treaty but by design and steady decline. Meanwhile, in Asia the war machine of Imperial Japan prepared for offensive action to expand territorial control and prestige throughout the region.

French Forces: North Africa
1920–39

European influence in North Africa was heavily contested in Morocco as Spain, later joined by France, sought to consolidate rule over tribal regions east of their mountainous holdings.

THE TREATY OF FEZ was concluded in 1912, and like other treaties of its time became the basis for future conflict. As a portion of Morocco became a French protectorate, the government of Spain was given territory in the mountainous western region of the country. Subsequently, it was decided that the Spanish would extend their rule into eastern areas populated by the Rif and Jabala tribes.

Although the Spanish troops deployed were better armed and equipped, the natives under the leadership of Abd el-Krim (1882–1963) resisted resolutely and five years of insurgency, counter-insurgency and open

warfare ensued. Eventually, the Spanish were joined by French troops and succeeded in asserting control in the region. However, Abd el-Krim proved to be a resourceful tactician and builder of consensus among the various native factions taking part in the resistance to European rule, sowing the seeds of pan-North African nationalism that was to rise with great force a half-century later.

Another unintended consequence of the Rif Wars was the emergence of Francisco Franco (1892–1975), a leader of Spanish troops who distinguished himself during the fighting in Morocco and gained a

▲ **Fusil Mle 1886**

French Army / 2nd Foreign Legion Regiment, Morocco, 1920

The bolt-action Lebel Model 1886 was the standard French Army rifle from the late nineteenth century until the 1930s. Nearly three million were produced, and it remained in service alongside other weapons intended as replacements.

Specifications

Country of Origin: France	Overall Length: 1303mm (51.3in)
Date: 1886	Barrel Length: 798mm (31.4in)
Calibre: 8mm (.314in) Lebel	Muzzle Velocity: 725m/sec (2379ft/sec)
Operation: Bolt action	Feed/Magazine: 8-round tubular magazine
Weight: 4.245kg (9.375lb)	Range: 400m (1312ft)

▲ **Fusil Automatique Modèle 1917**

French Army / 4th Foreign Legion Regiment, Morocco, 1925

Intended to supplant the Lebel Model 1886 rifle in the French Army, the Modèle 1917 entered production late in World War I and eventually saw service in the Rif Wars. Its semiautomatic operation was aided by gas cartridge ejection.

Specifications

Country of Origin: France	Overall Length: 1331mm (52.4in)
Date: 1917	Barrel Length: 798mm (31.4in)
Calibre: 8mm (.314in) Lebel	Muzzle Velocity: 853m/sec (2800ft/sec)
Operation: Gas, rotating bolt	Feed/Magazine: 5-round box magazine
Weight: 5.25kg (11.6lb)	Range: 300m (984ft)

following among military personnel who had become disenchanted with the instability of government at home. By the end of the Rif Wars in 1926, Franco had become the youngest general in any European army and gained additional notoriety suppressing labour unrest. The emergence of a left-wing Popular Front government precipitated a failed coup d'etat by Franco and members of the Falange Party, bringing about the bloody Spanish Civil War.

French firepower

A pair of French rifles were prominent during the Rif Wars and beyond. The Lebel Model 1886 and its successor, the Fusil Automatique Modèle 1917, were available in large numbers among the French regular troops and Foreign Legionnaires who took part in the Moroccan fighting. The Lebel 1886 was an 8mm (.314in) bolt-action rifle that entered service in large numbers with French forces in the spring of 1887. Fed by an eight-round tubular magazine, the Lebel was the primary shoulder arm of the French Army during World War I.

During the course of the weapon's production from 1887 to 1920, more than 2.8 million Lebel Model 1886 rifles were produced by state-run arms-manufacturing facilities in Châtellerault, Saint-Etienne and Tulle. The rifle was distributed in large quantities to French colonial troops during World War I; therefore, thousands of them found their way into the hands of rebels, insurgents, and militia that later fought the French and Spanish militaries during the Rif Wars. Early setbacks for European forces also resulted in the capture of many of these weapons.

The Fusil Automatique Modèle 1917 was the result of a French attempt to replace the Lebel rifle and became operational with units of the French Army in the spring of 1916. The rifle was also known as the Modèle 1917 RSC, for its design collaboration team of Ribeyrolles, Sutter, and Chauchat. By the end of World War I in November 1918, approximately 86,000 of these had been built by the French government at its Manufacture d'armes de Saint-Etienne facility. The Modèle 1917 fired an 8mm (.314in) cartridge and was operated by bolt action with a long recoil and gas-operated ejection assistance for spent cartridges, which provided some benefits of semiautomatic operation. Its internal box magazine was fed by a five-round clip. Although it appeared late in World War I, French troops rapidly formed a negative opinion of the Modèle 1917, particularly because its length of 1331mm (52.4in) was too cumbersome for trench warfare.

A substantial improvement to the design was completed in 1918 and included the change from a proprietary ammunition clip to the universal Berthier clip. About 4000 of the 1918 variant were produced, and many of these performed satisfactorily during the Rif Wars.

▲ **Fusil Mitrailleur Mle 24/29**

French Army / 21st Colonial Infantry Regiment, Morocco, 1924

An improvement over the Mle 1915 of World War I, the Modèle 24/29 served with the French armed forces into the 1950s and was the army's principal light machine gun of World War II.

Specifications

Country of Origin: France	Barrel Length: 500mm (19.75in)
Date: 1924	Muzzle Velocity: 825m/sec (2707ft/sec)
Calibre: 7.5mm (.295in) M29	Cyclic Rate: 450rpm
Operation: Gas operated, air cooled	Feed/Magazine: 25-round box magazine
Weight: 9.25kg (20.25lb)	Range: 1000m (3280ft) +
Overall Length: 1080mm (42.5in)	

Spanish Civil War
1936–39

The bloody Spanish Civil War raged for three years and served as a harbinger of the global war that followed as Nazi Germany and Fascist Italy sent direct military aid to the forces of Francisco Franco.

FOR NEARLY A CENTURY prior to the outbreak of the Spanish Civil War on 17 July 1936, Spain had experienced periods of tumult and chaos as rival liberal and conservative factions vied for preeminence and the long-embattled monarchy endured despite numerous efforts to undermine or abolish it. The Republican government of Spain had attempted to quell right-wing discontent among the army leadership and demoted General Francisco Franco (1892–1975) to command in the Canary Islands. However, he was later able to escape capture and rally troops in North Africa for landings at Seville. The war dragged on until the conservative government, dominated by Franco and his Falange Party, consolidated power in April 1939.

Atrocities were widespread on both sides during the Spanish Civil War, and civilian deaths numbered in the hundreds of thousands. Both Nazi Germany and Fascist Italy sent military personnel, arms and equipment in support of Franco, while the Soviet Union provided limited support for the Republicans. Eventually, Franco controlled the country while the monarchy survived with limited authority.

During the Spanish Civil War, a flood of small arms from around the world equipped the forces of both the Nationalists and Republicans. In addition to the French Lebel, German Mauser, British Lee-Enfield and Austrian Mannlicher rifles that had been so prevalent during World War I, the American Springfield Model 1903 and numerous other shoulder arms such as the antiquated Norwegian Krag-Jørgensen saw service during the conflict.

Machine guns in Spain

Numerous types of machine gun were deployed during the Spanish Civil War. Prominent among them was the German Maschinengewehr 34, commonly known as the MG 34, which entered service with the German Army in great numbers following Hitler's repudiation of the Versailles Treaty in the spring of 1935. The MG 34 was tested in combat by German troops aiding Franco's Nationalists, and its characteristics as an automatic weapon with a heavy sustained rate of fire, providing substantial support to infantry in defensive positions but highly mobile as well, were demonstrated to the world in horrific fashion.

French machine guns, including improved versions of World War I-vintage Fusil Mitrailleur and Hotchkiss models, were deployed by both sides. At

▶ **Unceta Victoria**

Spanish Nationalist Army / 2nd CCNN Division Fiamme Nere (Black Flames), Guadalajara, 1937

Closely related to the Browning family of pistols, the Unceta Victoria was also closely associated with the Ruby pistol of the French Army during World War I. It was adopted by the French after entering service in 1911.

Specifications

Country of Origin: Spain	Barrel Length: 81mm (3.2in)
Date: 1911	Muzzle Velocity: 229m/sec (750ft/sec)
Calibre: 7.65mm (.301in)	Feed/Magazine: 7-round detachable box
Operation: Blowback	magazine
Weight: .57kg (1.25lb)	Range: 30m (98ft)
Overall Length: 146mm (5.75in)	

the end of World War I, the French military assessed the shortcomings of the Mitrailleur Modèle 1915 and determined to provide a more functional and reliable weapon to its soldiers. In competition with the newly developed American Browning Automatic Rifle (BAR), the French arms producer Manufacture d'Armes de Saint-Etienne (MAS) won a competitive bid to produce the Modèle 24/29.

This updated machine gun was to serve as the basic French light infantry support weapon for the next quarter-century and has surfaced as late as the last decade in the hands of various militia and paramilitary groups. It also remained in service with the French *Gendarmerie Nationale* until 2006. The Modèle 24/29 was known for its in-line stock, bipod mount and pistol grip, which was favoured by infantrymen for ease of aiming and control of the weapon's vibration. It was fed by a 25-round top-fitted magazine, and the bolt held itself open for reloading when the last round was fired. A Lieutenant-Colonel Reibel, credited with the weapon's design, recognized the need for a comparatively high cyclic rate of fire and achieved that at 450 rounds per minute.

The weapon first entered service as the Modèle 1924 and fired a 7.5mm (.295in) cartridge, a departure from the traditional 8mm (.314in) ammunition. Problems encountered through trying to use captured 8mm (.314in) rounds during the Rif Wars, though, led to the production of a modified version of the weapon, which became the Modèle 24/29. The machine gun armed French troops during the opening days of the Nazi offensive against France during the spring of 1940 and emerged as a prominent weapon during the Algerian war for independence in the 1950s. A further modification was accomplished in 1931 and included a heavier barrel and drum feed, increasing the rate of fire to 600 rounds per minute.

Another French light machine gun, the Hotchkiss M1922/26, suffered from a woefully underfunded French arms research and development industry in the 1920s. Although the design itself was promising, with a muzzle-climb compensator and an adjustable rate of fire, the weapon almost came to nothing and its production numbers were limited. A handful of these 6.5mm (.256in) machine guns with a cyclic rate of fire of 500 rounds per minute were in action during the Rif Wars and in the Spanish Civil War. Most of the production run was sold to the Greek armed forces.

Spanish export

The blowback-operated Unceta Victoria pistol fired a 7.65mm (.301in) cartridge and utilized a seven-round detachable box magazine. It was developed by the Spanish firm that later came to be known as Astra and entered service in 1911. The pistol initially saw action with Allied forces in 1914 and was officially adopted by the French Army. Patterned after the

▲ **Hotchkiss M1922/26**

Nationalist Army / Flechas Negras (Black Arrows) Division, Catalonia, 1938

An adjustable rate of fire and muzzle-climb compensator were two outstanding features of the Hotchkiss M1922/26; however, the weapon was produced in limited numbers due to French arms budget constraints. Most were exported to Greece, while a relative few were fielded during the Spanish Civil War.

Specifications

Country of Origin: France	Barrel Length: 575mm (22.75in)
Date: 1922	Muzzle Velocity: 745m/sec (2444ft/sec)
Calibre: 6.5mm (.256in)	Feed/Magazine: 25- or 30-round strip
Operation: Gas operated, air cooled	Cyclic Rate: 500rpm
Weight: 9.5kg (21lb)	Range: 1000m (3280ft) +
Overall Length: 1215mm (47.75in)	

Republican soldiers move up to the front lines in the Guadarrama Mountains, September 1936.

American Browning Model 1903, it is considered by many to be an almost identical copy of the Ruby pistol that was widely used by the French Army as a sidearm during World War I.

Automatic weapons

Although the Treaty of Versailles prohibited the deployment of submachine guns with the German armed forces, they had nevertheless utilized them during the waning months of World War I and recognized their tremendous firepower enhancement capabilities. Therefore, the Germans continued the development of the submachine gun during the interwar years, and its prowess on the battlefield was validated in combat in Spain. Typically, German submachine gun designations included the initials 'MP' for *Maschinenpistole*.

The German Erma MPE was one of the most widely used submachine guns of the Spanish Civil War and was exported in large numbers to several nations in Central and South America whose governments were right-wing. Designed in the 1920s by Heinrich Vollmer (1885–1961), the Erma MPE

was used by both French Foreign Legion and German troops during the 1930s and was eventually replaced by the MP 38. It was fed by a 32-round detachable box magazine that was loaded from the left side, and featured a wooden stock and pistol grip for control.

In another effort to circumvent the Treaty of Versailles, the German government facilitated the acquisition of the Swiss firm of Solothurn by Rheinmetall, and production of a prototype began on what came to be known as the MP 34. Rheinmetall in turn purchased a controlling interest in the Austrian arms manufacturer Steyr, and the result was a highly successful submachine gun that developed a reputation for operational excellence. The Austrian version of the MP 34 was known as the Steyr-Solothurn S1-100. The blowback-operated weapon fired a 9mm (.35in) cartridge and was fed by a detachable box magazine holding from 20 to 32 rounds. It featured a selective shot option, either single-round or fully automatic. Although the weapon was extremely well made, production of the MP 34/Steyr-Solothurn S1-100 was somewhat limited due to high materials costs.

▲ Erma MPE

Guardia Civil

Widely used during the Spanish Civil War, the Erma MPE began production in 1930. Its service life was extended by a significant export market for the submachine gun in Central and South America.

Specifications

Country of Origin: Germany

Date: 1930

Calibre: 9mm (.35in) Parabellum

Operation: Blowback

Weight: 4.15kg (9.13lb)

Overall Length: 902mm (35.5in)

Barrel Length: 254mm (10in)

Muzzle Velocity: 395m/sec (1300ft/sec)

Feed/Magazine: 32-round box magazine

Cyclic Rate: 500rpm

Range: 70m (230ft)

Specifications

Country of Origin: Austria

Date: 1930

Calibre: 9mm (.35in)

Operation: Blowback

Weight: 4.48kg (9.88lb)

Overall Length: 850mm (33.46in)

Barrel Length: 200mm (7.87in)

Muzzle Velocity: 418m/sec (1370ft/sec)

Feed/Magazine: 20- or 32-round box magazine

Cyclic Rate: 500rpm

Range: 100m (328ft)

▲ Steyr-Solothurn S1-100

Army of Africa / Spanish Foreign Legion, 1937

The Austrian version of the extraordinarily well-engineered MP 34 submachine gun, the Steyr-Solothurn S1-100 was a successful effort to circumvent the Treaty of Versailles.

▲ Star S135

Spanish Republican Army / 3rd Mixed Brigade, Catalonia, 1937

The Star S135 submachine gun was a complicated design that eventually was discarded for simpler and less expensive models. Originating in Spain, it did offer selective rates of fire and a mechanism that held the bolt open for easy reloading of an empty magazine.

Specifications

Country of Origin: Spain

Date: 1935

Calibre: 9mm (.35in) Largo

Operation: Delayed blowback

Weight: 3.74kg (8.25lb)

Overall Length: 900mm (35.45in)

Barrel Length: 269mm (10.6in)

Muzzle Velocity: 410m/sec (1345ft/sec)

Feed/Magazine: 10-, 30- or 40-round detachable box magazine

Cyclic Rate: 300 or 700rpm

Range: 50m (164ft)

Sino-Japanese War
1937–45

Japanese expansion on the mainland of Asia was set in motion in a series of violent clashes with the Chinese; however, the vastness of China plus Allied aid prevented Japan from achieving complete victory.

JAPAN AND CHINA had fought intermittently since the turn of the twentieth century, and modern conflict had developed in 1931 with the Japanese using a trumped-up incident in Manchuria as a pretext for the invasion of this northern region of China. The Japanese secured control of Manchuria, installed a puppet regime, and renamed the province Manchukuo.

Fighting continued sporadically for several more years until another armed incident at the Marco Polo Bridge near Beijing marked the beginning of the Sino-Japanese War between Imperial Japan and the Republic of China. The war officially commenced on 7 July 1937, and lasted until Japan's defeat by the Allies in August 1945. The war was spawned by an insatiable Japanese hunger for land and raw materials on the Asian mainland and a political desire to dominate the affairs of their giant neighbour to the west. Following the Japanese attack on Pearl Harbor and US entry into World War II, the Sino-Japanese War effectively merged into the greater global conflict and formed the largest component of the China-Burma-India theatre.

With its victory over Russia in the Russo-Japanese War of 1904–05, Japan established itself as the preeminent power in East Asia. In 1910, the Japanese were granted a mandate over the Korean peninsula and effectively ruled that country for the next 35 years. Influenced heavily by the military technology of the West, the Japanese built an army which was equivalent in size and strength to many of those of the European powers. Its support of the Allies during World War I resulted in further territorial influence in Asia during the interwar years.

An increasingly imperialistic Japan provided its troops with an array of small arms, including the Arisaka series of rifles and the pistols and machine guns manufactured to the specifications of prolific arms designer Kijiro Nambu (1869–1949). European influence was further apparent in the design and manufacture of several of these key small arms.

Type 38

The primary Japanese shoulder arm of the early twentieth century was the Arisaka 38th Year rifle, simply known as the Type 38 and named for the weapon's adoption during the 38th year of the Meiji restoration. It entered service in 1905 and was intended as a replacement for the Type 30 rifle that had served with the Japanese Army for a brief seven years. The Type 38 fired a 6.5mm (.256in) cartridge which was underpowered by many Western

▲ **Chinese Gew 88 (Hanyang 88)**

Chinese National Revolutionary Army / 127th Infantry Brigade, Shanghai, 1937

The Gew 88 was more commonly known as the Hanyang 88 and equipped large numbers of Chinese infantrymen during the Sino-Japanese War. Patterned after the German Mauser design, it was produced at Hanyang Arsenal.

Specifications

Country of Origin: China	Overall Length: 1110mm (43.7in)
Date: 1895	Barrel Length: 600mm (23.6in)
Calibre: 7.92mm (.312in)	Muzzle Velocity: 810m/sec (2657ft/sec)
Operation: Bolt action	Feed/Magazine: 5-round box magazine
Weight: 4.08kg (9lb)	Range: 500m (1640ft)

standards, and the rifle's length of 1280mm (50.39in) presented challenges in handling to the average Japanese soldier of the period, who stood but 1.6m (5ft 3in) tall.

By 1939, the Japanese had embarked on a programme to replace the Type 38 with the new Type 99 rifle; however, the outbreak of World War II impeded the progress of this initiative. A total of 3.4 million of the bolt-action Type 38 were produced, and the weapon was prominent among Japanese forces during the Pacific War. It was fed by a five-round box magazine, and a skilled rifleman was said to be capable of firing 30 rounds per minute.

Mauser copy

Like its Japanese Type 38 counterpart, the Chinese Gew 88 rifle was influenced by the German Mauser design. The Republic's forces depended on the Gew,

or Gewehr 88, heavily during the Sino-Japanese War. Those weapons in Chinese service were often referred to as the Hanyang 88 in reference to their production at the Hanyang Arsenal. A virtual copy of the Gewehr 88, the Hanyang 88 fired a 7.92mm (.312in) Mauser round and its external box magazine was fed by a five-round clip.

The Hanyang 88 was relatively inexpensive to produce and rather well suited for China's weak industrial posture in relation to its Japanese adversary. One distinct advantage over its Japanese counterpart was the fact that the Hanyang 88 fired a heavier round than the 6.5mm (.256in) Japanese Arisaka, which tipped the scales slightly towards the Chinese in early close-quarters fighting. Although it had been in service since 1895 and pre-dated the most recent Japanese rifles, the Hanyang 88 performed well during the Sino-Japanese War. Despite the fact that its

▲ Arisaka 38th Year rifle

Japanese Tenth Army / 6th Infantry Division, Nanjing, 1937

The Type 38 rifle entered service in 1905, and plans to replace it with the updated Type 99 were only partially completed. The Type 38 remained in service through to the end of World War II.

Specifications

Country of Origin: Japan	Overall Length: 1280mm (50.7in)
Date: 1905	Barrel Length: 800mm (31.5in)
Calibre: 6.5mm (.256in)	Muzzle Velocity: 765m/sec (2509ft/sec)
Operation: Bolt action	Feed/Magazine: 5-round internal magazine
Weight: 3.95kg (8.7lb)	Range: 500m (1640ft)

◀ Baby Nambu

Imperial Japanese Army / Central China Expeditionary Army / 14th Independent Brigade, September 1939

The Baby Nambu pistol fired an underpowered 7mm (.275in) cartridge and has become the most recognized of the Nambu series of pistols adopted as sidearms for Japanese officers.

Specifications

Country of Origin: Japan	Overall Length: 230mm (9.06in)
Date: 1906	Barrel Length: 117mm (4.61in)
Calibre: 7mm (.275in)	Muzzle Velocity: 289.6m/sec (950ft/sec)
Operation: Recoil spring	Feed/Magazine: 8-round box magazine
Weight: .9kg (1.98lb)	Range: 50m (164ft)

rate of fire was relatively slow, the Hanyang remained in production until 1947, and over 1.1 million were built during the course of more than 50 years.

A principal Japanese heavy machine gun of the Sino-Japanese War was the Type 3, also referred to as the Taisho 14 machine gun. Patterned after the French Hotchkiss Model 1914, the Type 3 was produced in Japan under licence and fired the 6.5mm (.256in) standard Arisaka cartridge rather than the heavier 8mm (.314in) ammunition of the Hotchkiss.

The air-cooled Type 3 was adapted by Japanese designer Kijiro Nambu in 1914 and was fed by a 30-round ammunition strip. It was capable of a rate of fire up to 450 rounds per minute.

The Nambu nemisis

A career officer of the Japanese Army, Nambu rose to the rank of lieutenant-general and founded the Nambu Arms Manufacturing Company in Tokyo in 1927. He was responsible for the design and

Specifications

Country of Origin: Japan	Barrel Length: 750mm (29.5in)
Date: 1914	Muzzle Velocity: 760m/sec (2500ft/sec)
Calibre: 6.5mm (.256in) Arisaka	Feed/Magazine: Strip fed
Operation: Gas operated, air cooled	Cyclic Rate: 400rpm
Weight: 28kg (62lb)	Range: 1500m (4921ft)
Overall Length: 1155mm (45in)	

▲ **Taisho 14**

Japanese Tenth Army / 6th Infantry Division, Nanjing, 1937

The Taisho 14 heavy machine gun was built in Japan under licence as a duplicate of the French Hotchkiss Model 1914. Designer Kijiro Nambu modified the French weapon to fire the Japanese 6.5mm (.256in) cartridge.

▶ **94 Shiki Kenju (Type 94)**

Japanese Northern China Area Army / 2nd Independent Mixed Brigade, northern China, 1940

Issued primarily to the crewmen of aircraft and vehicles, the Type 94 pistol was intended for cheap manufacture but eventually became prohibitively expensive. Like most other Japanese pistols, it fired an underpowered 8mm (.314in) round.

Specifications

Country of Origin: Japan	Overall Length: 183mm (7.2in)
Date: 1934	Barrel Length: 96mm (3.78in)
Calibre: 8mm (.314in)	Muzzle Velocity: 305m/sec (1000ft/sec)
Operation: Not known	Feed/Magazine: 6-round box magazine
Weight: .688kg (1.52lb)	Range: Not known

production of a number of Japanese small arms carried through the Sino-Japanese War and the duration of World War II. Among his most famous weapons designs is the Baby Nambu pistol, one of a series of pistols that were common sidearms of Japanese officers and soldiers.

The Baby Nambu was officially known as the Type A Model 1902 Modified and fired a 7mm (.275in) round compared with the larger 8mm (.314in) round of the Type A Model 1902 Grandpa Nambu. Essentially a scaled-down version of the Grandpa, the Baby Nambu included modifications to the sights, grip, safety and magazine finger pad along with a swivelling lanyard ring and an aluminium magazine base. Both pistols were fed by an eight-round box magazine. The Grandpa Nambu was notorious for misfiring due to weak magazine springs, while the Baby Nambu has become one of the most highly sought-after Japanese firearms. Slightly more than 10,000 Baby Nambu pistols were built, and a small number of these were produced by Tokyo Gas and Electric.

Production of the Nambu series of pistols was begun in 1906, and in 1925 the Type A was replaced by the Type 14, which was produced through to the end of World War II in numbers that eventually exceeded 250,000. The Type 14 short-recoil semiautomatic fired an 8mm (.314in) Nambu cartridge and was fed by an eight-round detachable box magazine. It was an improvement over earlier models with an enlarged trigger guard. The Nambu series proved to be accurate pistols; however, they fired substantially underpowered rounds with inferior knockdown capability and remained prone to misfiring throughout their service lives.

▲ **Invasion and occupation**

Bayonets fixed on their Arisaka rifles, a Japanese infantry battalion marches through a town somewhere in China during the Sino-Japanese War.

◀ **Nambu Type 14**

Japanese Twelfth Army / 115th Infantry Division, Zhengzhou, 1939

Replacing the Type A series in 1925, the semiautomatic Nambu Type 14 pistol provided some limited improvements such as an enlarged trigger guard but remained prone to misfiring.

Specifications

Country of Origin: Japan	Barrel Length: 121mm (4.76in)
Date: 1925	Muzzle Velocity: 335m/sec (1100ft/sec)
Calibre: 8mm (.314in) Nambu	Feed/Magazine: 8-round detachable box
Operation: Short recoil	magazine
Weight: .9kg (1.98lb)	Range: 30m (98ft)
Overall Length: 227mm (8.93in)	

Czechoslovakian Arsenal
1920–45

Prior to the collapse of the Austro-Hungarian Empire, the provinces that would constitute the nation of Czechoslovakia were known for their production of quality small arms.

CONSIDERED one of the premier producers of arms in Europe, the Skoda manufacturing works at Plzen turned out the Model 1909 machine gun for the Austro-Hungarian Army, and by that time the company was a half-century old. Although the firm was better known for its production of heavy artillery and even turrets for battleships, the reputation of Skoda and other Czech arms producers enticed Hitler to assert control over the Central European nation prior to World War II.

At the end of World War I, another Czech arms manufacturer, Zbrojovka Brno, was established and began to produce the ZB-53 medium machine gun, which fired the 7.92mm (.312in) Mauser cartridge at a rate of up to 800 rounds per minute, fed by a 225-round metal-link belt. Copied by the British and built under licence as the Besa machine gun, the weapon was primarily mounted on vehicles. By the late 1930s, the ZK-383 submachine gun was being produced by Zbrojovka Brno, and many entered service with the German Army. Although production volume was low, it continued until 1966.

The company's Lehky Kulomet ZGB vz.33 light machine gun also served with the German Army and was exported to many countries. Capable of a rate of fire of up to 500 rounds per minute, it was fed by a 30-round detachable box magazine. It shared a similar lineage and was virtually identical to the fabled British Bren Gun, a derivative of the earlier ZB vz.26, which entered production in 1924.

Initially ordered by the Czech Army, the blowback-operated CZ Model 38 pistol was designed by Frantisek Myska and underwent field testing in 1938. A few of the weapons were shipped to Bulgaria; however, the majority of the 10,000 produced wound up in service with various German security forces. The pistol fired a 9mm (.35in) cartridge and was fed by a eight-round magazine.

▲ **Lehky Kulomet ZGB vz.33**

German Army Group Centre / 1st SS Infantry Brigade, Zhitomir, Belorussia, 1942

Virtually identical in design to the British Bren Gun, the ZGB vz.33 entered service just prior to the Bren and was one of many highly successful Czech light machine guns.

Specifications

Country of Origin: Czechoslovakia	Barrel Length: 635mm (25in)
Date: 1933	Muzzle Velocity: 730m/sec (2400ft/sec)
Calibre: 7.92mm (.312in) Mauser	Feed/Magazine: 30-round box magazine
Operation: Gas operated, air cooled	Cyclic Rate: 500rpm
Weight: 10.25kg (22.5lb)	Range: 1000m (3280ft)
Overall Length: 1150mm (45.25in)	

◀ CZ Model 38

German police unit, 1939

The CZ Model 38 pistol was a failure in the field due to a heavy trigger pull and its weak 9mm (.35in) short cartridge. Due to a shortage of handguns, the German Army and police pressed the Model 38 into service.

Specifications

Country of Origin: Czechoslovakia	Overall Length: 198mm (7.8in)
Date: 1938	Barrel Length: 119mm (4.69in)
Calibre: 9mm (.35in) Short	Muzzle Velocity: 296m/sec (970ft/sec)
Operation: Short recoil	Feed/Magazine: 8-round box magazine
Weight: .909kg (2lb)	Range: 30m (98ft)

▲ ZK-383

German Army Group North / 4th SS Polizei Division, Luga, August 1941

Large numbers of the ZK-383 submachine gun were exported from Czechoslovakia prior to World War II. Following the German occupation of Czech territory, most of the weapons were issued to the *Waffen*-SS.

Specifications

Country of Origin: Czechoslovakia	Overall Length: 875mm (34.45in)
Date: 1938	Barrel Length: 325mm (12.8in)
Calibre: 9mm (.35in) Parabellum	Muzzle Velocity: 365m/sec (1200ft/sec)
Operation: Blowback	Feed/Magazine: 30-round box magazine
Weight: 4.83kg (10.65lb)	Range: 100m (328ft)

▲ Besa

British Army / 2nd Royal Tank Regiment, Tobruk, Libya, 1942

The British version of the Czech ZB-53 medium machine gun, the Besa was commonly mounted on armoured vehicles. It was chambered for the 7.92mm (.312in) Mauser cartridge and could fire captured German ammunition.

Specifications

Country of Origin: Czechoslovakia	Barrel Length: 736mm (29in)
Date: 1936	Muzzle Velocity: 825m/sec (2700ft/sec)
Calibre: 7.92mm (.312in) Mauser	Feed/Magazine: 225-round belt
Operation: Gas operated, air cooled	Cyclic Rate: 750–850rpm
Weight: 21.5kg (47lb)	Range: 2000m (6560ft) +
Overall Length: 1105mm (43.5in)	

Chapter 4

World War II: Poland and Western Theatre

World War II raged in the West for five years,
from the campaign against France in 1940 to VE Day. It
spanned the Low Countries, the deserts of North Africa and
the boot of Italy. Throughout the period, millions of soldiers
fought with countless varieties of small arms, some
antiquated and others actually ahead of their time. While
bolt-action rifles ruled the day, the semiautomatic shoulder
arm made its combat debut and automatic weapons became
regular issue for some units, increasing the firepower of the
individual soldier substantially. A new generation of heavy
machine guns provided devastating fire from fixed positions,
while lighter models were transportable and highly
effective with infantry on the move.

◀ Ship's armoury
A US naval rating examines a row of Springfield M1903 rifles during a visit to England, 1944. Although
superseded by the Garand M1 for many frontline troops, the Springfield was in service with other branches
of the US military.

Introduction

From static warfare to rapid mobility, World War II in the West was characterized by the attack and defence of small infantry units employing offensive and defensive tactics to cope with the increasing firepower of the enemy.

WHEN THE GERMAN ARMY executed Case Yellow in May 1940, and the Phoney War in the West, derisively referred to as the 'Sitzkrieg', became a shooting war, the swift advance of the *Blitzkrieg* carried German armour from the French frontier to the coast of the Channel in a matter of days. While the tanks rolled westwards, risking the threat of counterattack against open flanks, it was the German infantry that secured and held the ground gained and eventually came to grips with the British Expeditionary Force evacuating at Dunkirk.

In many respects, the battle between the Germans and the defending British and French forces was a renewal of the conflict of a generation earlier. However, this time there would be no prolonged war of attrition in the trenches. In just over a month,

France had surrendered and the British had been ejected from the European continent. German soldiers patrolled the streets of Paris with their Mausers slung over their shoulders.

The British Expeditionary Force had evacuated northern France with little of its precious equipment intact. Thousands of Vickers machine guns and Lee-Enfield SMLE rifles were left lying on the beaches at Dunkirk. The legions of French prisoners of war turned over their arms to the Germans. Rearming and re-equipping many of the 350,000 Allied soldiers evacuated at Dunkirk was a formidable task, and for more than a year Great Britain stood alone against the Nazis, forced to content itself with an ill-fated foray into Greece and an ultimately unsuccessful attempt to maintain control of the island of Crete.

▲ **Defensive fire**

Armed with a mixture of Garand M1 rifles and M1 carbines, a US infantry anti-tank crew returns fire on German troops who machine-gunned their vehicle somewhere in the Netherlands, November 1944.

◀ *Wehrmacht* **firepower**
German soldiers man an MG 34 during the invasion of Denmark and Norway, April 1940.

planning a cross-Channel invasion of the Nazi-occupied European continent almost immediately.

US forces relied heavily on their World War I-era weapons, including the Springfield Model 1903 bolt-action rifle and the Browning Model 1917 machine gun, which had undergone some improvements in the 1930s. By 1937, the M1 Garand rifle and the smaller M1 carbine had been adopted by the US Army and were gradually coming into service with American troops. The M1 was the first semiautomatic rifle officially to enter service with any army and proved a decided advantage for US soldiers in combat.

German designers, however, had not called a halt to their innovative weapons design programmes and continued to deploy the stalwart Maschinengewehr 34, or MG 34, with its high rate of fire and reasonable mobility, in large numbers. In addition, the Germans improved the MG 34 design and deployed the Maschinengewehr 42 (MG 42) in substantial numbers. Although the durable and simply constructed MG 42 was intended to replace the MG 34, both continued in widespread production throughout the war.

Perhaps the most significant harbinger of the future of ground warfare was the German development of the Sturmgewehr 44, a fully automatic rifle that was capable of tremendous firepower in the hands of a single soldier and bolstered the long-serving Mauser bolt-action Karabiner 98k rifle. Although initially available in relatively low quantities, it was a shock to Allied soldiers battling in the hedgerows of Normandy following the D-Day landings on 6 June 1944. The Sturmgewehr 44 is considered by many to be the first fully operational assault rifle to see combat.

By 1945, the Allies had driven deep into Germany from the west and threatened the Reich from the south as they drove through mountainous northern Italy. While the Soviets pressed from the east, US and British forces halted their advance along the Elbe River and met the vanguard of the Red Army there. Along with the fighting stamina of the Allied soldiers in the West, the arms they carried proved sufficient to win the victory, even in the face of German innovation.

Pressing needs to supply the armed forces in Crete and North Africa stretched both fronts thin, limiting the successes in North Africa and dooming the defence of Crete to failure.

America's arsenal

The Nazi invasion of the Soviet Union in June 1941 brought an unlikely ally into the war, and Hitler's declaration of war on the United States at the end of the year finally buoyed British hopes for a reversal of fortune. Although the US had been savagely attacked by the Japanese at Pearl Harbor, it was agreed by President Franklin D. Roosevelt and Prime Minister Winston Churchill that the defeat of Nazi Germany was to take precedence over the war in the Pacific. The commitment of American troops and arms was tremendous, substantially exceeding the lifeline of Lend-Lease that had helped keep Britain in the war during the dark days of 1940–41. Although Allied forces for such an undertaking were deemed to be insufficient for some time, the US and Britain began

Polish Army
SEPTEMBER 1939

The overmatched Polish Army fought heroically to stem the German *Blitzkrieg*; however, it was overwhelmed by the *Wehrmacht* and the Red Army in a matter of weeks.

DURING THE 1930S, THE POLISH GOVERNMENT and its military commanders became increasingly concerned with the possibility of war with Germany and formulated plans for the defence of their country. Organized into six field armies with several additional units of corps size known as operational groups, the Polish Army consisted of up to 30 infantry divisions, 11 cavalry brigades, nine reserve divisions, three mountain brigades and two motorized brigades. During the years immediately following World War I, the Poles had received military assistance and training from a cadre of French officers.

The swiftness of the German advance into Poland prevented the coordinated defensive effort envisioned by the Polish high command, and mutual support of Polish operations of division size or greater was quite limited. Nevertheless, by 1 September 1939, the Polish Army numbered 700,000 troops. Although heavy weapons and armoured vehicles were relatively few in number, the Poles possessed more than three battalions of French-made Renault light tanks and 11 armoured car battalions, each with eight armoured cars and 13 tankettes.

The Polish infantry battalion of 1939 included three rifle companies and a machine-gun company. The rifle company included a complement of 232 troops organized in three rifle platoons. Each of the platoons included three rifle sections of 19 men. The primary shoulder arm of the Polish infantry was the Karabinek wz.29, a bolt-action rifle based on the German Mauser-designed Karabiner Model 1898, a close relative of the German standard rifle of World War II, the Mauser Karabiner 98k. The Karabinek wz.29 fired the 7.92mm (.312in) cartridge that was standard for Mauser rifles.

The Karabinek was fed by a five-round internal box magazine, and an average rate of fire was 15 rounds per minute. It entered production at the Polish National Arms Factory in Radom in 1930, and 264,000 were manufactured. It remained in service with Polish resistance units and in some organized units of Polish origin that fought with the Allies.

A machine-gun company consisted of 12 Ckm wz.30 heavy machine guns, and a platoon of three machine guns was typically assigned by battalion command to support each infantry company. The Ckm wz.30 was a Polish-made copy of the American Browning Model 1917 water-cooled machine gun. It was chambered to fire the 7.92mm (.312in) Mauser cartridge. Only about 7800 were built between 1930 and 1939. Although an agreement had been reached with Colt to produce the Model 1917, confusion arose between the American company and Fabrique Nationale, its European liaison, and the patent was never authorized in Poland. Therefore, Polish designers moved forward with their own version of the weapon.

In each 19-man rifle section, one soldier was armed with an Rkm wz.28 rifle, a licence-built version of the American Browning Automatic Rifle (BAR), which added some limited mobile firepower to the formation. The rifle company also fielded nine light machine guns, three anti-tank rifles and three light mortars.

▲ **Horse power**
These Polish lancers carry Karabinek wz.29 rifles across their backs. The Polish Army used their cavalry as mounted infantry, rather than in a purely cavalry role.

▲ Karabinek wz.29 (Kbk wz.29)

Polish Army / 55th Infantry Regiment, Lodz, September 1939

Based on the German Mauser Karabiner Model 1898, the bolt-action Karabinek was the standard rifle of the Polish Army in September 1939. It was chambered to fire the 7.92mm (.312in) Mauser cartridge.

Specifications

Country of Origin: Poland
Date: 1930
Calibre: 7.92mm (.312in) Mauser M98
Operation: Bolt action
Weight: 3.9kg (8.6lb)

Overall Length: 1110mm (43.7in)
Barrel Length: 600mm (23.62in)
Muzzle Velocity: 845m/sec (2772ft/sec)
Feed/Magazine: 5-round integral box magazine
Range: 500m (1640ft) + with iron sights

▲ Pistolet maszynowy wz.39 Mors

Polish Army / 36th Infantry Regiment, Lublin, September 1939

Following trials with the German Erma, Polish designers developed the Mors wz.39 between 1937 and 1939. Production was begun in 1939; however, only about 40 were manufactured before the German invasion of Poland.

Specifications

Country of Origin: Poland
Date: 1939
Calibre: 9mm (.35in)
Operation: Blowback
Weight: 4.25kg (9.37lb) (without magazine)
Overall Length: 970mm (38in)

Barrel Length: 300mm (11.8in)
Muzzel Velocity: 400m/sec (1312ft/sec)
Feed/Magazine: 24-round magazine
Range: 440m (1444ft) + with adjustable iron
  sights

▶ Radom wz.35

Polish Army / Wilenska Cavalry Brigade, Warsaw, September 1939

The 9mm (.35in) Radom wz.35 was developed for the Polish Army in 1935, and more than 360,000 were manufactured. Also known as the Vis pistol, the semiautomatic handgun was utilized by the Germans following their invasion of Poland.

Specifications

Country of Origin: Poland
Date: 1935
Calibre: 9mm (.35in) Parabellum
Operation: Short recoil
Weight: 1.022kg (2.25lb)
Overall Length: 197mm (7.76in)

Barrel Length: 115mm (4.53in)
Muzzle Velocity: 350m/sec (1150ft/sec)
Feed/Magazine: 8-round detachable box
  magazine
Range: 30m (98ft)

Wehrmacht
SEPTEMBER 1939 – JUNE 1940

The German Army that rolled to victory in Poland and then crushed French and British forces the following spring demonstrated tremendous speed and coordination.

WHEN ADOLF HITLER (1889–1945) came to power in January 1933, the German Army had already taken steps to circumvent the Treaty of Versailles. By autumn, the Nazi chancellor had taken his country out of the League of Nations and quietly authorized a build-up of the army to 300,000 soldiers, triple the strength authorized by the treaty. In concert with that build-up of troop strength, training proceeded under the guise of sports leagues and Nazi youth development programmes.

Following the *Anschluss* with Austria, the annexation of the Sudetenland and the occupation of the remainder of Czechoslovakia, and the acquisition of other territory during the full flower of the Allied appeasement doctrine, Hitler turned to war and invaded Poland on 1 September 1939. When war broke out, the German Army hurled more than 60 infantry and armoured divisions against the Polish Army, which was outnumbered 10 to one.

When German forces attacked Poland on 1 September 1939, the standard field army, or *Feldheer*, infantry division averaged a strength of about 17,500 troops including support personnel. The combat infantry element of the division consisted of three regiments, each commanded by a

GERMAN INFANTRY BATTALION, *CIRCA* 1939–40		
Unit	Officers	Men
Battalion Headquarters	5	15
Communications Platoon		19
Battle Train	2	17
Rations Train		8
Baggage Train		7
Machine Gun Company	4	173
Company HQ	1	20
Battle Train		11
Rations Train		3
Mortar Platoon	1	67
Two Machine-Gun Platoons, each	1	36
Three Rifle Companies, each	4	186
Company HQ	1	11
Battle Train		18
Rations and Baggage Trains		6
Machine-Gun Section		16
Three Rifle Platoons, each	1	45
Platoon HQ	1	3
Light Mortar Section		3
Three Rifle Squads, each		13
Total Strength of 820 all ranks	23	797

▶ **Parabellum M1908**

German Army / 50th Infantry Division, Poland, September 1939

Popularly known as the Luger after its designer, the semiautomatic Parabellum M1908 utilized a toggle-locking system rather than a slide, and its magazine was located in the handgrip. Although newer handguns were introduced, the weapon was popular with German officers throughout World War II.

Specifications

Country of Origin: Germany

Date: 1908

Calibre: 9mm (.35in)

Operation: Toggle locked, short recoil

Weight: .96kg (2.125lb)

Overall Length: 222mm (8.8in)

Barrel Length: 127mm (5in)

Muzzle Velocity: 351m/sec (1150ft/sec)

Feed/Magazine: 8-round detachable box
  magazine

Range: 30m (98ft)

colonel who reported to the general in command of the division. Based on an organizational alignment from 1938, the regiments consisted of approximately 3100 officers and men.

Each regiment consisted of three battalions, while each of these included three infantry companies with light and heavy machine gun and light mortar components. An infantry company typically comprised up to 200 troops, with a battalion populated by 825 officers and soldiers. A separate heavy weapons company contained additional mortars and heavy machine guns that could be deployed at the discretion of the battalion commander. The small-arms complement of the German infantry division of 1939 included nearly 650 machine guns along with rifles, submachine guns

▼ German Infantry Rifle Squad, 1940

Intended for effective fire and manoeuvre, the German rifle squad of 1940 included 13 soldiers. Seven of these were riflemen carrying the Mauser K98k shoulder arm, while three soldiers made up the machine-gun section. The squad leader or assistant squad leader was often armed with an MP 40 submachine gun capable of firing up to 550 rounds of 9mm (.35in) ammunition per minute. Augmented by the powerful MG 34 machine gun, the squad was capable of a significant volume of fire.

Rifle Squad (1 x MP 40 SMG, 9 x K98k rifle)

Machine-gun Section (1 x machine-gunner with pistol and MG 34, 1 x loader with pistol, 1 x loader with K98k rifle)

▲ Mauser Karabiner 98k

German Army / 213th Infantry Division, Poland, September 1939

The iconic Mauser K98k was the standard rifle of the German Army throughout World War II. Its bolt action had been modified from the earlier Gewehr 98, and its average rate of fire was 15 rounds per minute. The rifle remains popular with marksmen today.

Specifications

Country of Origin: Germany	Overall Length: 1110mm (43.7in)
Date: 1935	Barrel Length: 600mm (23.62in)
Calibre: 7.92mm (.312in) Mauser M98	Muzzle Velocity: 745m/sec (2444ft/sec)
Operation: Bolt action	Feed/Magazine: 5-round internal box magazine
Weight: 3.9kg (8.6lb)	Range: 500m (1640ft) + with iron sights

and pistols to equip the individual soldiers. During the course of the war, the composition of the infantry division was changed, as was the strength of the standard infantry squad, which was reduced from 13 to 10 men following the combat experience in Poland.

The backbone of the German Army in World War II was the infantry platoon. In 1939, the platoon comprised just under 50 soldiers in three squads of 13 riflemen. A 50mm (2in) light mortar section was organic, and one officer armed with a pistol and three soldiers with rifles who normally performed courier duties served as the headquarters element.

Two noncommissioned officers served as squad leader and assistant squad leader in each of the three squads, while each squad fielded seven riflemen and four soldiers who manned an MG 34 machine gun. Usually one noncommissioned officer carried an MP 40 submachine gun. Two members of the machine-gun section carried pistols, and one was usually armed with a rifle.

▶ **Landser**

A young German soldier poses for the camera during the invasion of France, May 1940. He is armed with the ubiquitious Karabiner 98k rifle and the famous Model 24 stick grenade.

Specifications	
Country of Origin: Germany	Barrel Length: Not known
Date: 1930	Muzzle Velocity: 890m/sec (2919.2ft/sec)
Calibre: 7.92mm (.312in) Mauser	Feed/Magazine: 25-round box magazine or
Operation: Short recoil	75-round saddle drum magazine
Weight: 13.3kg (29.32lb)	Cyclic Rate: 600rpm
Overall Length: 1443mm (56.8in)	Range: 2000m (6560ft)

▲ **Maschinengewehr 13 (MG 13)**

German Army / 301st Infantry Regiment, Poland, September 1939

Modified from a water-cooled weapon of World War I, the MG 13 was air-cooled and capable of firing 600 rounds per minute. It continued in service although it was intended to be replaced by the MG 34.

Long-serving Mauser

In 1935, the German Army adopted the most recent rifle in the long Mauser line as its standard shoulder arm. The Mauser Karabiner 98 Kurz, which is also abbreviated as the K98k or K98, was a bolt-action rifle that was chambered for the standard Mauser 7.92mm (.312in) cartridge. During its decade-long production run from 1935 to 1945, the rifle was produced in great numbers, with over 14.6 million entering service.

The K98k was fed by a five-round stripper clip and an internal magazine. It was developed from the Mauser Gewehr 98, which had first appeared in great numbers with German forces around the turn of the century and was the primary infantry weapon of the German Army in World War I. During the years between the wars, variants of the Gewehr 98

appeared, and the K98k was intended to incorporate the best elements of each of these. It was lighter at 3.9kg (8.6lb) and shorter at 1110mm (43.7in) than the original Gewehr 98 and designated as a 'short carbine'. The right to manufacture the K98k was licensed to several other countries, including Czechoslovakia and Turkey.

The Mauser M98 bolt-action system of the Gewehr 98 was modified from a straight bolt to a turn-down bolt in the K98k for easier operation and better placement of the iron sights, which were accurate up to 500m (550 yards). The K98k was known for its ruggedness and reliability in action. Accessories included mounts for the standard infantry bayonet and a grenade launcher intended for clearing fortified buildings or other strongpoints. An average rate of fire was 15 rounds per minute. The

Specifications

Country of Origin: Germany	Barrel Length: 627mm (24.75in)
Date: 1936	Muzzle Velocity: 762m/sec (2500ft/sec)
Calibre: 7.92mm (.312in) Mauser	Feed/Magazine: 50- or 75-round drum magazine
Operation: Recoil, air cooled	or up to 250-round belt
Weight: 12.1kg (26.67lb)	Cyclic Rate: 800–900rpm
Overall Length: 1219mm (48in)	Range: 2000m (6560ft) +

▲ **Maschinengewehr 34 (MG 34)**

German Army / 207th Infantry Division, Holland, May 1940

The MG 34 became the standard by which other machine guns of the early World War II period were measured. It was an excellent weapon with a high rate of fire and ease of operation; however, its high cost and precision manufacturing process limited the number available for service by 1939.

▲ **Solothurn Maschinengewehr 30 (MG 30)**

German Army / 69th Infantry Division, Norway, April 1940

Designed by Rheinmetall, the MG 30 entered service with the Swiss Army and was subsequently adopted by the German military. Mauser designer Heinrich Vollmer modified the weapon and developed the iconic MG 34.

Specifications

Country of Origin: Germany	Barrel Length: 595mm (23.42in)
Date: 1930	Muzzle Velocity: 800m/sec (2650ft/sec)
Calibre: 7.5mm (.295in) Schmidt-Rubin	Feed/Magazine: 25-round detachable box
Operation: Recoil, air cooled	magazine
Weight: 7.7kg (17lb)	Cyclic Rate: 500rpm
Overall Length: 1175mm (46.25in)	Range: 2000m (6560ft) +

Germans deployed a sniper variant on all fronts, and 132,000 of these were produced.

Infantry support

The versatile Maschinengewehr 34, or simply MG 34, was arguably the finest machine gun in the world at the time of its adoption and deployment with the German Army in 1934–35. The MG 34 was based initially on a Rheinmetall design, the Solothurn MG 30, which had entered service with the Swiss military a few years earlier. The MG 30 was adapted and modified by Heinrich Vollmer (1885–1961) of Mauser. Vollmer moved the feed mechanism to the left of the breech and introduced a shroud for the barrel. Improvements to the operating mechanism resulted in an astonishing rate of fire of 800 to 900 rounds per minute.

The recoil-operated MG 34 served both in the light machine gun role, fed by a drum magazine that held 50 or 75 rounds of 7.92mm (.312in) ammunition, and in a somewhat heavier and more stationary defensive role, mounted on a bipod or tripod and fed by an ammunition belt. Belts were carried in boxes of five with each belt containing 50 rounds, and these lengths could be linked together for sustained fire. Changing barrels was a rapid process for the trained operator and involved disengaging a latch and swinging the receiver to the right for the insertion of the new barrel. The gun's double crescent trigger dictated either semiautomatic or fully automatic firing modes.

The MG 34 was well known for its precision engineering and high production costs. Although it was reliable and dominant on the battlefield, it was prohibitively expensive and too few were available to supplant the older MG 13 and other models when war broke out in 1939. It was manufactured from 1934 until the end of the war.

Defending Norway, France and the Low Countries
APRIL–MAY 1940

The swift German advance across Western Europe in the spring of 1940 overran the smaller armies of several neighbouring countries and forced the capitulation of France within weeks.

FOLLOWING THE DEFEAT OF POLAND in the East, Hitler bided his time before launching offensive operations against France, the Low Countries and Scandinavia in the spring of 1940. Although the French Army, consisting of 133 divisions, appeared to be a formidable foe on paper, the French military establishment shuddered to contemplate a repeat of the bloodbath of 1914–18 and contented itself with constructing the imposing fortifications of the Maginot Line across the frontier with Germany.

Recalling images of massed infantry mown down before German machine-gun fire in World War I, the French abandoned their doctrine of heavy infantry assaults against entrenched enemy positions and considered the defences of the Maginot Line a deterrent to direct German invasion. On the other hand, a repeat of the Schlieffen Plan of 1914, with large infantry formations pivoting through Belgium, was expected by some as the logical offensive stroke by the Germans. Therefore, continuing cooperation with Belgium was another linchpin of French military thinking on the eve of World War II.

The French infantry platoon in 1940 consisted of a commanding officer, three squads of 10 men each armed with rifles, and two sections of grenade launchers. Light machine guns were deployed at squad level and operated by a gunner and a loader.

French deployment of updated shoulder arms lagged behind that of other nations, and with the outbreak of war most French soldiers carried the Berthier rifle, a bolt-action firearm of World War I that entered service in 1907 and was modified in

▶ Browning Hi-Power 35

Belgian Army / 11th Infantry Division, May 1940

Known as Hi-Power because of its 13-round magazine, the Browning HP 35 short-recoil semiautomatic pistol has become one of the most successful handguns in history and influenced many other models.

Specifications

Country of Origin: Belgium/United States	Barrel Length: 118mm (4.65in)
Date: 1935	Muzzle Velocity: 335m/sec (1100ft/sec)
Calibre: 9mm (.35in) Parabellum	Feed/Magazine: 13-round detachable box
Operation: Short recoil	magazine
Weight: .99kg (2.19lb)	Range: 30m (98ft)
Overall Length: 197mm (7.75in)	

▲ Krag-Jørgensen

Norwegian Army / 4th Infantry Regiment, Oslo, April 1940

A Norwegian design that entered production in the late 1880s, the Krag-Jørgensen rifle was fed by an integral magazine that could be loaded prior to the last round being expended. At the turn of the twentieth century it equipped US Army units.

Specifications

Country of Origin: Norway	Overall Length: 986mm (38.8in)
Date: 1886	Barrel Length: 520mm (20.5in)
Calibre: 7.62mm (.3in)	Muzzle Velocity: 580m/sec (1900ft/sec)
Operation: Bolt action	Feed/Magazine: 5-round magazine
Weight: 3.375kg (7.4lb)	Range: 500m (1640ft)

▲ Fusil Automatique Modèle 1917

French Army / 104th Infantry Division, Maginot Line, June 1940

The Fusil Automatique Modèle 1917 was adapted to semiautomatic operation from the Model 1886 Lebel rifle. It used the same ammunition and was fed by a five-round box magazine.

Specifications

Country of Origin: France	Overall Length: 1331mm (52.4in)
Date: 1917	Barrel Length: 798mm (31.4in)
Calibre: 8mm (.314in) Lebel	Muzzle Velocity: 853m/sec (2800ft/sec)
Operation: Gas, rotating bolt	Feed/Magazine: 5-round box magazine
Weight: 5.25kg (11.6lb)	Range: 300m (984ft)

1915. The Fusil Automatique Modèle 1917, a semiautomatic gas-operated rifle that fired an 8mm (.314in) Lebel cartridge, was introduced in 1917, and its short production run that ended a year later resulted in 86,000 weapons. The Fusil Automatique Modèle 1917 proved unpopular with frontline troops during World War I, and many of the rifles were withdrawn from service by the end of the Rif Wars in 1926. At the time of the German invasion in the West on 10 May 1940, a few of these weapons were still in service.

By 1936, the shortcomings of antiquated rifles in French service were noted, and plans were made to re-equip French infantry units with the MAS-36, a bolt-action design that would finally retire the bulk of the Berthier and Lebel weapons remaining in service. However, budget constraints resulted in a relative few examples of the MAS-36 being manufactured, and only a handful produced by the government-run Manufacture d'Armes de Saint-Etienne were available in 1940. The Lebel Modèle 1886/93 did remain in service as the principal weapon of the grenade-launcher sections.

The standard French light machine gun remained the 7.5mm (.295in) Fusil Mitrailleur 24/29, which had been designed in the 1920s and entered service during the interwar years. The FM 24/29 had a rate of fire of 450 rounds per minute and a 25-round box magazine feed, and performed well enough to serve into the 1960s before being replaced.

The standing Belgian Army comprised 100,000 soldiers, and this could be expanded to 550,000 with mobilization. Among the 18 infantry and two cavalry divisions available to defend Belgium in 1939, however, there were only about 160 machine guns, 52 of these considered heavy weapons.

The Belgian infantry platoon of 1940 included a headquarters section of the commanding lieutenant, a noncommissioned officer and an orderly. The officer typically carried a 9mm (.35in) Browning pistol, while the NCO and orderly were armed with the elderly 7.65mm (.301in) FN Modèle 1889 rifle, a Mauser design built under licence in Belgium. Four infantry sections each included a machine-gun squad of a sergeant, five riflemen and a single machine-gunner with a Browning FM 30 light machine gun (which has also been described as an automatic rifle similar to the more famous BAR) plus a rifle squad of five riflemen and a noncommissioned officer.

The small Norwegian Army was taken by surprise when the Germans invaded in April 1940 and was only partially able to mobilize, with just four battalions of its six divisions deploying to defend the country. The Norwegian infantry battalion included a machine-gun company of 12 machine guns, either the outdated Hotchkiss Mitraljöse Model 1898 or the newer Colt Mitraljöse Model 29 that was utilized as an infantry and anti-aircraft weapon.

Norwegian infantry platoons included four 10-man light-machine-gun sections, each of which consisted of a sergeant, the machine-gun support and five riflemen armed with the Krag-Jørgensen Model 1894 bolt-action rifle. The Krag-Jørgensen had equipped infantry units of the US Army until replaced by the Springfield Model 1903. Its performance during the Spanish-American War had

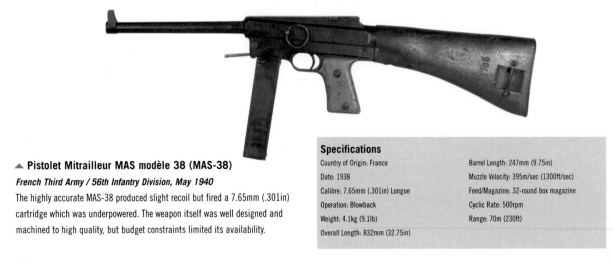

▲ **Pistolet Mitrailleur MAS modèle 38 (MAS-38)**
French Third Army / 56th Infantry Division, May 1940
The highly accurate MAS-38 produced slight recoil but fired a 7.65mm (.301in) cartridge which was underpowered. The weapon itself was well designed and machined to high quality, but budget constraints limited its availability.

Specifications

Country of Origin: France	Barrel Length: 247mm (9.75in)
Date: 1938	Muzzle Velocity: 395m/sec (1300ft/sec)
Calibre: 7.65mm (.301in) Longue	Feed/Magazine: 32-round box magazine
Operation: Blowback	Cyclic Rate: 500rpm
Weight: 4.1kg (9.1lb)	Range: 70m (230ft)
Overall Length: 832mm (32.75in)	

been considered inferior to that of the Mauser rifles carried by Spanish infantrymen. Nevertheless, more than 700,000 variants of the Krag-Jørgensen were manufactured during more than half a century of production. The 6.5mm (.256in) weapon was a Norwegian design that bore the names of its originators, Ole Herman Johannes Krag

(1837–1916) and Erik Jørgensen (1848–1896). It was fed by a five-round integral magazine.

British Expeditionary Force

Four infantry divisions of the British Army were on the ground in France within a week of the British declaration of war against Nazi Germany on

▲ Bren Mk I

British Expeditionary Force / 1st Battalion Welsh Guards, Dunkirk, May 1940

Adapted from a proven Czechoslovakian design, the Bren I light machine gun was capable of only a relatively low rate of fire. However, it was highly accurate and was modified in five major variants that served with British forces in combat as late as the Falklands War of 1982.

Specifications

Country of Origin: United Kingdom	Barrel Length: 635mm (25in)
Date: 1937	Muzzle Velocity: 730m/sec (2400ft/sec)
Calibre: 7.7mm (.303in)	Feed/Magazine: 30-round box magazine
Operation: Gas operated, air cooled	Cyclic Rate: 500rpm
Weight: 10.25kg (22.5lb)	Range: 1000m (3280ft)
Overall Length: 1150mm (45.25in)	

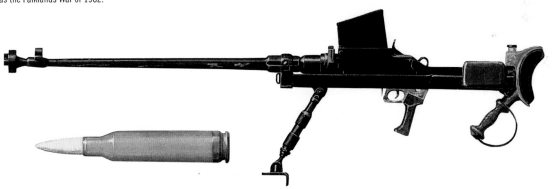

Specifications

Country of Origin: United Kingdom	Barrel Length: 910mm (36in); 762mm (30in)
Date: 1937	airborne version
Calibre: 13.97mm (.55in)	Muzzle Velocity: 747m/sec (2450ft/sec)
Operation: Bolt action	Feed/Magazine: 5-round detachable box
Weight: 16kg (35lb)	Range: 90m (295ft) against 16–19mm
Overall Length: 1575mm (62in)	(.63–.75in) armour

▲ Boys Mk I Anti-Tank Rifle

British Expeditionary Force / 143rd Brigade / Royal Warwickshire Regiment, May 1940

The heavy Boys Anti-Tank Rifle weighed 16kg (35lb) and was steadied with a bipod and padded butt. A new generation of shoulder-fired anti-tank weapons made the Boys obsolete soon after its debut in 1937.

3 September 1939. By the following spring, 400,000 troops organized in 10 divisions had arrived. These troops generally fought well in northern France and Belgium but were victimized by a German feint to the north and cut off by a *Wehrmacht* thrust through the Ardennes, finally retreating to the beaches of Dunkirk for evacuation. Thousands of tonnes of arms and equipment were abandoned; however, more than 350,000 Allied soldiers escaped to fight the Nazis another day.

The British infantry platoon of 1940 included headquarters personnel and three rifle sections of eight soldiers each, totalling about 30 men. Each section was commanded by a corporal or lance-corporal and included seven riflemen armed with the Short Magazine Lee-Enfield Rifle (SMLE). The section's single light machine gun, the Bren, was serviced by a gunner and loader, who also carried rifles.

The Mark III Short Magazine Lee-Enfield was introduced in 1907 and remained the principal shoulder arm of the British military for half a century, with more than 17 million variants produced. It remains in limited service today with some specialized units, and the line traces its origin to 1895 when the Magazine Lee-Enfield (MLE) rifle was adopted by the British Army. The weapon was named for its designer, James Paris Lee (1831–1904) and the Royal Small Arms Factory at Enfield, where it was originally manufactured. The SMLE fired the 7.7mm (.303in) cartridge and was fed by a 10-round magazine loaded with five-round charger clips. The

▲ **Street fighting**
German infantrymen armed with a drum-fed MG 34 squad machine gun advance through the streets of Oslo during the invasion of Norway, April 1940.

rifle was modified to accept the new high-velocity spitzer ammunition, while improved sights were mounted and the magazine improved.

The Bren light machine gun, which provided mobile fire support to small groups of infantrymen, had been adapted from the Czechoslovakian ZB vz.26 and entered service with the British Army in 1938. Following competitive trials with Browning

Specifications

Country of Origin: United Kingdom	Barrel Length: 196mm (7.7in)
Date: 1941	Muzzle Velocity: 365m/sec (1198ft/sec)
Calibre: 9mm (.35in) Parabellum	Feed/Magazine: 32-round detachable box
Operation: Blowback	magazine
Weight: 3.1kg (7lb)	Range: 60m (196ft)
Overall Length: 760mm (29.9in)	

▲ **Sten Mk I**

Eastern Command / 61st Infantry Division, Colchester, August 1941
Developed from captured examples of the German MP 40 submachine gun, the Sten is easily recognized with its crude metal stock and 32-round box magazine that loaded from the left side. About 100,000 were made before production switched to the Mark II.

and Vickers models in the early 1930s, the British Army adopted the Czech weapon, which was modified to accept the 7.7mm (.303in) cartridge and nicknamed Bren after its original place of manufacture in the Czech city of Brno. Fed from detachable magazines of 20, 30 or 100 rounds, the Bren had a relatively low rate of fire at about 500 rounds per minute. Nevertheless, it proved to be a durable weapon and remains in service today.

The initial British submachine gun of World War II was the 9mm (.35in) Lanchester, generally a copy of the German Bergmann MP 28. Since the Lanchester was complicated and could not be produced in large numbers, a few American Thompsons were procured. By 1941, several captured German MP 40 submachine guns had been copied and designated Sten, incorporating the first letters of the names of its designers, Sheffield and Turpin, along with the first two letters of the Enfield small-arms facility. The Sten also fired the 9mm (.35in) cartridge. It was fed by a 32-round detachable box magazine.

▲ **Lanchester Mk I**

Royal Navy, July 1941

The Lanchester was a copy of the German Bergmann MP 28 submachine gun. Many of its components were common with the Lee-Enfield rifle; however, such construction made the weapon's production lengthy and expensive. It was first deployed by Royal Navy units.

Specifications

Country of Origin: United Kingdom	Barrel Length: 203mm (8in)
Date: 1941	Muzzle Velocity: 380m/sec (1247ft/sec)
Calibre: 9mm (.35in) Parabellum	Feed/Magazine: 50-round box magazine
Operation: Blowback	Cyclic Rate: 600rpm
Weight: 4.34kg (9.56lb)	Range: 70m (230ft)
Overall Length: 850mm (33.5in)	

Specifications

Country of Origin: United Kingdom	Barrel Length: 558mm (22in)
Date: 1940	Muzzle Velocity: 730m/sec (2300ft/sec)
Calibre: 7.7mm (.303in)	Feed/Magazine: 30-round box magazine
Operation: Gas operated, air cooled	Cyclic Rate: 600rpm
Weight: 9.75kg (20.5lb)	Range: 2000m (6560ft) +
Overall Length: 1185mm (46.75in)	

▲ **Besal Mk II**

British Army / Undeployed

The Besal Mk II light machine gun was intended to supplement the British Army's supply of Bren Guns. It was constructed to fire the same ammunition and utilize the same magazine and was lighter and easier to produce. As the war progressed it was deemed unnecessary to produce the Besal in quantity.

Special Ops: Behind Enemy Lines
1941–45

British and US intelligence organizations supported covert operations by resistance groups and launched their own clandestine missions, while the Germans conducted raids and undercover efforts of their own.

WHEN THE DARK GREEN, open-topped Mercedes carrying 37-year-old Reinhard Heydrich (1904–42), *Reichsprotektor* of Bohemia and Moravia and top lieutenant of *Reichsführer*-SS Heinrich Himmler (1900–45), turned a sharp corner in downtown Prague and the driver lurched into second gear, an unobtrusive man dressed in civilian clothes suddenly pulled a Sten submachine gun from beneath his coat, pointed it at the Nazi officer and pulled the trigger. Nothing happened. The Sten had jammed.

An accomplice tossed a pair of grenades at the vehicle and seriously wounded Heydrich, who later died in a Czech hospital. The assailants were Czech operatives, trained in Scotland and equipped with weapons supplied by British intelligence. Josef Gabcik (1912–42) and Jan Kubis (1913–42) were the cornerstones of Operation Anthropoid, an assassination attempt against Heydrich. The pair had been parachuted into Nazi-occupied Czechoslovakia and once on the ground connected with a resistance network that facilitated the covert operation.

▲ **Sten in action**

A French resistance fighter poses with a Sten Mk II submachine gun during the battle for Paris, August 1944. The Sten was widely supplied to resistance fighters across Europe, because of its easy assembly and simple operation.

▲ **Welrod**

British Special Operations Executive / SO2 Operations, Occupied France 1943

The Welrod assassination pistol was a short-range precision weapon that included an integral silencer. Although the pistol included an eight-round magazine, reloading was manual rather than automatic, so a user could only expect to get off one round at a time.

Specifications

Country of Origin: United Kingdom	Overall Length: 310mm (12in)
Date: 1940	Barrel Length: 95mm (less silencer)
Calibre: 9mm (.35in), 8.1mm (.32in)	Muzzle Velocity: Not known
Operation: Rotary bolt	Feed/Magazine: 6- or 8-round magazine
Weight: 1.090kg (2.4lb)	Range: 20m (65ft)

Of course, when the Sten failed, the back-up plan succeeded in killing Heydrich and loosing a vengeful bloodbath against the Czech civilian population. The village of Lidice was thoroughly destroyed and its people massacred in reprisal. Gabcik and Kubis were cornered in the burial chamber beneath a church and finally killed.

With covert operations, necessity is often the mother of invention, and innovative weapons systems were deployed with intelligence agents and resistance fighters across Europe during World War II. Like Gabcik and Kubis, those willing to undertake such hazardous operations realized that it was likely they would not survive the mission. Nevertheless, the agents who were willing to participate were deployed

in attempts to kill enemy military and political figures, and weapons were developed for them, some of which could be easily concealed or broken down for transport.

Surprise and silence

Among the most innovative weapons developed for covert missions was the Welrod assassination pistol, a 9mm (.35in) or 8.1mm (.32in), manually reloaded bolt-action weapon with an integral silencer and a six- or eight-round magazine. Developed by the British Special Operations Executive (SOE), the Welrod was intended for close-quarters, single-opportunity action. The chambering of a new round from the magazine was slow, and it was likely that the

▶ Liberator M1942

French Resistance / Maquis Forces, Lyon, 1944

Cheaply made and often air-dropped to resistance fighters in Nazi-occupied Europe, the Liberator, or FP-45, was meant for close-in killing. It was difficult to operate, and clearing spent cases required the insertion of a dowel peg or a stick.

Specifications

Country of Origin: United States	Overall Length: 141mm (5.55in)
Date: 1942	Barrel Length: 102mm (4in)
Calibre: 11.4mm (.45in)	Muzzle Velocity: 250m/sec (820ft/sec)
Operation: Manual	Feed/Magazine: Single shot
Weight: .454kg (1lb)	Range: 8m (26.2ft)

▲ Sten Mk II 'Silent Sten'

British Special Operations Executive / SO2 Operations, Occupied France 1943

The Silent Sten was a variant of the British submachine gun with a suppressor to reduce the weapon's report. After 10 rounds were fired, the effectiveness of the suppressor was significantly degraded.

Specifications

Country of Origin: United Kingdom	Barrel Length: 196mm (7.7in)
Date: 1942	Muzzle Velocity: 380m/sec (1247ft/sec)
Calibre: 9mm (.35in) Parabellum	Feed/Magazine: 32-round detachable box
Operation: Blowback	magazine
Weight: 2.95kg (6.5lb)	Range: 70m (230ft)
Overall Length: 762mm (30in)	

agent would get off one shot only. To chamber a second round, a cap at the rear of the barrel was twisted and pulled back and then pushed forward. Reloading was accomplished only by removing the entire grip.

In the United States, the smoothbore 11.4mm (.45in) Liberator Model 1942 pistol was manufactured for the purpose of equipping resistance fighters. American intelligence officers reasoned that a quantity of crude, inexpensively made pistols could be manufactured and delivered quickly to resistance groups on the European continent, and the Liberator was cheaply made of stamped components. Although it was fitted with a single-shot magazine, each Liberator was packaged with 10 rounds of ammunition. Reloading was accomplished only after a suitable implement such as a stick was utilized to poke the spent shell casing from the weapon to clear the chamber. The Liberator was cocked by pulling the cocking piece to the rear; turning the piece sideways enabled reloading and ejecting spent casings.

The Special Operations Executive developed a silent version of the Sten Mk II for use by its agents. While the Sten itself was widely distributed to resistance fighters in Europe, the Silent Sten was identical to the original version with the exception that the muzzle report was suppressed. Although it was quiet for approximately the first 10 rounds, carbon build-up made the Silent Sten progressively louder as the 32-round 9mm (.35in) magazine was emptied.

The Hudson M3A1 was an improved version of the M3 submachine gun, popularly known as the 'Grease Gun'. Like the M3, the M3A1 was cheaply made. However, it was not approved for production until December 1944, and issued to few US troops during the waning months of World War II. The US Office of Strategic Services (OSS) requested a modification of the M3A1 with an integral sound suppressor. The suppressor was designed by Bell Laboratories, and approximately 1000 were ordered. The effectiveness of the suppressor was considerably below that of the British Sten. The M3A1 was capable of a rate of fire of 45 rounds per minute, although the low muzzle velocity retarded knockdown capability.

Another silenced weapon was intended specifically for assassination or long-distance killing. The De Lisle carbine was developed in the early 1940s and entered service in 1943. Designer William De Lisle based the weapon on the Short Magazine Lee-Enfield rifle, modifying the receiver to accept the 11.4mm (.45in) cartridge, replacing the barrel with a modified Thompson submachine gun barrel, and using modified magazines from the Model 1911 pistol.

A single-shot bolt-action weapon, the De Lisle was, in contrast to other silenced weapons of the time, extremely quiet. The single-shot feature was considered an advantage over semiautomatic operation, which might alert sentries or other enemy personnel when silence was required for a successful operation. The De Lisle was manufactured in quite limited numbers, and only 129 were produced from 1943 to 1945. Most of these were placed in the hands of British Commandos.

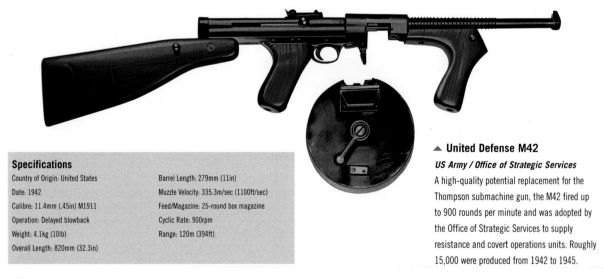

▲ **United Defense M42**

US Army / Office of Strategic Services

A high-quality potential replacement for the Thompson submachine gun, the M42 fired up to 900 rounds per minute and was adopted by the Office of Strategic Services to supply resistance and covert operations units. Roughly 15,000 were produced from 1942 to 1945.

Specifications

Country of Origin: United States	Barrel Length: 279mm (11in)
Date: 1942	Muzzle Velocity: 335.3m/sec (1100ft/sec)
Calibre: 11.4mm (.45in) M1911	Feed/Magazine: 25-round box magazine
Operation: Delayed blowback	Cyclic Rate: 900rpm
Weight: 4.1kg (10lb)	Range: 120m (394ft)
Overall Length: 820mm (32.3in)	

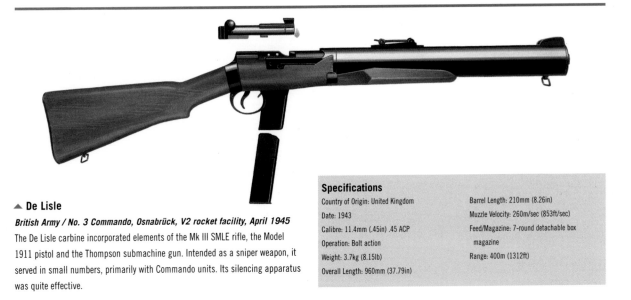

▲ De Lisle

British Army / No. 3 Commando, Osnabrück, V2 rocket facility, April 1945
The De Lisle carbine incorporated elements of the Mk III SMLE rifle, the Model
1911 pistol and the Thompson submachine gun. Intended as a sniper weapon, it
served in small numbers, primarily with Commando units. Its silencing apparatus
was quite effective.

Specifications

Country of Origin: United Kingdom	Barrel Length: 210mm (8.26in)
Date: 1943	Muzzle Velocity: 260m/sec (853ft/sec)
Calibre: 11.4mm (.45in) .45 ACP	Feed/Magazine: 7-round detachable box
Operation: Bolt action	magazine
Weight: 3.7kg (8.15lb)	Range: 400m (1312ft)
Overall Length: 960mm (37.79in)	

North Africa: British & Commonwealth Forces
1940–43

The seesaw struggle for supremacy on the African continent was waged across thousands of kilometres of arid desert, and British and Commonwealth forces fought tenaciously to win the final victory over their Axis adversaries.

CONTINUALLY PLAGUED by shortages of supplies and manpower, the British and Commonwealth armed forces in the desert won significant early victories against Mussolini's Italian Army. Outnumbered 10 to one, General Sir Archibald Wavell (1883–1950) authorized an offensive action against the Italians in late 1940. Operation Compass, intended as a five-day raid against Italian bases, turned into a two-month string of Commonwealth victories. Under the command of Lieutenant-General Richard O'Connor (1889–1981), 31,000 troops, 275 tanks and 120 field guns succeeded in forcing a break in Italian lines, routing the enemy.

In eight weeks of fighting, O'Connor's force, which consisted primarily of the 7th Armoured Division and the 4th Indian Infantry Division, killed 3000 Italian soldiers while capturing 115,000 enemy

troops, 400 tanks and nearly 1300 artillery pieces. The crowning victory of Operation Compass took place at Beda Fomm, just south of the major Libyan city of Benghazi. The remnants of the Italian Tenth Army were cut off and forced to surrender. O'Connor pleaded for the resources necessary to fight on to the Libyan capital of Tripoli, but Wavell had already turned his focus on the defence of Greece and Crete – primarily at the behest of Prime Minister Winston Churchill.

Within days of the Axis disaster at Beda Fomm, two German divisions, the vanguard of the *Afrika Korps* and what would become the vaunted Panzer Army Afrika in combination with Italian formations, landed at Tripoli. The German commander, Major-General Erwin Rommel (1891–1944), soon engineered a spectacular reversal of fortune, pushing

Commonwealth forces across kilometres of territory and eventually crossing the Egyptian frontier. Rommel's only major setback was the failure to capture the Libyan port of Tobruk, stubbornly

ANZAC INFANTRY BATTALION, 1941	
Unit	Strength
Battalion HQ	
Regimental Aid Post	1
Headquarters Company	1
Signals Platoon	1
Anti-aircraft Platoon	1
Mortar Platoon	1
Pioneer Platoon	1
Administration Platoon	1
Carrier Platoon	1
Rifle Companies	4
Rifle Company HQ	
Platoons	3
Rifle Platoon HQ	
Rifle sections	3
Anti-tank rifle	1
50mm (2in) mortar	1
Rifle Section	
Bren light machine gun	1
Thompson submachine gun	1

defended in the spring of 1941 primarily by soldiers of the Australian 9th Division, who were relieved during Operation Crusader after a 240-day siege. Rommel was plagued by shortages of supplies due to the great distances from bases and the continuing Allied interdiction of shipping and road transport.

During his second North African offensive, Rommel did capture Tobruk in June 1942. By this time, he had achieved fame as the 'Desert Fox', threatening the Egyptian capital of Cairo, Egypt's great port of Alexandria, and the security of the Suez Canal, the lifeline of Commonwealth supply to troops in the Middle East. In October 1942, Axis forces reached their high-water mark. The reinforced British Eighth Army under Lieutenant-General Bernard Montgomery (1887–1976) attacked at El Alamein and drove Rommel westwards. El Alamein is considered the turning point in the Desert War and one of the great Allied victories of World War II.

Meanwhile, Operation Torch, the Allied invasion of North Africa from the west, began on 8 November 1942, with landings at Casablanca, Oran and Algiers. Rommel was fighting on two fronts, and the fate of Axis forces in North Africa was sealed. Hitler recalled Rommel from the African continent, and more than

▼ Australian Infantry Rifle Section, 1941

Australian troops deployed to the North African desert bore a significant burden during the fighting of the first two years against Erwin Rommel's Panzer Army Afrika. The Australian infantry rifle section was organized in similar fashion to those of other Commonwealth forces and included a rifle group and a gun group. In the rifle group, one automatic weapon, usually a Thompson submachine gun handled by the section leader, supported eight riflemen armed with the Lee-Enfield Mk III. The gun section included a Bren light machine gun and two riflemen.

Rifle Group (section leader, six riflemen), 1 x Thompson SMG, 6 x SMLE rifles

Gun Group (lance-corporal, loader, gunner), 2 x SMLE rifle, 1 x Bren light machine gun

300,000 Axis troops remaining surrendered in Tunisia in May 1943.

Weapons of the Desert War

The British and Commonwealth troops who fought the Germans and Italians in the North African desert came from all areas of the British Empire, particularly Australia, New Zealand and India. The riflemen were equipped with the Mark III Short Magazine Lee-Enfield (SMLE) rifle, the principal rifle of the British Army and all Commonwealth forces for more than half a century.

Among the personal automatic weapons carried in the desert was the Sten Mk II submachine gun, of which nearly two million examples were produced during World War II. The Sten was constructed of just 47 parts, and these were stamped from steel, then welded or pressed together rapidly. The only machined parts of the weapon were the barrel and the bolt. Firing a 9mm (.35in) cartridge, the Sten was fed by a side-mounted, 32-round magazine and could actually accept captured German ammunition. The weapon could be dismantled quickly for cleaning in the harsh desert environment, but it was sometimes prone to jamming.

The Thompson submachine gun was developed by American inventor John T. Thompson (1860–1940) in 1919 as a means of possibly breaking the stalemate of trench warfare after the heavy bloodshed of World War I. Thompson reasoned that such a weapon could

Specifications

Country of Origin: United Kingdom	Barrel Length: 640mm (25.2in)
Date: 1907	Muzzle Velocity: 634m/sec (2080ft/sec)
Calibre: 7.7mm (.303in)	Feed/Magazine: 10-round box, loaded with
Operation: Bolt action	5-round charger clips
Weight: 3.93kg (8.625lb)	Range: 500m (1640ft)
Overall Length: 1133mm (44.6in)	

▲ **Lee-Enfield Rifle No. 1 Mk III SMLE**

British Eighth Army / 7th Support Group / 1st King's Royal Rifle Corps, Operation Battleaxe, June 1941

The Lee-Enfield Mk III became the primary infantry weapon of Commonwealth forces during World War II. The bolt-action rifle was one of a series of weapons that served through the 1950s with specialized variants still active today.

▲ **Thompson M1**

British Eighth Army / 6th Battalion Durham Light Infantry, El Alamein, November 1942

The American Thompson submachine gun was issued to British and Commonwealth troops early in the Desert War and was later complemented by the Sten Mk II.

Specifications

Country of Origin: United States	Barrel Length: 267mm (10.5in)
Date: 1942	Muzzle Velocity: 280m/sec (920ft/sec)
Calibre: 11.4mm (.45in) M1911	Feed/Magazine: 20- or 30-round box magazine
Operation: Delayed blowback	Cyclic Rate: 700rpm
Weight: 4.74kg (10.45lb) loaded	Range: 120m (394ft)
Overall Length: 813mm (32in)	

provide the firepower to literally sweep enemy soldiers from their trenches. Hence, the moniker 'Trench Broom' was among its many nicknames.

The Thompson did not achieve its greatest fame on the battlefield, but during the Prohibition era of the 1920s and 1930s in the United States. The Thompson became symbolic of the fighting between law enforcement officers and organized crime and was used by both. The weapon fired the 11.4mm (.45in) cartridge and was blowback-operated; it featured the Blish Lock breech-locking system designed by US naval officer John Bell Blish (1860–1921). The Thompson was fed by stick or box magazines of 20 or

30 rounds or by 50- or 100-round drums.

The Thompson was adopted by the US Army in 1938 and made available to British and Commonwealth forces through Lend-Lease. Many examples were placed in the hands of Commando units from Britain and Canada.

As the war progressed, the British Sten and the Australian Owen submachine gun, officially known as the Owen Machine Carbine, began appearing on the battlefield in greater numbers.

Complementing the Vickers Mk I machine gun was the lighter but hefty Vickers-Berthier, a weapon weighing 11.1kg (24.4lb) and firing a 7.7mm

Specifications

Country of Origin: United Kingdom	Barrel Length: 196mm (7.7in)
Date: 1942	Muzzle Velocity: 380m/sec (1247ft/sec)
Calibre: 9mm (.35in) Parabellum	Feed/Magazine: 32-round detachable box
Operation: Blowback	magazine
Weight: 2.95kg (6.5lb)	Cyclic Rate: 500rpm
Overall Length: 762mm (30in)	Range: 70m (230ft)

▲ **Sten Mk II**

South African 2nd Infantry Division / 2nd Infantry Brigade, Tobruk, May 1942
Constructed of only 47 parts, the Sten Mk II submachine gun was stamped and generally pressed together for rapid deployment to Commonwealth forces. The weapon proved popular due to its firepower and ease of disassembly.

Specifications

Country of Origin: United Kingdom	Overall Length: 1156mm (45.5in)
Date: 1932	Barrel Length: 600mm (23.6in)
Calibre: 7.7mm (.303in)	Muzzle Velocity: 745m/sec (2450ft/sec)
Operation: Gas operated	Feed/Magazine: 30-round box magazine
Weight: 11.1kg (24.4lb)	Range: 550m (1805ft)

▲ **Vickers-Berthier**

Western Desert Force / 6th Rajputana Rifles, Egypt, 1940
The Vickers-Berthier was based on a French design of World War I and adopted by the British Indian Army in 1932. It proved heavy and deficient in comparison to the Bren Gun.

◀ **Foxholes**

Australian troops man foxholes in the hard ground of the Western Desert, 1942. All are armed with the Mk III Short Magazine Lee-Enfield, bayonets fixed.

▲ **Bren Mk II**

British Eighth Army / 51st Highland Division, El Alamein, November 1942

Although a very accurate light machine gun, the Bren's limited magazine capacity could make sustained fire problematic, especially when laying down suppressing fire. However, the Bren proved key to British Army doctrine in World War II and every infantryman was expected to know how to use the section's Bren.

Specifications

Country of Origin: United Kingdom	Barrel Length: 625mm (25in)
Date: 1941	Muzzle Velocity: 730m/sec (2400ft/sec)
Calibre: 7.7mm (.303in)	Feed/Magazine: 30-round box magazine
Operation: Gas operated, air cooled	Cyclic Rate: 500rpm
Weight: 10.25kg (22.5lb)	Range: 1000m (3280ft)
Overall Length: 1150mm (45.25in)	

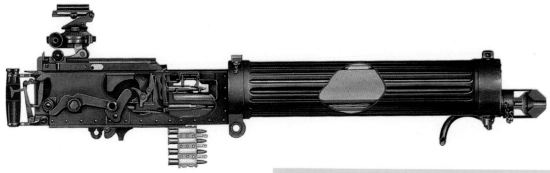

▲ **Vickers Mk I**

British Eighth Army / 10th Armoured Division / 5th Battalion Royal Sussex
Regiment, Tunisia, March 1943

The venerable Vickers Mk I was based on the old Maxim design and had served in
World War I. It fired the same cartridge, the 7.7mm (.303in), as lighter machine
guns and the Lee-Enfield Mk III rifle.

Specifications

Country of Origin: United Kingdom	Barrel Length: 725mm (28.5in)
Date: 1912	Muzzle Velocity: 600m/sec (1970ft/sec)
Calibre: 7.7mm (.303in)	Feed/Magazine: Belt fed
Operation: Recoil, water cooled	Cyclic Rate: 600rpm
Weight: 18kg (40lb)	Range: 2000m (6560ft) + ; later 3000m
Overall Length: 1155mm (40.5in)	(9842ft)

(.303in) cartridge. Based on a French design of the
World War I era, the weapon was licence-built in
Britain as a replacement for the Lewis Gun. The
British Indian Army adopted the Vickers-Berthier in
1932, while the British Army opted for the famous
Bren Gun. The Vickers-Berthier, or VB, was welcome
in the desert for its firepower of 450 to 600 rounds
per minute; however, the weapon was about a
kilogram (2.2lb) heavier than the Bren and was less
portable. As a result, despite the VB's simpler design,
the British Army chose the Bren.

The Vickers Mk I medium machine gun fired the
same cartridge as the lighter Vickers-Berthier, the
7.7mm (.303in) round, but was water-cooled and
significantly heavier at 18kg (40lb), and required a
team of as many as six soldiers to service it. The
Vickers was a veteran of World War I and based on
the venerable Maxim design. Although the British
military establishment had made plans to replace it
between the world wars, the Vickers remained in
service throughout World War II and was not retired
until the late 1960s.

Italian Army
1940–43

**Although its ranks included some elite formations such as the Bersaglieri who fought heroically
in the desert, the Italian Army was badly outclassed early in the Desert War and depended on its
German allies for support and leadership.**

FOLLOWING THE DEBACLE of the Italian Tenth Army
during Operation Compass, Mussolini continued
to send reinforcements to North Africa, and when
Major-General Erwin Rommel (1891–1944) and the
German *Afrika Korps* arrived in Libya, the Germans
were nominally under senior Italian command. Often
the performance of Italian forces during
World War II, and particularly in North Africa, has

been maligned by historians. The Italians suffered
from a pronounced lack of command and control
and proved inexperienced at large-scale military
operations.

Infantry and armoured formations were typically
equipped with small arms of Italian manufacture, and
the quality of many of these weapons has been
criticized, both with reason and also unfairly. Variants

of the Fucile Modello 91 rifle were commonly used by Italian troops during World War II. A veteran of service in World War I, the Modello 1891 was fed by an integral six-round magazine and loaded with an en-bloc clip. It entered service with the Italian Army in 1892 and was originally chambered for a 6.5mm (.256in) rimless cartridge.

However, reports of inadequate performance at both short and long ranges during the Italian expeditions into Africa during the 1930s prompted the government to authorize a new weapon, the Modello 1938, chambered for a more powerful 7.35mm (.29in) cartridge. Problems with

manufacture and supply of the new weapon thwarted the progress and compelled the Italians to revert to 6.5mm (.256in) ammunition and weapons. For a time, the Italian Army deployed a shorter version of the Modello 1891, but by 1941 the longer Carcano M91/41 was in use. It remained slightly shorter than the original Modello 1891. The sojourn of the Modello 1891 is somewhat indicative of the travails of the Italian arms industry of the interwar and World War II period.

The principal light machine gun of the Italian forces from 1940 to 1943 was the Fucile Mitragliatore Breda Modello 30. Although it was

Specifications

Country of Origin: Italy	Barrel Length: 520mm (20.5in)
Date: 1930	Muzzle Velocity: 610m/sec (2000ft/sec)
Calibre: 6.5mm (.256in) M95 and others	Feed/Magazine: 20-round integral box magazine
Operation: Blowback, air cooled	Cyclic Rate: 475rpm
Weight: 10.2kg (22.5lb)	Range: 1000m (3280ft)
Overall Length: 1230mm (48.5in)	

▲ **Fucile Mitragliatore Breda Modello 30**

Italian Tenth Army / 63rd Infantry Division, Sidi Barrani, September 1940

The standard light machine gun of the Italian Army, the Modello 30 developed a reputation for high maintenance and unreliability in combat. Nevertheless, it was deployed with Italian forces for the duration of the war.

▲ **Fucile Modello 91**

64 Infantry Division Catanzaro, Buq Buq, December 1940

The long-serving Modello 91 was the primary shoulder arm of the Italians in World War I. Variants continued in service through World War II despite problems with performance during African campaigns of the 1920s and 1930s.

Specifications

Country of Origin: Italy	Overall Length: 1285mm (50.6in)
Date: 1891	Barrel Length: 780mm (30.7in)
Calibre: 6.5mm (.256in)	Muzzle Velocity: 630m/sec (2067ft/sec)
Operation: Bolt action	Feed/Magazine: 6-round box magazine
Weight: 3.8kg (8.375lb)	Range: 500m (1640ft)

innovative, with a hinged magazine that was opened and filled with 20-round rifle chargers of 6.5mm (.256in) ammunition for reloading, the weapon was less than robust and prone to battlefield damage, which often rendered it useless. The closed-bolt, blowback-operated machine gun also utilized a small mechanism that oiled each cartridge for firing. During combat this process sometimes resulted in the premature 'cooking-off' of a round. The weapon was manufactured by Breda Meccanica Bresciana and is considered inferior to contemporary light machine

guns fielded by other armies due to a low rate of fire at 475 rounds per minute, low ammunition capacity, lack of a handle to facilitate changing of barrels, a propensity for jamming, and susceptibility to damage. The early allocation of machine guns to Italian infantry companies was inadequate, with only a single weapon apportioned to a pair of squads, resulting in a maximum of eight Modello 30 guns per company, which was therefore somewhat undergunned. Later, this number was increased to a single gun per squad.

Specifications

Country of Origin: Italy	Barrel Length: Not known
Date: 1915	Muzzle Velocity: 301.82m/sec (990ft/sec)
Calibre: 9mm (.35in)	Feed/Magazine: 25-round detachable box
Operation: Blowback	magazine
Weight: 3.62kg (8lb)	Range: 70m (230ft)
Overall Length: 901.69mm (35.5in)	

▲ **Villar-Perosa OVP M1918**

1st Blackshirt Division 23 Marzo, Bardia, Libya, January 1941

The OVP M1918 submachine gun was an adaptation of an earlier twin-barrelled weapon with a high rate of fire of 900 rounds per minute. It entered service late in World War I and was still in use more than two decades later.

Specifications

Country of Origin: Italy	Barrel Length: 198mm (7.79in)
Date: 1938	Muzzle Velocity: 395m/sec (1295ft/sec)
Calibre: 9mm (.35in)	Feed/Magazine: 10-, 20- or 40-round detachable
Operation: Blowback	box magazine
Weight: 2.72kg (6lb)	Range: 70m (230ft)
Overall Length: 798mm (31.4in)	

▲ **Moschetto Automatico Beretta Modello 38 (MAB 38)**

132 Armoured Division Ariete, Battle of Gazala, May 1942

The successful MAB 38 was a sturdy submachine gun that was originally issued to elite units and compared favourably with its Allied and German counterparts. The weapon fired in either semiautomatic or fully automatic modes with separate triggers.

▶ **Alpine aim**
An Italian mountaintrooper aims a Beretta Modello 1934 pistol during training in the Alps. The Modello 1934 was a reliable handgun, although its 9mm (.35in) short cartridge was underpowered.

Submachine guns

Italian troops deployed a pair of submachine guns, the Villar-Perosa OVP M1918 and the Moscheto Auto Beretta MAB 38. The former was developed during World War I and was an improvement on an earlier version – a twin-barrelled weapon designated the M1915. The M1918 fired a 9mm (.35in) cartridge and was capable of an impressive rate of fire of 900 rounds per minute fed by a top-mounted box magazine with a 25-round capacity. A shoulder stock was added for stability in sustained combat situations.

The Moschetto Automatico Beretta Modello 38 (MAB 38) was a 9mm (.35in) submachine gun manufactured at the Beretta Works in Gardone Valtrompia, Brescia, and firing the same ammunition as Beretta pistols. It was capable of firing a maximum of 500 rounds per minute and was fed by a detachable box magazine of 10, 20 or 40 rounds. This gas-operated submachine gun was capable of semiautomatic or fully automatic firing, with two triggers. Until 1943, the MAB 38 was primarily issued to elite airborne and Carabineri units and some formations deployed to Africa. It was recognized as a formidable weapon and was sought after by Allied soldiers who faced it in combat. As the war progressed, the weapon was issued to Italian troops fighting with the Allies.

◀ **Fiat Modello 35**
German-Italian Panzer Army / Italian 17th Infantry Division Pavia, Tunisia, 1943
The Fiat-Revelli 35 was a revised version of the Modello 1914, which had equipped the Italian Army during World War I. It proved to be an unreliable weapon, especially in desert conditions.

Specifications

Country of Origin: Italy	Barrel Length: 680mm (26.75in)
Date: 1935	Muzzle Velocity: 790m/sec (2600ft/sec)
Calibre: 8mm (.314in)	Feed/Magazine: 50-round belt
Operation: Gas operated, air cooled	Cyclic Rate: 450rpm
Weight: 19.5kg (43lb)	Range: 2000m (6560ft)
Overall Length: 1270mm (50in)	

Sicily and Italian Campaign
1943–45

The bitter fighting through Sicily and up the boot of Italy was characterized by close-quarters combat in rugged terrain with small arms dealing death from caves, fortified positions and house to house in towns and villages.

IN EARLY JULY 1943, the Allies landed in force on the southern tip of the island of Sicily. Operation Husky launched the Italian campaign, one of the most arduous and prolonged actions of World War II. Within six weeks, the British Eighth Army, commanded by General Sir Bernard Montgomery (1887–1976), had pushed northwards from the southern tip of the island and joined the spearhead of the American Seventh Army, under General George S. Patton Jr. (1885–1945), that had landed to the east at Gela, advanced to the northwest capturing Palermo, and pressed the Axis defenders into a perimeter around the city of Messina in the island's northeast corner.

Although Sicily had been secured by late August, the cooperative Allied offensive had failed to close the trap on the island and allowed thousands of Axis troops to escape to the Italian mainland across the narrow Strait of Messina. German and Italian forces braced for the coming invasion of Italy.

Montgomery's Eighth Army executed Operation Baytown on 3 September 1943, landing in southern Italy, and the US Fifth Army, commanded by General Mark W. Clark (1896–1984), landed at Salerno on 9 September to undertake Operation Avalanche. More than 15 months of costly fighting ensued as the Eighth Army pushed up the east coast along the Adriatic Sea and the Fifth Army doggedly advanced up the west coast near the Tyrrhenian Sea.

The Italian campaign was marked by stubborn German defence, which stiffened following the surrender of Fascist Italy just as Allied forces were poised to invade the country. The Germans constructed a series of lengthy defensive lines stretching for kilometres across the mountainous spine of Italy. The most formidable of these was the Gustav Line. Allied attempts to breach it precipitated the horrendous battle for Monte Cassino and the epic fight for its abbey, as well as the amphibious Allied landing at Anzio, Operation Shingle, that was intended to rapidly seize Rome but instead degenerated into a months-long stalemate.

The first Axis capital to fall into Allied hands, Rome was liberated on 4 June 1944. Two days later, the Allied invasion of Normandy relegated the Italian campaign to a sideshow. Fighting continued in the north of the country until the end of the war in May 1945.

Specifications

Country of Origin: Germany
Date: 1942
Calibre: 7.92mm (.312in) Mauser
Operation: Gas operated
Weight: 4.53kg (9.99lb)
Overall Length: 940mm (37in)

Barrel Length: 502mm (19.76in)
Muzzle Velocity: 761m/sec (2500ft/sec)
Feed/Magazine: 20-round detachable box
  magazine
Range: 400m (1312ft) +

▲ **Fallschirmjägergewehr 42 (FG 42)**

German I Parachute Corps / 1st Parachute Division, Monte Cassino, March 1944

Intended to provide firepower for lightly armed airborne troops, the FG 42 combined elements of a machine gun and a bolt-action rifle and could be considered an early assault rifle.

COLT M1911A1 MILITARY PRODUCTION FIGURES	
Period	Total
1924–39	17,281
1940	4695
1941	34,756
1942	100,266
1943	752,529
1944	134,317
1945	136,000

COLT COMMERCIAL PRODUCTION: MODEL 1911A1		
Serial Numbers	Date	Total
S/N C135000 to C139999	1924	5000
S/N C140000 to 144999	1925	5000
S/N C145000 to C150999	1926	6000
S/N C151000 to C151999	1927	1000
S/N C152000 to C154999	1928	3000
S/N C155000 to C155999	1929	1000
S/N C156000 to C158999	1930	3000
S/N C159000 to C160999	1931	2000
S/N C161000 to C164799	1932	3800
S/N C164800 to C174599	1933	9800
S/N C174600 to C177999	1934	3400
S/N C178000 to C179799	1935	1800
S/N C179800 to C183199	1936	3400
S/N C183200 to C188699	1937	5500
S/N C188700 to C189599	1938	900
S/N C189600 to C198899	1939	9300
S/N C198900 to C199299	1940	400
S/N C199300 to C208799	1941	9500
S/N C208800 to C215018	1942	6219

King of the hill

A few of the elite German *Fallschirmjäger*, or airborne troops, who turned the rubble of the abbey of Monte Cassino into a virtually impregnable redoubt that stood against repeated assaults, were armed with the light Fallschirmjägergewehr 42 (FG 42), developed specifically for the lightly armed and equipped paratroopers. It was first in action during the daring raid by SS troops under the command of Major Otto Skorzeny (1908–75) to rescue Mussolini (1882–1945) from captivity in the Italian Alps in September 1943.

The FG 42 was conceived as a weapon that could provide sustained fire support on the ground, displaying the characteristics of the machine gun with the ease of transport of the basic infantry rifle. Therefore it may truly be classified as an early assault rifle. It weighed only 42kg (9.3lb) and fired the 7.92mm (.312in) cartridge. It was fed by a detachable box magazine of 10 or 20 rounds and was capable of selective semiautomatic or fully automatic firing modes. Intended to supplant the bolt-action

Mauser Karabiner 98k rifle and the submachine guns then in wide use, it was designed by Louis Stange and manufactured by Rheinmetall. One complication led to quite low production numbers. Manganese, which was used in making the barrels for the weapon, was in short supply, and after the production of only 2000 guns the limited supply of

▶ **Browning M1911A1**

US VI Corps / 3rd Infantry Division, Anzio, March 1944

One of the most popular small arms of the modern era, the 11.4mm (.45in) Browning M1911A1 pistol set a standard for modern pistols in both design and longevity of service.

Specifications

Country of Origin: United States

Date: 1911

Calibre: 11.4mm (.45in)

Operation: Short recoil

Weight: 1.1kg (2.425lb)

Overall Length: 216mm (8.5in)

Barrel Length: 127mm (5in)

Muzzle Velocity: 262m/sec (860ft/sec)

Feed/Magazine: 7-round magazine

Range: 50m (164ft)

manganese was designated for other projects and other materials were substituted.

Once the FG 42 reached the field, several modifications were requested, including a relocation of the bipod from near the hand guard to the muzzle for greater control, a reduction in the weapon's propensity to overheat by changing the stock from metal to wood, and slanting the handgrip to a nearly vertical position.

When the weapon was in fully automatic mode, the power of the rifle cartridge made it a challenge to maintain control and any degree of accuracy. Later versions reduced the rate of fire from 900 rounds per minute to 750. The muzzle was modified to help with recoil and muzzle flash but this resulted in a much louder report. Due to the great expense of manufacturing the FG 42, only about 7000 were produced from 1943 to 1945.

Browning dominance

The Browning M1911A1 pistol was a common sight on the hips of US Army personnel during the Italian campaign and indeed around the globe during World War II. This robust single-action, semiautomatic pistol fired an 11.4mm (.45in) cartridge and was fed by a seven-round detachable box magazine. It was reputed to have tremendous knockdown capability in the hands of a skilled user and replaced earlier potential standard issue pistols such as the German-made Luger for this reason. The M1911A1 has

▲ **Browning M2HB**

US Fifth Army / 135th Infantry Regiment, Rome, June 1944

The 12.7mm (.5in) Browning M2HB heavy machine gun was an air-cooled variant of the original weapon that entered service in the 1930s. Its proven success on the battlefield has resulted in its remaining in the NATO arsenal.

Specifications

Country of Origin: United States	Barrel Length: 1143mm (45in)
Date: 1933	Muzzle Velocity: 898m/sec (2950ft/sec)
Calibre: 12.7mm (.5in)	Feed/Magazine: 110-round belt
Operation: Short recoil, air cooled	Cyclic Rate: 450–575rpm
Weight: 38.5kg (84lb)	Range: 1800m (5905ft) effective
Overall Length: 1655mm (65in)	

Specifications

Country of Origin: United States	Barrel Length: 266mm (10.5in)
Date: 1921	Muzzle Velocity: 280m/sec (920ft/sec)
Calibre: 11.4mm (.45in) M1911	Feed/Magazine: 18-, 20-, 30-round detachable
Operation: Delayed blowback	box, or 50-, 100-round drum magazine
Weight: 4.88kg (10.75lb)	Cyclic Rate: 800rpm
Overall Length: 857mm (33.75in)	Range: 120m (394ft)

▲ **Thompson 1921**

1st Special Service Force, Monte Majo, January 1944

The Thompson submachine gun was developed in World War I as a means of breaking the stalemate of trench warfare with sustained fire support. It was adopted by the US Army in 1938 and made available to allies through Lend-Lease.

become one of the most famous firearms in modern history and remains popular today with a service life that has extended a full century.

The M1911 Browning pistol was the brainchild of prolific firearms designer John Browning (1855–1926), whose work led to some of the most highly produced firearms of the twentieth century. During his lifetime, Browning worked for his own arms company as well as Colt, Winchester, Remington, Savage and the Belgian company Fabrique Nationale. The M1911 is quite probably his best known design, although others include the Browning Automatic Rifle (BAR) and the 12.7mm (.5in) M2 heavy machine gun.

From 1911 to 1985, the M1911 was the standard issue sidearm for the US military. The handgun was chosen after a series of rigorous field tests, particularly in competition with a rival Savage model. Although officially replaced by the M9 pistol by 1990, it remains in service and is popular with civilian gun enthusiasts. It was officially adopted by the US Army on 29 March 1911, and the US Navy and Marine Corps followed suit two years later. Manufacturing was solely undertaken by Colt until the demand for the weapon grew and the US government's Springfield Armory took up production during World War I.

Combat experience during World War I prompted slight modifications to the original design and resulted in a new designation, M1911A1. The most prominent of these alterations included a shorter trigger, new grip chequering, cutouts behi the trigger, a longer grip safety spur, shorter hamm spur and wider front sight. Several companies produced the M1911A1 during World War II, including Colt, Remington Rand, Union Switch and Signal, Ithaca Gun Company, and Singer. More than 1.9 million were ordered by the US military during the period.

Browning machine guns

Browning's M2 12.7mm (.5in) heavy machine gun was developed during World War I and remains in service today, with more than three million manufactured since its adoption by the US Army in the early 1920s. The HB variant refers to the heavier air-cooled barrel that was introduced in 1933 to offer a lighter, more transportable weapon at 38.5kg (84lb) compared with 55kg (121lb) for the older water-cooled version. The short-recoil-operated M2HB was mounted on a tripod for infantry use, belt-fed and capable of a rate of fire of up to 635 rounds per minute.

Variants of the original Browning M2 machine gun have been mounted aboard fighter and bomber aircraft, tanks and other armoured vehicles, and naval vessels. The weapon's variety of heavy ammunition has proved effective against enemy personnel, light vehicles and aircraft in a multipurpose career. It is second only to the M1911 pistol in length of service with US forces and remains a primary weapon of US and NATO troops in Afghanistan and Iraq.

▲ **Hudson M3A1 with silencer**

US Office of Strategic Services / 2671st Special Recon Battalion, Naples-Foggia, November 1944

The M3A1 submachine gun was an improved version of the original M3 'Grease Gun' that was capable of further modification with a suppressor. An order for 1000 of these was placed by the OSS.

Specifications

Country of Origin: United States	Overall Length: 762mm (30in)
Date: 1944	Barrel Length: 203mm (8in)
Calibre: 9mm (.35in) or 11.4mm (.45in)	Muzzle Velocity: 275m/sec (900ft/sec)
.45 ACP	Feed/Magazine: 30-round detachable box mag
Operation: Blowback	Cyclic Rate: 450rpm
Weight: 3.7kg (8.15lb)	Range: 50m (164ft)

▲ **Sten Mk V**

British Eighth Army / 8th Battalion Royal Fusiliers, Gustav Line, May 1944

The Sten Mk V submachine gun reached British troops in 1944 and was of higher quality manufacture than the Mk II, the most common of the Sten guns. The Mk V included improvements such as a wooden pistol grip and stock.

Specifications

Country of Origin: United Kingdom	Barrel Length: 196mm (7.7in)
Date: 1944	Muzzle Velocity: 380m/sec (1247ft/sec)
Calibre: 9mm (.35in) Parabellum	Feed/Magazine: 32-round detachable box
Operation: Blowback	magazine
Weight: 3.86kg (8.5lb)	Cyclic Rate: 500rpm
Overall Length: 762mm (30in)	Range: 70m (230ft)

British Army: Normandy to the Rhine
1944–45

From three invasion beaches in Normandy, British and Commonwealth troops slugged their way to the frontier of the Third Reich against stubborn resistance as small-unit engagements often spelled the difference between victory and defeat.

BITTER FIGHTING LAY AHEAD for the British and Commonwealth troops who stormed ashore on Gold, Juno and Sword Beaches on D-Day, 6 June 1944. The liberation of Western Europe would prove to be an arduous task, culminating in the surrender of all German forces the following spring. However, during the weeks following the invasion of Normandy the issue was very much in doubt.

Although the Germans were taken by surprise, they quickly rebounded, organized counterattacks and slowed the Allied pace considerably. The important crossroads and communications centre of Caen, an objective that had been projected for capture on D-Day itself, was not taken for another month. Attempts to break out of the hedgerow country were initially stymied. In mid-July, the successful Operation Goodwood followed the failures of Operation Epsom and Operation Charnwood,

which had cost the British VIII Corps several hundred tanks.

The British Army soldier relied on his rifle, the Short Magazine Lee-Enfield, along with the additional firepower of the Sten series of submachine guns and the infantry machine gun, the Bren. Sustainable fire support was particularly important during airborne operations. Following their deployment by parachute or glider, the airborne troops were typically assigned tasks of seizing and holding key objectives until relieved by heavier units. Due to logistical constraints and the need for rapid movement, airborne units were often equipped with the lightest of weapons.

On D-Day, elements of the 6th Airborne Division executed near-perfect glider landings near the bridge that spanned the Caen Canal north of Sword and Juno beaches. Within minutes, the paras had secured the objective. Their precision operation resulted in Allied control of a key route inland from the invasion beaches. Subsequently, the span was renamed Pegasus Bridge in reference to the mythical winged horse depicted on the airborne unit's shoulder patch.

Arnhem ambition

During the autumn of 1944, Field Marshal Sir Bernard Montgomery (1887–1976) devised a combined airborne and ground assault through the Netherlands to seize key bridges over the Maas, Waal and Neder Rhine Rivers to facilitate a rapid advance across the German frontier and into the Ruhr, the industrial heart of the Reich. Along with the American 101st and 82nd Airborne Divisions, the British 1st Airborne Division would supply the rapid stroke from above, while the veteran XXX Corps would race up a narrow highway to link with the airborne troops, relieve them and hold the corridor open for a major Allied advance.

In the event, the parachute operations were hampered by stubborn German resistance, particularly at Arnhem, where two SS panzer divisions had been located for rest and refitting after

being mauled in Normandy. Only the British 2nd Parachute Battalion under Lieutenant-Colonel John D. Frost (1912–93) reached the bridge across the Rhine at Arnhem. Frost's 745 lightly armed paras were not intended to hold positions for indefinite periods. After several days, Frost was compelled to surrender, and Operation Market-Garden ended in failure, forever to be known by the moniker of 'A Bridge Too Far'.

PIAT potential

When confronted by German armour or engaged in house-to-house fighting, the heaviest weapon available to the men of the 2nd Parachute Battalion was the PIAT (Projector, Infantry, Anti-Tank). The PIAT operated on the same principle as the spigot mortar, utilizing a cocked spring to hurl a bomb tipped with a shaped charge a distance of up to 340m (1115ft). The weapon was front loaded, and the hollow-charge bomb carried explosive filling that weighed 1.1kg (2.5lb).

The origin of the PIAT pre-dates the turn of the twentieth century, and by 1940 it was apparent that older anti-tank rifles were inadequate against the

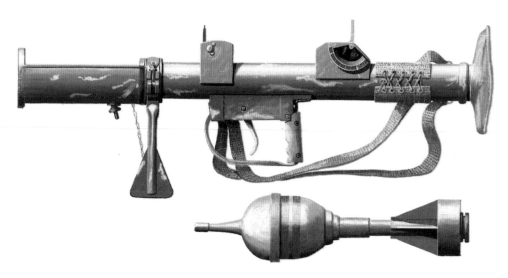

Specifications

Country of Origin: United Kingdom	Overall Length: 990mm (3ft)
Date: 1942	Muzzle Velocity: 76–137m/sec (250–450ft/sec)
Calibre: 89mm (3.5in)	Feed/Magazine: Front loaded
Operation: Firing spring	Range: 100m (328ft) combat; 340m (1115ft)
Weight: 14.51kg (32lb) launcher;	maximum
1.36kg (3lb) grenade	

▲ PIAT

British 6th Airborne Division, Pegasus Bridge, Normandy, June 1944

The PIAT (Projector, Infantry, Anti-Tank) entered service with the British Army in 1943 as an infantry anti-tank weapon. The spring-fired launcher operated in similar fashion to the spigot mortar, igniting propellant in a bomb that carried a hollow charge of 1.1kg (2.5lb).

increasing armour thickness of German vehicles. Major Millis Jefferis (1899–1963) is credited with reconfiguring prototype weapons and combining the hollow-charge ammunition, perfected in the 1930s, to produce the shoulder-fired weapon that became the functional PIAT. The weapon consisted of a tube with a spring and trigger apparatus and was usually serviced by two soldiers. The spring was quite difficult to cock, particularly in combat conditions, and the PIAT was well known for its hefty recoil that required heavy padding for the shoulder piece.

The PIAT entered service with British and Commonwealth forces in 1943, and 115,000 were produced from 1942 through to the end of the war.

▲ **Reliable rifle**

British troops move warily through a village somewhere in the Netherlands, winter 1944–45. All are armed with the Lee-Enfield Rifle No. 4 Mk I.

Although the weapon was bulky and fairly inaccurate, estimates of its performance in Normandy revealed that approximately seven per cent of the German tanks destroyed had been dispatched by the PIAT.

Sophisticated sniping

Along with improved versions of their standard issue Sten submachine guns and Bren machine guns, British troops in Western Europe also received the Lee-Enfield Rifle No. 4 Mk I and its sniper version, designated the No. 4 Mk I (T). Both prior to the war and as World War II progressed, the need for improvements in rifle performance and utility, not to mention ease of mass production, were noted. As early as 1939, the No. 4 Mk I was issued to some

troops. However, this new version of the ubiquitous Lee-Enfield was not formally adopted by the British military until 1941.

The No. 4 was easily distinguished from the Mk III SMLE, because the former's barrel protruded beyond the end of the stock and was somewhat heavier than that of the Mk III. By 1942, the design had been simplified further with the introduction of an indentation on the bolt track to replace the more complex bolt release catch. This version was produced only in Canada and the United States.

The No. 4 Mk I (T) was configured with the highly accurate standard No. 4 rifle being fitted with a wooden cheek rest and sniper sight. These conversions were produced primarily by the British

▲ **Lee-Enfield Rifle No. 4 Mk I**

7th Armoured Division / 1st Battalion The Rifle Brigade, Normandy, July 1944

The No. 4 Mk I formally entered service with the British Army in 1941 and provided improvements over earlier versions of the standard issue bolt-action Lee-Enfield rifles.

Specifications

Country of Origin: United Kingdom

Date: 1939

Calibre: 7.7mm (.303in) British Service

Operation: Bolt action

Weight: 4.11kg (9.06lb)

Overall Length: 1128mm (44.43in)

Barrel Length: 640mm (25.2in)

Muzzle Velocity: 751m/sec (2464ft/sec)

Feed/Magazine: 10-round detachable box
    magazine

Range: 1000m (3280ft) +

▲ **Lee-Enfield Rifle No. 4 Mk I (T)**

2nd Canadian Division / 1st Battalion Royal Winnipeg Rifles, Netherlands, October 1944

The sniper version of the No. 4 Mk I rifle was fitted with a cheek rest and telescopic sight. This weapon served for decades following the end of World War II.

Specifications

Country of Origin: United Kingdom

Date: 1942

Calibre: 7.7mm (.303in) British Service

Operation: Bolt action

Weight: 4.11kg (9.06lb)

Overall Length: 1128mm (44.43in)

Barrel Length: 640mm (25.2in)

Muzzle Velocity: 751m/sec (2464ft/sec)

Feed/Magazine: 10-round detachable box
    magazine

Range: 1000m (3280ft) +

firm of Holland and Holland, while some were retooled in Canada. The sniper variant served with British forces through the 1960s.

New submachine gun

By 1944, the British Army had adopted another submachine gun to complement the supply of Stens already in service. The Patchett Mk 1, like the Sten, fired the 9mm (.35in) Parabellum round and could accept the detachable magazine of the Sten. It could fire at a rate of up to 550 rounds per minute and was

constructed through a higher-quality process than the Sten, which was largely of stamped components due to the exigencies of war.

Named after George Patchett, the chief designer of the Sterling Armaments Company, the Patchett was also known as the Sterling submachine gun and was capable of semiautomatic or fully automatic fire using the blowback, open-bolt system. It was in the hands of some British paras during Operation Market-Garden following rapid trials with just over 100 weapons in use. In fact, it may be said that the

▲ **Sten Mk II**

British Second Army / 2nd Battalion The King's Shropshire Light Infantry, France, August 1944

The mass-produced Sten Mk II equipped thousands of British and Commonwealth troops during World War II. Its reputation for excellent fire support capability was somewhat tarnished by a tendency to jam.

Specifications

Country of Origin: United Kingdom	Barrel Length: 196mm (7.7in)
Date: 1942	Muzzle Velocity: 380m/sec (1247ft/sec)
Calibre: 9mm (.35in) Parabellum	Feed/Magazine: 32-round detachable box
Operation: Blowback	magazine
Weight: 2.95kg (6.5lb)	Cyclic Rate: 500rpm
Overall Length: 762mm (30in)	Range: 70m (230ft)

▲ **Patchett Mk 1**

I British Airborne Corps / 1st Airborne Division / 2nd Parachute Battalion, Arnhem, September 1944

Although largely unproven in combat, a few Patchett submachine guns were issued to airborne troops for Operation Market-Garden. The Patchett eventually replaced the famous Sten Gun.

Specifications

Country of Origin: United Kingdom	Barrel Length: 195mm (7.75in)
Date: 1944	Muzzle Velocity: 395m/sec (1295ft/sec)
Calibre: 9mm (.35in) Parabellum	Feed/Magazine: 32-round detachable box
Operation: Blowback	magazine
Weight: 2.7kg (6lb)	Cyclic Rate: 550rpm
Overall Length: 685mm (27in)	Range: 70m (230ft)

combat experience at Arnhem served as a trial for the weapon as well. The Patchett Mk 1 was assessed as reasonably accurate and capable of withstanding the rigours of prolonged combat with relatively little maintenance.

After the war, the surplus of Sten guns slowed conversion to the Patchett. However, the British Army officially adopted the newer weapon in 1953, and it was in common use until the late 1980s. It has been in service with the armies of more than 40 countries.

Specifications

Country of Origin: United Kingdom	Barrel Length: 625mm (25in)
Date: 1941	Muzzle Velocity: 730m/sec (2400ft/sec)
Calibre: 7.7mm (.303in) British	Feed/Magazine: 30-round box magazine
Operation: Gas operated, air cooled	Cyclic Rate: 500rpm
Weight: 10.25kg (22.5lb)	Range: 1000m (3280ft)
Overall Length: 1150mm (45.25in)	

▲ **Bren Mk II**

British Second Army / 6th Airlanding Brigade / 2nd Battalion The Royal Ulster Rifles, Operation Varsity, March 1945

The simplified Bren Mk II infantry machine gun was introduced in 1941 and included a modified bipod, fixed cocking handle and fewer steps in the fabrication of the weapon's wooden components.

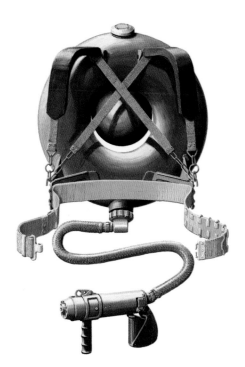

◄ **No. 2 Flamethrower**

British Second Army / 1st Airborne Division / 2nd Parachute Battalion, Arnhem, September 1944

The No. 2 version of the Mk 1 flamethrower proved the most effective and entered service with the British Army in 1944. Known for its rounded tank and nicknamed the Lifebuoy, the flamethrower was in action at Arnhem during Operation Market-Garden.

Specifications

Country of Origin: United Kingdom	Fuel Capacity: 18.2 litres (4 gallons)
Date: 1943	Duration of Fire: 10 seconds
Weight: 29kg (64lb)	Range: 27–36m (89–118ft)

US Forces
1944–45

Rising from a peacetime strength of scarcely 100,000 soldiers, the US Army developed into a fighting force of millions and supplied essential manpower during the liberation of North Africa, Italy and Western Europe.

ROUGHLY HANDLED DURING its combat debut against battle-hardened German troops at Kasserine Pass in Tunisia in 1943, the US Army gained experience and developed into a potent fighting force that joined its British and Commonwealth allies in successfully pushing northwards through Italy and eastwards across Europe to link up with the Soviet Red Army at the Elbe, splitting Germany in two, in the spring of 1945. The strength of the common 'triangular' US infantry division of World War II neared 20,000 men and included organic infantry, artillery, tank destroyer and support elements.

The infantry regiment consisted of three battalions of combat infantrymen totalling a strength of 600 to 900 troops and included more than 50 Browning M2 12.7mm (.5in) heavy machine guns along with a complement of lighter 7.62mm (.3in) machine guns of Browning design. The infantry company typically was composed of about 200 troops armed with the

▲ **Flushing out a sniper**
US infantrymen armed with M1 carbines attempt to draw fire during the battle for Normandy, July 1944.

standard issue M1 Garand rifle or M1 carbine, two 7.62mm (.3in) machine guns, a single 12.7mm (.5in) machine gun, and 15 Browning Automatic Rifles (BAR) firing the 7.62mm (.3in) rifle cartridge. A platoon of 41 soldiers was upgunned with three BAR men, and a standard squad of 12 soldiers included two men equipped with automatic weapons.

The soldiers of the 4th Infantry Division who landed at Utah Beach on 6 June 1944 actually came ashore in the wrong location; however, Brigadier-General Theodore Roosevelt Jr. (1887–1944), assistant division commander, resolved to 'start the war from here'. Elements of the 4th Division linked up with airborne units behind Utah Beach to begin the fight through hedgerow country, across France and into Germany.

Soldiers of the 1st and 29th Infantry Divisions assaulted Omaha Beach and encountered the stiffest German resistance on D-Day. Some units suffered 70 per cent casualties in the opening minutes of Operation Overlord, their landing craft taken under German machine-gun fire as soon as the ramps were lowered. Individual acts of heroism eventually turned the tide at Omaha Beach, although senior Allied commanders had considered the issue in doubt for

US INFANTRY RIFLE PLATOON, 1944		
Unit	Officers	Men
Headquarters	3	2
Squad 1	2	10
Squad 2	2	10
Squad 3	2	10
Medical Aidman	–	1
Bazooka Team 1	–	3
Bazooka Team 2	–	3
Bazooka Team 3	–	3
Bazooka Team 4	–	3
Bazooka Team 5	–	3

several hours and contemplated the withdrawal of the troops from their tenuous foothold.

Raising the rifle

Those US soldiers wading ashore on D-Day had their rifles wrapped in plastic to prevent fouling by seawater and sand. At times holding them above their heads to avoid the surf, the soldiers sought cover among anti-tank and landing craft obstacles,

▼ US Infantry Rifle Squad

The US Army infantry squad of 1944 was capable of delivering a high volume of small-arms fire. Containing 12 soldiers, the squad was equipped with the M1 Garand rifle, the Browning Automatic Rifle and the M3 submachine gun. Although German units were equipped with highly effective submachine guns throughout the war, the semiautomatic US M1 Garand could fire up to 50 rounds per minute, superior to any other rifle in service, since the shoulder arms of other forces continued to operate on bolt action.

Squad (1 x M3 'Grease Gun', 1 x BAR, 10 x M1 Garand)

hurriedly unwrapping their weapons and returning fire as they could, subsequently advancing across metres of open beach.

M1 Garand

The standard issue rifle of the US Army in World War II was the M1 Garand, a gas-operated rotating-bolt weapon that was actually the first semiautomatic rifle to enter regular service with any army in the world. The M1 Garand was designed by Canadian-born John C. Garand (1888–1974), who had moved to Connecticut with his family as a child. Garand enjoyed shooting and designing firearms and worked to develop a light machine gun. After his machine-gun design was adopted by the US Army, he was employed by the US Bureau of Standards and retained as a consultant with the army's Springfield Armory after World War I. In this capacity, he began to consider a design for a semiautomatic rifle.

For 15 years, Garand worked to perfect his design according to army specifications. By 1934, he had received a patent, and two years later production of the M1 began. It was officially adopted by the US Army in 1936 and entered service the following year. The M1 replaced the bolt-action Springfield Model 1903 and remained in service until the early 1960s, partially replaced by the selective-fire M14.

Through nearly 30 years of manufacture, approximately 6.5 million M1 Garand rifles were produced. The weapon fired the 7.62mm (.3in) cartridge and was fed by an eight-round en-bloc clip through an internal magazine. It was effective up to 402m (1326ft), and in the hands of a skilled rifleman was capable of firing 40 to 50 accurate shots in one minute, by far the highest sustained rate of fire of any standard issue rifle in World War II. A sniper version, the Garand M1C, was also produced.

A smaller and lighter version of the M1 Garand, the M1 carbine, was designed by a group of engineers during a three-year period from 1938 to 1941. Its shorter length made it suitable for issue to support troops, armoured troops, airborne units and some officers. Like the Garand, it was a semiautomatic, gas-operated, rotating-bolt rifle. It fired .30 calibre carbine ammunition from a detachable box magazine of 15 or 30 rounds. The carbine was manufactured in similar numbers to the Garand and remained in service with the US Army from the summer of 1942 into the mid-1970s.

The Greaser

Early in World War II, the automatic weapons available to the individual US soldier consisted of the Thompson submachine gun and the Browning Automatic Rifle. By 1942, it was determined that a more cost-effective and easily produced alternative to the older Thompson was needed. US observers had recognized the merits of such automatic weapons as the German MP 40 and the British Sten and commissioned General Motors designers to come up with a suitable US weapon.

The result was the M3 submachine gun, popularly known as the Grease Gun or simply the Greaser. The M3 and its successor the M3A1 were 11.4mm (.45in)

▲ **M1 carbine**

US Army / 101st Airborne Division / 501st Parachute Infantry Regiment, Normandy, June 1944

The M1 carbine was shorter than the standard M1 Garand rifle and therefore easier to carry and deploy in combat for troops who often operated in confined spaces or were required to perform specialized functions.

Specifications

Country of Origin: United States	Barrel Length: 457mm (18in)
Date: 1942	Muzzle Velocity: 595m/sec (1950ft/sec)
Calibre: 7.62mm (.3in) 0.30 calibre carbine	Feed/Magazine: 15- or 30-round detachable box
Operation: Gas operated	magazine
Weight: 2.5kg (5.47lb)	Range: c.300m (984ft)
Overall Length: 905mm (35.7in)	

▶ Remington M1911 pistol

US Seventh Army / 36th Infantry Division / 141st Infantry Regiment,
Operation Dragoon, Cannes, France, August 1944

The demand for the M1911 pistol was so great that numerous manufacturers produced the weapon for the US Army. Among these was Remington Rand, which made more than 900,000 during World War II.

Specifications

Country of Origin: United States	Barrel Length: 127mm (5in)
Date: 1911	Muzzle Velocity: 262m/sec (860ft/sec)
Calibre: 11.4mm (.45in)	Feed/Magazine: 7-round magazine
Operation: Short recoil	Range: 50m (164ft)
Weight: 1.1kg (2.425lb)	
Overall Length: 216mm (8.5in)	

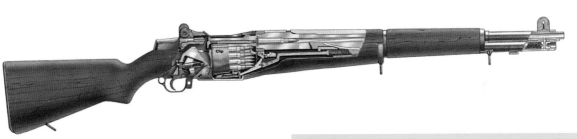

▲ M1 Garand

US First Army / 29th Infantry Division / 116th Regiment, Omaha Beach,
Normandy, June 1944

The M1 Garand was the first semiautomatic shoulder arm to become standard issue to any army in the world. Its service life spanned four decades.

Specifications

Country of Origin: United States	Overall Length: 1103mm (43.5in)
Date: 1936	Barrel Length: 610mm (24in)
Calibre: 7.62mm (.3in) US .30-06	Muzzle Velocity: 853m/sec (2800ft/sec)
Operation: Gas operated	Feed/Magazine: 8-round internal box magazine
Weight: 4.37kg (9.5lb)	Range: 500m (1640ft) +

▲ Garand M1C

US First Army / 1st Infantry Division / 16th Regiment, Normandy, July 1944

The sniper version of the M1 Garand rifle, the M1C was adopted by the US Army as its standard issue sniper rifle in June 1944, complementing the Springfield M1903A4.

Specifications

Country of Origin: United States	Barrel Length: 610mm (24in)
Date: 1944	Muzzle Velocity: 853m/sec (2800ft/sec)
Calibre: 7.62mm (.3in) US .30-06	Feed/Magazine: 8-round internal box
Operation: Gas operated	magazine
Weight: 4.37kg (9.5lb)	Range: 1000m (3280ft) +
Overall Length: 1103mm (43.5in)	

▲ Armoured cover

A US infantry squad take cover behind an M4A3 Sherman tank somewhere in Normandy, July 1944. All are armed with M1 Garand rifles, except the last man, who is carrying a BAR automatic rifle, the squad's heavy firepower.

Specifications

Country of Origin: United States

Date: 1943

Calibre: 7.62mm (.3in) M1906

Operation: Bolt action

Weight: 3.94kg (8.68lb)

Overall Length: 1097mm (43.19in)

Barrel Length: 610mm (24in)

Muzzle Velocity: 853m/sec (2800ft/sec)

Feed/Magazine: 5-round internal box magazine

Range: 1000m (3280ft) +

▲ Springfield M1903A4

US First Army / 9 Infantry Division, Ardennes, December 1944

Intended primarily as a sniper rifle, the old Springfield M1903A4 was fitted with a Weaver 2.5x 330C hunting telescope and incorporated stamped metal parts to expedite production. Other alterations included a modified grip and stock. The rifle entered service in 1943.

blowback, open-bolt automatic weapons with a rate of fire of up to 450 rounds per minute. Due to complications with production, the M3 did not enter service with US frontline troops until late 1944. A relative few were fielded during the weeks-long battles of the Hürtgen Forest and the reduction of the pocket created by the German Ardennes Offensive, popularly known as the Battle of the Bulge. The M3A1 was introduced in December 1944; however, very few of these saw service during World War II. The M3A1 did incorporate several improvements, including a more reliable cocking lever assembly.

Due to the late arrival of the M3, most American squad-level operations were dependent on the

Specifications

Country of Origin: United States

Date: 1942

Calibre: 11.4mm (.45in) .45 ACP

Operation: Blowback

Weight: 4.65kg (10.25lb) loaded

Overall Length: 745mm (29.33in)

Barrel Length: 203mm (8in)

Muzzle Velocity: 280m/sec (920ft/sec)

Feed/Magazine: 30-round detachable box magazine

Cyclic Rate: 450rpm

Range: 90m (295ft)

▲ **M3 'Grease Gun'**

US Third Army / 28th Infantry Division / 112th Infantry Regiment, Ardennes, December 1944

The M3 submachine gun was developed to replace the Thompson submachine gun but did not enter service with US troops until late 1944. An improved version, the M3A1, was not in service in quantity until the war was over.

Specifications

Country of Origin: United States

Date: 1928

Calibre: 11.4mm (.45in) M1911

Operation: Delayed blowback

Weight: 4.88kg (10.75lb)

Overall Length: 857mm (33.75in)

Barrel Length: 266mm (10.5in)

Muzzle Velocity: 280m/sec (920ft/sec)

Feed/Magazine: 18-, 20-, 30-round detachable box magazine

Cyclic Rate: 700rpm

Range: 120m (394ft)

▲ **Thompson 1928**

US First Army / 2nd Ranger Battalion, Battle of Hürtgen Forest, September–December 1944

The Thompson submachine gun was designed during World War I and intended to breach enemy trench networks with heavy, mobile fire. Instead, it gained fame during the Prohibition Era of the 1920s. The Thompson 1928 was adopted by the US military in 1938 with modifications to the original design.

Thompson and the BAR for the duration of the war. An assessment of the M3's performance concluded that it was prone to malfunction due to dust, mud and grime build-up and that the single-feed, 30-round magazine was difficult to load manually, particularly under combat conditions.

Another submachine gun, the M2 Hyde-Inland, had competed with the M3 during trials; however, an initial order for more than 160,000 of these 11.4mm (.45in) blowback-operated SMGs was cancelled in the spring of 1943. Although its rate of fire was near 500 rounds per minute and the M2 shared the same ammunition box magazine feed system as the famed Thompson submachine gun, only 400 of these weapons were produced by Marlin Firearms during 1942–43.

▲ M2 Hyde-Inland

US Army / Aberdeen Proving Ground, Maryland, 1944

The M2 Hyde-Inland submachine gun was produced in limited numbers and did not enter service with the US Army. An order was cancelled in favour of the M3 'Grease Gun'.

Specifications

Country of Origin: United States	Barrel Length: 305mm (12in)
Date: 1942	Muzzle Velocity: 292m/sec (960ft/sec)
Calibre: 11.4mm (.45in) .45 ACP	Feed/Magazine: Detachable box magazine
Operation: Blowback	(Thompson)
Weight: 4.19kg (9.24lb)	Cyclic Rate: 500rpm
Overall Length: 813mm (32in)	Range: 50m (164ft)

▲ M9 Bazooka

US Third Army / 106th Infantry Division / 424th Infantry Regiment, central Germany, April 1945

A basic anti-tank weapon, the M9 Bazooka was essentially a tube that fired a shaped-charge warhead at short range and was most effective from the flanks or rear of an enemy armoured vehicle.

Specifications

Country of Origin: United States	Weight: 5.98kg (13.18lb)
Date: 1943	Overall Length: 1545mm (61in)
Calibre: 60mm (2.36in) high-explosive (HE)	Muzzle Velocity: 83m/sec (270ft/sec)
and high-explosive anti-tank (HEAT) warheads	Feed/Magazine: Breech-loader
Operation: Solid rocket motor	Range: 640m (2010ft)

Defending the Reich: German Army 1944–45

The introduction of advanced automatic weapons was too little too late as the German Army, extended to fight on three major fronts, suffered from diminished manpower and resources in the final months of World War II.

BY 1944, THE INFANTRY DIVISIONS of the German Army had been reduced in strength to around 12,500 men, although they retained the same basic structure. The number of heavy machine guns had been reduced somewhat, and senior German commanders reasoned that the introduction of automatic weapons such as the Sturmgewehr 44 assault rifle, capable of a much higher rate of fire than the Karabiner 98k bolt-action weapon, might compensate at least partially for the waning availability of trained and veteran soldiers as casualties mounted.

Inevitably, in the early months of 1945 some divisions had been so drastically reduced in strength that they constituted few more soldiers than a normal regiment or battalion. Following the 1943 reorganization of the infantry squad, the workhorse infantry platoon of the German Army included four squads of 10 soldiers along with a light 50mm (2in) mortar section and a headquarters section of six men, one of them the officer in command.

Out of necessity and also due to the availability of advancing technology, the German Army of World

▲ **Tank killer**
An SS panzergrenadier armed with a Panzerfaust hollow-charge anti-tank weapon waits for an Allied armour attack, Normandy, July 1944.

War II was one of the first to deploy semiautomatic weapons in significant numbers. These included the Sturmgewehr 44 (StG 44) assault rifle, which was capable of semiautomatic and fully automatic firing modes. The StG 44 was the eventual result of a project to develop a *Maschinenkarabiner*, or machine carbine. At one point, Hitler would not sanction any new weapons types, so to disguise the project, it was labelled the MP 43, then the MP 44, where 'MP' stood for *Maschinenpistole*, a type of firearm that already existed. Hitler eventually approved the project and the designation of Sturmgewehr 44 became official when the weapon entered full production.

Storm of fire

The Sturmgewehr 44 is recognizable with its sleek lines and long, curved magazines which held up to 30 rounds of 7.92mm (.312in) ammunition. Many firearms experts conclude that the Sturmgewehr 44 was the world's first actual assault rifle to enter combat. It was capable of firing at a cyclic rate of 500 rounds per minute with a range of up to 300m (984ft). The weapon was gas-operated with a tilting bolt and was designed in the early 1940s. Hitler's

interference delayed production, which did not begin until October 1943, although it might have proceeded months earlier. Nearly 425,000 were manufactured. The majority of the Sturmgewehr 44s produced were sent to the Eastern Front.

Had the Sturmgewehr 44 entered production sooner, it might indeed have altered the course of the war. However, earlier submachine guns, most of them designed by the prolific Hugo Schmeisser (1884–1953), served throughout the conflict. The MP 38 and MP 40 were both high-profile weapons of the German infantry. When captured, they were often placed in service with Allied soldiers who were impressed with their performance.

Walther pistols

Throughout the war, the Walther PP series of pistols was popular with Nazi Party officials, army officers, police units and *Luftwaffe* personnel. The series entered production in 1929 and continues under licence with various companies today. The most popular of the series, the PPK and its variants, followed the original PP pistol into production in 1931. The PPK was carried by Adolf Hitler

▲ **Granatbüchse 39**

272nd Infantry Division / 981st Infantry Regiment, Battle of Verrières Ridge, July 1944

The Grantabüchse 39 was a modified anti-tank rifle that could fire anti-personnel or anti-tank grenades. Its threaded launcher was screwed to a rifle barrel.

Specifications

Country of Origin: Germany	Overall Length: Not known
Date: 1942	Barrel Length: 590mm (23.23in)
Calibre: N/A	Muzzle Velocity: N/A
Operation: Bolt action	Feed/Magazine: Single shot
Weight: Not known	Range: 125m (410ft)

(1889–1945), who committed suicide while biting down on a cyanide capsule and simultaneously firing a 7.65mm (.301in) bullet from his PPK into the side of his head. It has also become famous as the handgun of choice of fictional superspy James Bond.

The PP series was one of the first semiautomatic double-action pistols to gain wide popularity around the world. The weapons are further distinguished by their exposed hammer and single-column magazine. The PPK was slightly smaller and lighter than the original PP and more easily concealed, thereby increasing its popularity with clandestine operatives and civilian law enforcement personnel.

In 1942, the German Army deployed a variant of its original Panzerbüchse 39 anti-tank rifle. The Granatbüchse 39 was modified to shorten the original barrel of the Panzerbüchse 39, while the

bipod, sling band, carrying sling and handle were moved to different locations on the weapon. A threaded launcher was screwed to the barrel. The Granatbüchse 39 was actually capable of firing three types of grenade: anti-personnel, small anti-tank and large anti-tank. Each was propelled by a blank 7.92mm (.312in) cartridge.

Meanwhile, a new generation of purpose-built anti-tank weapons emerged. The RPzB Panzerschreck was based on the design of a captured American M1 Bazooka and was often manufactured with a blast shield to protect the operator. However, a significant backblast typically betrayed the location of the weapon and drew return fire. The Panzerschreck entered service with the German Army in 1943, and nearly 300,000 were made. Later versions fired a heavy 88mm (3.5in) rocket-propelled round.

▶ Walther PP

Luftwaffe / VIII Fliegerkorps / Jagdgeschwader 27, March 1945

The Walther PP series of semiautomatic double-action pistols entered production in 1929 and remains popular today, having been manufactured in numerous countries. During World War II it was popular with Nazi Party officials.

Specifications

Country of Origin: Germany	Barrel Length: 98mm (3.9in)
Date: 1935	Muzzle Velocity: 256m/sec (840ft/sec)
Calibre: 7.65mm (.301in)	Feed/Magazine: 7-round detachable box
Operation: Straight blowback	magazine
Weight: .665kg (1.46lb)	Range: 30m (98ft)
Overall Length: 170mm (6.7in)	

▲ Gewehr 43

German First Army / 198th Infantry Division, OB West, April 1945

The semiautomatic gas-operated Gewehr 43 was a victim of its own complex engineering and produced in limited numbers late in World War II. A sniper version was highly accurate.

Specifications

Country of Origin: Germany	Barrel Length: 546mm (21.5in)
Date: 1943	Muzzle Velocity: 853.6m/sec (2800ft/sec)
Calibre: 8mm (.314in) IS	Feed/Magazine: 10-round detachable box
Operation: Gas operated	magazine
Weight: 4.1kg (9.7lb)	Range: 500m (1640ft); 800m (2620ft) with
Overall Length: 1130mm (44.49in)	scope

▲ **RPzB Panzerschreck**

XLVII Panzer Corps / 21st Panzer Division / 125th Panzergrenadier Regiment,
Normandy, August 1944

The anti-tank Panzerschreck was fashioned from a captured American M1
Bazooka; however, it was subsequently modified to fire a much more powerful
round capable of destroying virtually any Allied armoured vehicle.

Specifications

Country of Origin: Germany	Overall Length: 1640mm (64.5in)
Date: 1943	Muzzle Velocity: 110m/sec (360ft/sec)
Calibre: 88mm (3.5in) high-explosive (HE)	Feed/Magazine: Breech-loader
and high-explosive anti-tank (HEAT) warheads	Range: 150m (492ft)
Operation: Solid rocket motor	
Weight: 11kg (24.25lb) empty	

Volkssturm: Hitler's Home Guard
1945

**As the perimeter of the Third Reich shrank steadily during the last years of World War II,
Germany was compelled to enlist old men and boys in the defence of the nation.**

HITLER'S LAST LINE OF DEFENCE against the Allies closing in on Germany were the *Volkssturm* formations, which included the old and infirm, the very young and even some women. Boys aged as young as 12 and men in their sixties were called up, given short periods of training and placed in uniform. Their weapons were those that had been in service with the German Army for the duration of the war, such as the Karabiner 98k rifle, the Model 24 hand grenade (a stick grenade known to Allied soldiers as the 'potato masher' due to its construction), the Model 39 and Model 43 hand grenades, the few available MG 34 and MG 42 machine guns, and various submachine guns. Older rifles such as the Gewehr 98 and Gewehr 71 were also issued. There was no standardization of weapons from one *Volkssturm* unit to another.

The basic operational formation of the *Volkssturm* was a battalion of just under 650 troops. Uniforms were often incomplete or unavailable, and those who received training were somtimes led by veterans of World War I or soldiers who had been previously wounded and deemed unfit for further combat duty.

Early in 1945, Germany undertook production of the MP 3008 machine pistol primarily intended to equip *Volkssturm* units with automatic weapons. The MP 3008 was based on captured models of the successful British Sten Gun. It was also known as the 'People's Machine Gun' because of its designation for the *Volkssturm*.

The MP 3008 was a blowback-operated, open-bolt submachine gun that fired up to 450 rounds per minute. It fired the 9mm (.35in) Parabellum cartridge and was fed by a 32-round detachable box magazine. Its production run was short and ceased prior to the end of the war, with only about 10,000 guns actually completed. Undertaken as an emergency solution to the shortage of automatic weapons, the MP 3008 was cheaply produced, with many of its parts stamped from steel plate.

The finish of the weapons was rough. Early versions were made without a handgrip, and the wire stock was welded to the frame. A few examples were actually manufactured with wooden stocks in the final days of production, as supplies of steel were virtually nonexistent.

Prolific Panzerfaust

The anti-tank Panzerfaust is, for many, symbolic of the last days of the Third Reich. Images of middle-aged women training to fire the tube weapon are indicative of the desperation in Germany in 1945. The Panzerfaust was inexpensive to produce, was preloaded and required only one individual to operate it. Therefore, more than six million were manufactured from 1943 to 1945.

The Panzerfaust consisted of a disposable launching tube that fired a 2.9kg (6.4lb) hollow-charge round with .8kg (1.8lb) of high explosive. Range depended on the variant, with a maximum of 100m (328ft). It was the first anti-tank weapon to include a disposable launcher, and its heavy backblast often gave away the concealed position of its operator. As the war progressed, some untrained German soldiers were given only the Panzerfaust and sent into combat. The number of Allied tanks engaged and destroyed by these weapons exceeded 30 per cent of the total losses in Western Europe.

▲ MP 3008

German Army / Volkssturm Battalion 20, March 1945

The MP 3008 was a cheaply made submachine gun issued to *Volkssturm* units in the last days of World War II. The weapon was produced only in the early months of 1945, and about 10,000 were manufactured.

Specifications

Country of Origin: Germany	Barrel Length: 196mm (7.7in)
Date: 1945	Muzzle Velocity: 365m/sec (1198ft/sec)
Calibre: 9mm (.35in) Parabellum	Feed/Magazine: 32-round detachable box
Operation: Blowback	magazine
Weight: 3.2kg (7.05lb)	Cyclic Rate; 500rpm
Overall Length: 760mm (29.9in)	Range: 70m (230ft)

▲ Panzerfaust

German Army / Volkssturm Battalion 301, March 1945

The anti-tank Panzerfaust was fired from a disposable tube and created significant backblast. As more powerful versions emerged during World War II, some were emblazoned with the warning 'Attention! Fire Jet'.

Specifications

Country of Origin: Germany	Overall Length: 1000mm (39.4in)
Date: 1943	Muzzle Velocity: 30m/sec (98ft/sec)
Calibre: 100mm (3.9in)	Feed/Magazine: N/A
Operation: Recoilless gun	Range: 30m (98ft)
Weight: 1.475kg (3.3lb) total	

Chapter 5

World War II: Eastern Front

Hitler's invasion of the Soviet Union on 22 June 1941 opened a two-front war for the German Army and sealed the fate of the Third Reich. The vastness of Russia, the resilience of the peoples of the Soviet Union and harsh winter weather provided the Red Army with the capacity to withstand tremendous losses and achieve ultimate victory four years later. Although German spearheads reached within 19km (12 miles) of the Soviet capital of Moscow, they were denied the prize. Hitler's redirection of his armies towards the south and the oilfields of the Caucasus led to the disaster at Stalingrad and losses from which the *Wehrmacht* could never recover. In the spring of 1945 the emblem of the hammer and sickle flew above the *Reichstag*.

◄ **Machine-gun squad**

Wehrmacht soldiers move carefully through corn fields in southern Russia during Case Blue, the German push towards Stalingrad and the Caucasus, August 1942. The soldier in the foreground is carrying an MG 34 squad machine gun, the standard German infantry support weapon for much of the war.

Introduction

From an uneasy alliance in their cooperative invasion of Poland, Nazi Germany and the Soviet Union became sworn enemies. World War II on the Eastern Front involved more men, machines, equipment, destruction and death than on any other.

SOVIET LEADER JOSEF STALIN (1878–1953) was astonished when German tanks and troops attacked his country in the predawn hours of 22 June 1941. Repeated warnings had gone unheeded, and in fact Stalin had continued to send shipments of grain and other resources to the Third Reich on a regular basis. More than 160 German divisions assaulted the Soviets without warning on a 1600km (1000-mile) front, and the Red Army was sent reeling from the hammer blows.

Ironically, the Soviets had contributed to their own perilous situation. Since the 1920s, they had secretly facilitated German circumvention of the Versailles Treaty, allowing German troops to train and test new weapons from small arms to tanks on Soviet territory. The Soviets had also entered into a non-aggression pact with the Nazis that provided Stalin with too much assurance that German intentions did not involve eastwards expansion that would extend beyond the agreed upon line of demarcation in a partitioned Poland.

As Hitler's troops advanced, killing and capturing hundreds of thousands of Soviet soldiers and committing countless atrocities, the Red Army also suffered from a shortage of experienced officers. Many of the most senior had been executed during

▲ **Soviet solidity**
Armed with the super-reliable 71-round-drum-magazine PPSh-41 submachine gun, Soviet partisans prepare to move during operations in Belorussia, March 1943.

▲ **MG 30**

A rare photograph showing Axis troops manning a Maschinengewehr Solothurn 1930 (MG 30) somewhere on the Eastern Front.

Stalin's purge of the Red Army officer corps during the mid-1930s.

To compound the problems faced by the Red Army high command, much of the Soviet Union's industrial capacity lay within reach of the German juggernaut. In response, entire factories were dismantled and relocated eastwards, some beyond the Ural mountains. The Soviets drew upon their vast resources in manpower and made good their staggering losses. Then, the winter of 1941 slowed the Germans to a standstill.

The resumption of German offensive operations the following spring offered opportunity for the Red Army. Hitler diverted his main thrust away from Moscow, besieged Leningrad in the north and ordered his spearheads to the south and the oil-rich Caucasus. At Stalingrad on the banks of the Volga River, Soviet forces encircled the German Sixth Army, annihilating it as a fighting force. Stalingrad was the turning point of the war on the Eastern Front, and when the five-month battle for the city ended in February 1943, the Germans had suffered nearly 850,000 killed, wounded or captured. These were casualties that could not be replaced. The Soviet propaganda machine labelled 1944 'The Year of 10 Victories' as a succession of Red Army offensive operations drove the *Wehrmacht* back towards Germany. Repeatedly, Hitler's senior commanders would issue orders to withdraw from hopeless defensive situations only to have the *Führer* countermand the order, demanding that the troops stand their ground and fight to the end. Continuing interference from Hitler prevented the stabilization of the Eastern Front, and Soviet forces were fighting in the suburbs of Berlin by the spring of 1945.

Early in World War II, the Soviet Union depended heavily on military aid from the United States, which shipped millions of tonnes of supplies and equipment through the Lend-Lease programme. Soviet industry did maintain productivity and manufacture improved weapons such as the legendary T-34 medium tank, as well as a number of small arms such as the standard issue semiautomatic SVT-40 rifle and the PPSh-41 submachine gun that carried the Red Army to victory.

Winter War
1939–40

The small but potent Finnish Army fought tenaciously against Red Army aggression during the brief but bitter Winter War. Although the Soviets sustained heavy casualties, the Finns were ultimately overwhelmed.

A TERRITORIAL DISPUTE between Finland and the Soviet Union erupted in war in November 1939, only weeks after World War II had begun and Red Army troops had invaded neighbouring Poland. Anticipating a quick victory, Soviet leader Josef Stalin (1878–1953) failed to comprehend the impact that his purges of the Red Army officer cadre during the mid-1930s would have on later operations. Up to 30,000 Soviet officers, many of them senior commanders, had been imprisoned or murdered to assuage Stalin's paranoia. As a result, when Soviet forces invaded Finland the gallant Finnish Army put up stubborn resistance and inflicted heavy casualties on the Red Army.

Inexperienced Soviet officers executed strategic and tactical blunders that the Finnish Army exploited regularly. The mobile Finnish troops regularly utilized skis for rapid movement in the deep snow and thick forests of their country. Soviet troop and supply columns were often trapped on icy roads and decimated. The result was an embarrassing prolonged war in which the Soviets lost more than 320,000 casualties, more than four times the losses incurred by the Finns.

Soviet victory

In the end, however, the weight of Soviet numerical superiority was too great, the Finns were forced to sue for peace and the war ended on 13 March 1940. Although the Soviets did not achieve the complete subjugation of Finland, they gained more than 10 per cent of the territory that had previously been claimed by the Finns. This included land near the Soviet city of Leningrad and Lake Ladoga, the Karelian Isthmus, islands in the Gulf of Finland and the Rybachy Peninsula. At the same time the Soviets also gained control of significant Finnish natural resources and centres of industry.

◄ **Ski troops**
Ski-mounted Finnish soldiers stop for a break during the Winter War, January 1940. Most Finnish troops were armed with a Finnish version of the Soviet Mosin-Nagant rifle.

Finnish Army
1939–44

The Finnish Army of 1939–40 was small but efficient and well disciplined and exuded a high degree of morale. When the Soviet Union invaded, the Finns fought a vigorous defence.

A S NEGOTIATIONS with the Soviet Union deteriorated in the autumn of 1939, the Finnish Army mobilized nine divisions and four separate brigades totalling slightly more than 200,000 men. In contrast, the Red Army eventually committed 1.2 million soldiers to the fighting in 1939–40. The battalion was the tactical unit most often employed, and for two months the Finns clung to the Mannerheim Line on the Karelian Isthmus while the poorly led Soviets became increasingly frustrated. The Finns themselves, meanwhile, developed a reputation as skilled fighters manoeuvring rapidly on skis across the snowy landscape, attacking Soviet positions and swiftly disappearing before an effective counterstroke could be organized.

Although the Finnish Army was inspired and defending its territory, the army was deficient in heavy weapons, with only 112 anti-tank guns reportedly available and just a handful of armoured vehicles. Nevertheless, in the far north the Finns employed their Motti tactics, fragmenting attacking Soviet divisions and surrounding the weakened elements, then systematically destroying them one at a time. During a series of battles near Suomussalmi from December 1939 to January 1940, the Finns severely mauled the Soviet 44th and 163rd Divisions.

When the Winter War ended in March 1940, the result was an uneasy peace that realistic observers knew would never last. With tensions between Nazi Germany and the Soviet Union growing, the Finns were caught in a vice and eventually drawn into the Continuation War of 1941–44, after which Finland ceded more territory to the Soviet Union but maintained its sovereignty. The Finns did cooperate with Nazi Germany in the planning and execution of Operation Barbarossa, the German invasion of the Soviet Union, and participated somewhat loosely in the 900-day siege of Leningrad.

The Finnish Army of 1939–40 was armed with a number of weapons, including the Mosin-Nagant Model 1891 rifle, many of which had been captured by the Germans and Austro-Hungarians during World War I and then sold to Finland after the war. The bolt-action, internal-magazine-fed Mosin-Nagant had been developed in Belgium prior to becoming the standard issue of the Czarist Army in Russia. It fired a 7.62mm (.3in) cartridge and eventually more than 37 million were manufactured in pre- and post-Soviet Russia and elsewhere. Several Finnish manufacturers subsequently produced variants of the Model 1891, including a carbine and a model with a heavier barrel for greater accuracy

▶ **Lahti L-35**

Finnish Army / 4th Division, Karelian Front, 1940

In overall appearance the Finnish Lahti L-35 pistol was similar to the German Luger; however, its bolt assembly was substantially different. The L-35 functioned well in the harsh Arctic climate of Finland.

Specifications

Country of Origin: Finland	Barrel Length: 107mm (4.21in)
Date: 1935	Muzzle Velocity: 335.3m/sec (1100ft/sec)
Calibre: 9mm (.35in)	Feed/Magazine: 8-round detachable box
Operation: Toggle locked, short recoil	magazine
Weight: 1.2kg (2.6lb)	Range: 50m (164ft)
Overall Length: 245mm (9.65in)	

known as the M24. Prior to the Winter War, the Finns experienced a shortage in small arms and ordered great numbers of rifles from Yugoslavia, Italy, Sweden, Belgium, France and Great Britain.

Designed by Aimo J. Lahti (1896–1970), the Suomi KP-31 ('KP' stands for *Konepistooli*: submachine gun) was a Finnish submachine gun that earned a reputation as an excellent infantry weapon. The original patent was granted in the early 1920s, and the early version was chambered for 7.65mm

(.301in) ammunition, but the standard weapon used the 9mm (.35in) Parabellum cartridge. The KP-31 was fed from a drum magazine of 71 rounds or a box magazine of 20 or 50 rounds. It was capable of semiautomatic or fully automatic fire, and its remarkable rate of fire exceeded 800 rounds per minute. Instances during the Winter War in which small numbers of Finnish troops held off Red Army forces several times their size with the skilful operation of the KP-31 have been documented.

Specifications

Country of Origin: Finland	Barrel Length: 319mm (12.52in)
Date: 1931	Muzzle Velocity: 400m/sec (1310ft/sec)
Calibre: 9mm (.35in) Parabellum	Feed/Magazine: 20- or 50-round detachable box
Operation: Blowback	magazine or 71-round drum magazine
Weight: 4.87kg (10.74lb)	Cyclic Rate: 800–900rpm
Overall Length: 870mm (34.25in)	Range: 100m (328ft) +

▲ **Suomi KP-31**

Finnish Army / Infantry Regiment 16, Suomussalmi, December 1939

The Suomi KP-31 was a blowback-operated submachine gun that proved a formidable adversary during the Winter War. Its high rate of fire and reliability made the KP-31 popular among Finnish troops.

Specifications

Country of Origin: Finland	Barrel Length: 247mm (9.72in)
Date: 1944	Muzzle Velocity: 395m/sec (1300ft/sec)
Calibre: 9mm (.35in) Parabellum	Feed/Magazine: 50-round box magazine or
Operation: Blowback	71-round drum magazine
Weight: 2.8kg (6.17lb)	Cyclic Rate: 650rpm
Overall Length: 825mm (32.48in)	Range: 70m (230ft)

▲ **Konepistooli M44**

Finnish Army / 13th Division, East Karelia, June 1944

A copy of the Soviet PPS-43 submachine gun, the M44 was capable of using the 71-round drum magazine of the KP-31 or a 50-round magazine. It was later modified for the 36-round magazine of the Carl Gustav submachine gun.

Defending the Motherland: Red Army 1941–42

Hard pressed in the early years of what the Soviets called the Great Patriotic War, the Red Army was resurgent. Despite absorbing tremendous losses, the Soviets halted the eastwards advance of German forces.

THE RAPID MOVEMENT of the German *Wehrmacht* across the open terrain of the Russian steppes resulted in the capture of hundreds of thousands of Red Army troops as they were encircled and cut off from retreat. As Soviet troops absorbed heavy losses and fell back, Communist Party commissars often were assigned to smaller units with orders to bolster the morale of the troops with party and patriotic doctrine along with the threat of being shot for desertion or fleeing in the face of the enemy.

As the summer of 1941 extended into winter, German armoured spearheads neared the Soviet capital of Moscow, and officers viewed the onion domes of the city through their binoculars. The citizens of Moscow dug tank traps and built fortifications to defend the city. Resistance stiffened, and Moscow was never occupied by German troops. As the harsh winter weather set in, the Germans found that their mechanized equipment failed to function in sub-zero temperatures. So sure had Hitler been of a quick victory that adequate provision had not been made to supply winter clothing to the troops. Frostbite disabled thousands, and combat efficiency eroded steadily.

Further complicating the situation for the Germans was the tremendous amount of supplies the *Wehrmacht* needed in the East as well as the great distances over which these supplies would have to be transported. While the Germans languished far from home, Soviet forces were augmented with substantial formations from Siberia and other areas untouched by the war. Many of these formations were released for deployment against the Germans after Stalin was assured that war with Japan was not imminent. These troops were to play a key role in the great victory at Stalingrad that followed the German spring and summer offensive of 1942.

When the weather improved sufficiently, Hitler resumed offensive operations and ordered substantial forces southwards toward the Caucasus and its precious oilfields. He further ordered his forces to split, and while a potent thrust continued into the Caucasus, another headed for the city of Stalingrad on the Volga River and a rendezvous with destiny.

Early in World War II the primary shoulder arm of Soviet forces was the venerable Mosin-Nagant Model 1891 bolt-action rifle. With the German invasion, production was stepped up. In 1932, the original

▶ **Tokarev TT30**

Soviet Third Army / 85th Rifle Division, Southwest Front, June 1941

The Tokarev TT30 pistol was intended as a replacement for earlier Nagant revolvers in service with the Red Army. The short-recoil pistol was fed by an eight-round box magazine.

Specifications

Country of Origin: USSR	Barrel Length: 116mm (4.57in)
Date: 1930	Muzzle Velocity: 420m/sec (1380ft/sec)
Calibre: 7.62mm (.3in)	Feed/Magazine: 8-round detachable box
Operation: Short recoil	magazine
Weight: .83kg (1.83lb)	Range: 50m (164ft)
Overall Length: 194mm (7.6in)	

Soviet Rifle Platoon, June 1941

The Soviet rifle platoon of 1941 was a substantial fighting force on paper, consisting of a 50mm (2in) mortar section and four rifle squads, each of 11 soldiers. Two men in each rifle squad were armed with PPD submachine guns. A gunner and loader serviced the single light machine gun available to each squad, the Degtyaryov DP-28, designed in 1927, introduced in 1928 and fed by a 47-round, top-mounted pan magazine.

Platoon HQ (1 Officer, 1 NCO, 1 other rank): 1 x pistol, 1 x SMG, 1 x rifle

Squad 1 (1 NCO, 10 other ranks): 1 x pistol, 2 x SMG, 8 x rifle, 1 x LMG

Squad 2

Squad 3

Squad 4

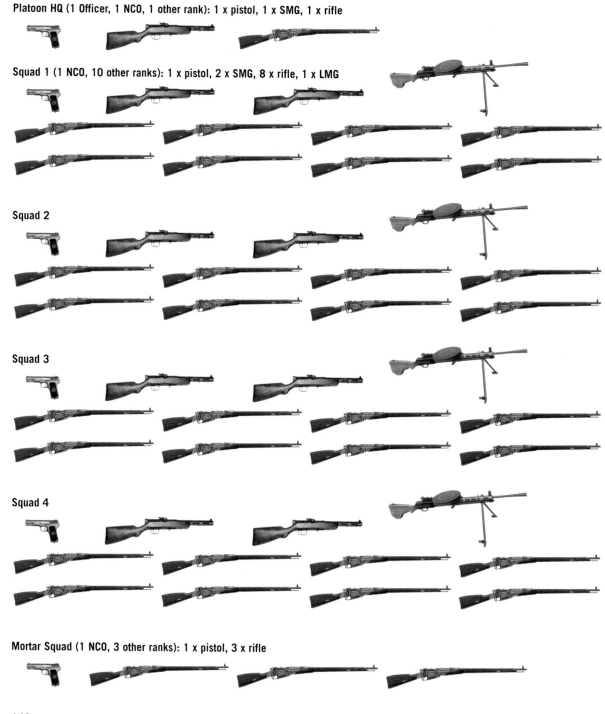

Mortar Squad (1 NCO, 3 other ranks): 1 x pistol, 3 x rifle

Mosin-Nagant was modified for use by snipers and designated the Model 91/31. Known for its accuracy, the Model 91/31 achieved fame along with Soviet snipers such as Vasily Zaitsev (1915–91), who was renowned as a Hero of the Soviet Union and was reported to have more than 225 kills to his credit. With a telescopic sight fitted above the bolt, the sniper version of the Mosin-Nagant included a longer and more curved bolt to facilitate the shooter's action.

By 1936, the Mosin-Nagant was again modified, this time for more rapid production. The receiver was simplified from an octagonal configuration to a rounded shape, and by the end of the war more than 17 million of the basic Model 91/30 had been manufactured. Known for rugged dependability in harsh conditions and extremes of weather, the Mosin-Nagant production rifles of the war years lacked the finish and overall quality of pre-war rifles due to the need for large numbers to be provided in a relatively short period of time.

Early Soviet submachine gun production borrowed heavily from German designs, as was the case with the PPD-1934/38, a virtual copy of the Bergmann MP 28. The PPD was a blowback, open-bolt weapon that fired the Soviet 7.62mm (.3in) round. It was developed by arms designer Vasily Degtyaryov (1880–1949), and it was fed either by a drum magazine that was copied from the Finnish Suomi KP-31 or a 25-round box magazine. The weapon entered service with the Red Army in 1935 but was soon deemed too expensive for mass production. Although more than 90,000 were manufactured, the cheaper PPSh-41 was already set to replace it by the end of 1941.

Specifications

Country of Origin: Russia	Barrel Length: 802mm (31.6in)
Date: 1891	Muzzle Velocity: 810m/sec (2657ft/sec)
Calibre: 7.62mm (.3in)	Feed/Magazine: 5-round box magazine
Operation: Bolt action	Range: 500m (1640ft); 750m (2460ft) + with
Weight: 4.37kg (9.625lb)	optics
Overall Length: 1305mm (51.4in)	

▲ Mosin-Nagant Model 1891

Soviet Eleventh Army / 184th Rifle Division, Northwest Front, June 1941

The Mosin-Nagant rifle was the standard issue weapon of the Soviet Red Army throughout World War II. A product of Belgian design, it has become an icon of Soviet weaponry.

▲ PPD-1934/38

Soviet Ninth Army / 5th Cavalry Division, Odessa Special Military District, August 1941

The recognition by Red Army personnel of the potential for the submachine gun on the modern battlefield resulted in the development of the PPD-1934/38, a copy of the German Bergmann MP 28.

Specifications

Country of Origin: USSR	Barrel Length: 269mm (10.60in)
Date: 1934	Muzzle Velocity: 488m/sec (1600ft/sec)
Calibre: 7.62mm (.3in) Soviet	Feed/Magazine: 25-round box magazine or
Operation: Blowback	71-round drum magazine
Weight: 5.69kg (12.54lb) loaded	Cyclic Rate: 800rpm
Overall Length: 780mm (30.71in)	Range: 100m (328ft) +

Designer Georgi Shpagin (1897–1952) developed the PPSh-41 as a blowback, open-bolt submachine gun that was chambered for a 7.62mm (.3in) round and could operate in semiautomatic or automatic firing modes. It was much more cost-effective to produce than its predecessor the PPD 1934/38 and remains in service today.

Following the Red Army encounters with formidable Finnish submachine guns during the Winter War of 1939–40, it became readily apparent that the concentrated, mobile firepower of such weapons could be decisive on the battlefield. In the

autumn of 1941, production of the PPSh-41 was undertaken in a number of factories in the Moscow area. During the first five months of 1942, more than 150,000 were manufactured, and as the war progressed more than 3000 per day were being turned out by Soviet production facilities. The simple construction of the PPSh-41 involved 87 components and simple stamping and tooling

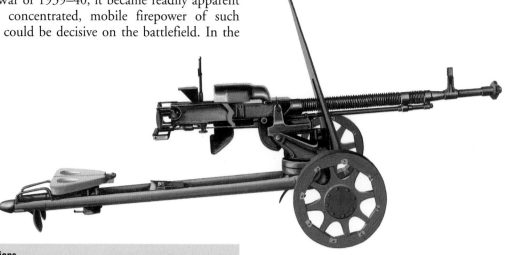

Specifications

Country of Origin: USSR	Barrel Length: 1066mm (42in)
Date: 1938	Muzzle Velocity: 850m/sec (2788ft/sec)
Calibre: 12.7mm (.5in) Soviet	Feed/Magazine: 50-round belt
Operation: Gas operated, air cooled	Cyclic Rate: 550rpm
Weight: 35.5kg (78.5lb)	Range: 2000m (6560ft) +
Overall Length: 1586mm (62.5in)	

▲ **DShK 1938**

Soviet Twentieth Army / 144th Rifle Division, Bryansk Front, October 1941

The heavy DK machine gun was originally fed by a drum magazine. Converted to a belt system as the DShK 1938, it was often mounted on a carriage and served as the primary heavy machine gun of the Red Army in World War II.

Specifications

Country of Origin: USSR	Barrel Length: 266mm (10.5in)
Date: 1941	Muzzle Velocity: 490m/sec (1600ft/sec)
Calibre: 7.62mm (.3in) Soviet	Feed/Magazine: 35-round box magazine or
Operation: Blowback	71-round drum magazine
Weight: 3.64kg (8lb)	Cyclic Rate: 900rpm
Overall Length: 838mm (33in)	Range: 120m (394ft)

▲ **PPSh-41**

Soviet Twentieth Army / 229th Rifle Division, Bryansk Front, December 1941

The PPSh-41 submachine gun was an easily produced and less expensive alternative to the earlier PPD model. More than six million of the highly successful weapon were manufactured during World War II.

Specifications

Country of Origin: USSR	Barrel Length: 273mm (10.7in)
Date: 1942	Muzzle Velocity: 500m/sec (1640ft/sec)
Calibre: 7.62mm (.3in) Soviet	Feed/Magazine: 35-round detachable box
Operation: Blowback	magazine
Weight: 2.95kg (6.5lb)	Cyclic Rate: 650rpm
Overall Length: 907mm (35.7in)	Range: 100m (328ft) +

▲ **PPS-42**

Soviet XXIV Tank Corps / 24th Motorized Rifle Brigade, Bryansk Front,
July 1942

The inexpensively produced PPS-42 submachine gun proved remarkably robust for its construction and filled a need for rapidly manufactured firepower at the Red Army squad level early in World War II.

Soviet Machine-Gun Platoon, April 1942

The four squads of the Soviet Red Army machine-gun platoon at the time of Operation Barbarossa in 1941 each fielded the DShK 1938 12.7mm (.5in) heavy machine gun with a crew of four. Easily distinguished by its two-wheeled carriage and gun shield, the DShK 1938 performed as an infantry support machine gun as well as an anti-aircraft weapon, similar to Allied counterparts such as the Browning M2. Other elements of the machine-gun platoon were soldiers armed with the Mosin-Nagant Model 1891/30 rifle and Tokarev TT30 sidearms.

Platoon HQ (1 officer): 1 x pistol

MG Squad 1 (1 NCO, 6 other ranks): 2 x pistol, 5 x rifle, 1 x MG

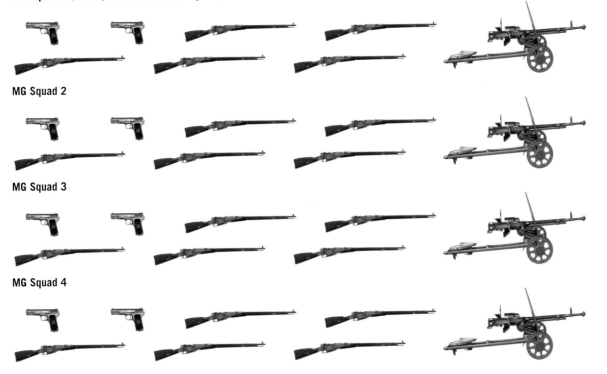

MG Squad 2

MG Squad 3

MG Squad 4

equipment. The machining for a single weapon could be accomplished in just over seven hours.

With tremendous production capacity, more than six million of the PPSh-41 were manufactured by the end of World War II, and the Red Army was eventually able to equip entire divisions with it while also supplying the weapon by air to partisan formations behind German lines. German soldiers also prized the PPSh-41 and pressed captured weapons into service. Conveniently, the Soviet and German 7.62mm (.3in) cartridges were similar, and the weapon could fire either one. In early 1943, yet another submachine gun, the PPS-42, designed by Alexey Sudayev (1912–46),

entered mass production and was even cheaper to produce. By the end of the year, production had increased to 350,000 weapons per month.

The primary Soviet infantry support heavy machine gun of World War II was the DShK 1938, which was developed in the late 1920s. The weapon was often mounted on a two-wheeled carriage and fitted with a shield. Firing a 12.7mm (.5in) round, the machine gun was originally drum fed and designated the DK. A modification to a belt-feed system resulted in the DShK 1938 designation. The weapon's rate of fire was 550 rounds per minute, and it served in an anti-aircraft role as well.

Specifications

Country of Origin: USSR	Overall Length: 2100mm (83in)
Date: 1941	Barrel Length: 1219mm (47in)
Calibre: 14.5mm (.57in)	Muzzle Velocity: 1114m/sec (3655ft/sec)
Operation: Gas operated	Feed/Magazine: 5-round magazine
Weight: 20.3kg (46lb)	Range: 800m (2620ft)

▲ **PTRS-41**

Soviet Third Shock Army / 54th Rifle Brigade, Kalinin Front, March 1942
Heavier than the PTRD-41, the PTRS-41 anti-tank rifle was fed by a five-round magazine and was easier to transport, having a detachable barrel. It fired a powerful round with a steel or tungsten core.

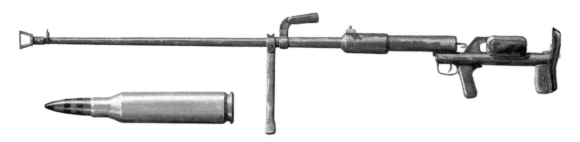

Specifications

Country of Origin: USSR	Overall Length: 2020mm (79.5in)
Date: 1941	Barrel Length: 1350mm (53.14in)
Calibre: 14.5mm (.57in)	Muzzle Velocity: 1114m/sec (3655ft/sec)
Operation: Single fire	Feed/Magazine: Single shot
Weight: 17.3kg (38.1lb)	Range: 1000m (3280ft)

▲ **PTRD-41**

Soviet Ninth Shock Army / Southern Front, June 1942
The PTRD-41 anti-tank rifle entered service with the Red Army in 1941, a time when most armies had opted for rocket- or spring-fired weapons to combat enemy armour. Later, Soviet troops used the PTRD-41 against entrenched infantry.

Soviet Anti-tank Rifle Squad, 1942

The Soviet anti-tank rifle squad of 1942 included three examples of the PTRS-41, capable of firing up to five steel- or tungsten-cored rounds without reloading, or a similar number of the single-shot PTRD-41. The anti-tank platoon consisted of three squads, totalling nine anti-tank rifles and 24 soldiers. The anti-tank rifles themselves were late in developing within the Soviet Union since Red Army commanders initially believed that early German tanks were too heavily armoured to be penetrated by such weapons. The rifles were also developed at a time when other armies were favouring rocket- or spring-propelled anti-tank weapons.

Squad (8 soldiers): 3 x PTRS-41 or PTRD-41

Germany and Allies
1941–42

Hitler's unbroken string of victories in the East came to an end in the autumn of 1942 as the Red Army and unfavourable weather halted the eastward march of the *Wehrmacht*.

WHEN HITLER launched Operation Barbarossa in June 1941, the German war machine had gained an aura of invincibility. From the Arctic Circle to the North African desert, Axis forces had the ascendancy. The *Führer* and his generals were afflicted with that most dangerous of military maladies – victory disease.

War with the Soviet Union was a gamble regardless of the apparent prowess of the German armed forces. Hitler was aware that fighting would one day resume in the West, creating a second front that had always been seen as the potential undoing of German military ambitions. Nevertheless, he was sure of a

quick victory and opined that the Soviet Union was in decay. Germany needed only to 'kick the door in and the whole house will come down!'

The German high command did have reason for optimism. The *Führer* appeared to be the master of the calculated risk. Besides, the German armed forces were the best trained and disciplined in the world and their equipment was of the highest quality.

The Germans and their allies, the Romanians, Hungarians, a contingent of Italian troops, and even a division of volunteers from Fascist Spain, failed to consider the vastness of the Soviet Union from the northern tundra to the steppes and the Crimea. They

◄ **Star Model B**

Spanish Blue Division / 250th Reconnaissance Battalion, Volkhov River, 1942

The Star Model B was a Spanish copy of the Colt Model 1911 pistol chambered for the 9mm (.35in) Parabellum cartridge. The pistol was carried on the Eastern Front by Spanish volunteers.

Specifications

Country of Origin: Spain	Overall Length: 215mm (8.46in)
Date: 1924	Barrel Length: 122mm (4.8in)
Calibre: 9mm (.35in) Parabellum	Muzzle Velocity: Not known
Operation: Short recoil	Feed/Magazine: Not known
Weight: 1.1kg (2.4lb)	Range: Not known

GERMAN INFANTRY BATTALION, *CIRCA* 1941–42		
Unit	Officers	Men
Battalion Headquarters	5	27
Communications Platoon		22
Battalion Train		32
Machine Gun Company	5	197
Company HQ	1	14
Battle Train		14
Rations Train		3
Mortar Platoon	1	61
Three Machine Gun Platoons, each	1	35
Three Rifle Companies, each	4	187
Company HQ	1	12
Battle Train		17
Rations and Baggage Trains		7
Anti-tank Rifle Section		7
Three Rifle Platoons, each		
Platoon HQ	1	5
Light Mortar Section		3
Four Rifle Squads, each		10
Total Strength of 861 all ranks	22	839

encircling and annihilating entire Soviet armies. However, they failed to win the decisive victory that would compel Stalin to sue for peace. Fighting literally at the gates of Moscow, the Germans were frustrated in their attempts to capture the Soviet capital. The price was horrific as the Red Army sustained more than a million casualties in several weeks of heavy fighting from October 1941 to January 1942.

Among the German small arms that were responsible for such grim Soviet losses was the outstanding Maschinengewehr 34, or MG 34, the mainstay of the German Army infantry support weapons since the beginning of the war. With a rate of fire of up to 900 rounds per minute and an easy exchange of barrels in combat, the MG 34 was both feared and respected by Allied soldiers. However, its precision manufacturing process was costly, particularly during wartime, and prompted German designers to seek an alternative that could be more rapidly and inexpensively produced.

Applying similar mass production techniques to those that had been used with the MP 38 submachine gun, the Germans developed the Maschinengewehr 42, or MG 42. The MG 42 was light and easily maintained and capable of producing an astonishing rate of fire of 1550 rounds per minute. Its distinctive report was similar to a ripping or shredding sound and is remembered to this day by Allied veterans who faced it in combat. Its 7.92mm (.312in) ammunition was fed from a 50-round belt, and the weapon was fired from a tripod or bipod mounting.

failed to comprehend the extent of Soviet resources in terms of manpower and machines. They failed to prepare for the cruel winter climate should their sensitive timetable stretch beyond the seasons of favourable weather.

The German advance across Russia in the summer of 1941 wreaked havoc on the Red Army, killing and capturing more than a million men. At times covering more than 160km (100 miles) in a single day, German spearheads pushed deep into Russia,

▲ **vz. 24**

Romanian Army / 11th Infantry Division, Odessa, August 1941

A rifle manufactured in Czechoslovakia shortly after the end of World War I, the vz. 24 was similar in design to the German Gewehr 98. However, it is not considered an identical copy, with a shorter barrel and other modifications.

Specifications

Country of Origin: Czechoslovakia

Date: 1938

Calibre: 7.92mm (.312in) Mauser M98

Operation: Bolt action

Weight: 4.2kg (9.2lb)

Overall Length: 1110mm (43.7in)

Barrel Length: 590mm (23.23in)

Muzzle Velocity: 760m/sec (2493ft/sec)

Feed/Magazine: 5-round integral box magazine

Range: 500m (1640ft) + with iron sights

▶ **Walther P38**

German Eighteenth Army / 21st Infantry Division, Army Group North, June 1941

The Walther P38 was one of a family of handguns that has been acknowledged as among the best pistols of the twentieth century. Always in short supply, it was nevertheless adopted in the 1930s as the official sidearm of the German Army.

Specifications

Country of Origin: Germany	Barrel Length: 127mm (5in)
Date: 1938	Muzzle Velocity: 350m/sec (1150ft/sec)
Calibre: 9mm (.35in) Parabellum	Feed/Magazine: 8-round detachable box
Operation: Short recoil	magazine
Weight: .96kg (2.11lb)	Range: 30m (98ft)
Overall Length: 213mm (8.38in)	

▲ **Karabiner 98k sniper rifle**

German Eleventh Army / 2nd SS Brigade, Army Group North, July 1942

Fitted with a precision telescopic sight, the sniper version of the standard issue German infantry rifle was extremely accurate up to 1000m (3280ft) in the hands of a skilled operator.

Specifications

Country of Origin: Germany	Overall Length: 1110mm (43.7in)
Date: 1935	Barrel Length: 600mm (23.62in)
Calibre: 7.92mm (.312in) Mauser M98	Muzzle Velocity: 745m/sec (2444ft/sec)
Operation: Bolt action	Feed/Magazine: 5-round integral box magazine
Weight: 3.9kg (8.6lb)	Range: 1000m (3280ft) +

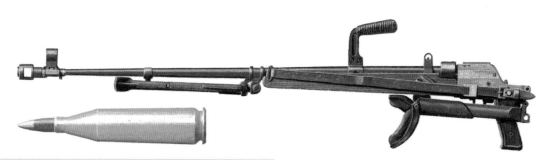

Specifications

Country of Origin: Germany	Barrel Length: 1085mm (42.7in)
Date: 1939	Muzzle Velocity: 1265m/sec (4150ft/sec)
Calibre: 7.92mm (.312in)	Feed/Magazine: Single shot
Operation: Bolt action	Range: 300m (984ft) against 25mm (.98in)
Weight: 11.6kg (25.57lb)	armour
Overall Length: 1620mm (63.8in)	

▲ **Panzerbüchse 39**

German Fourth Army / 331st Infantry Division, Army Group Centre, May 1942

The Panzerbüchse 39 anti-tank rifle was not highly effective against Soviet tanks; however, with the introduction of ammunition with a tungsten core, the unusually long weapon remained in service.

The MG 42 entered service on the Eastern Front and in North Africa in 1942, and more than 400,000 were produced during the war with the highest number per year at 212,000 in 1944. Its crew of six included a commander, gunner, bipod or tripod bearer, and three others who carried ammunition and spare barrels.

Like its predecessors the MP 38 and MP 40, the MP 41 submachine gun that emerged on the Eastern Front was conceived to provide the individual soldier with substantial firepower. It was intended to be carried by the crewmen of armoured vehicles, airborne troops and the commanders of small ground units, particularly at squad and platoon level. However, the MP 41 was never deployed by the German Army and was utilized mainly by SS and police units. The MP 41 was essentially the same weapon as the MP 40 with a wooden stock and selective-fire option. It fired the 9mm (.35in) Parabellum cartridge at a rate of up to 550 rounds per minute. One impediment to its wide acceptance was a legal battle over patent rights.

Specifications

Country of Origin: Germany	Barrel Length: 250mm (9.8mm)
Date: 1941	Muzzle Velocity: 381m/sec (1250ft/sec)
Calibre: 9mm (.35in) Parabellum	Feed/Magazine: 32-round box magazine
Operation: Blowback	Cyclic Rate: 500rpm
Weight: 3.87kg (8.5lb)	Range: 150-200m (492-656ft)
Overall Length: 860mm (33.8in)	

▲ **Maschinenpistole 41 (MP 41)**

307th Police Abteilung (Motorized), Army Group Centre, June 1942

The MP 41 was originally designed as a new infantry submachine gun but was instead deployed with police and SS units. Essentially the same weapon as the MP 40, it was manufactured with a wooden stock.

Specifications

Country of Origin: Germany	Barrel Length: 535mm (21in)
Date: 1942	Muzzle Velocity: 800m/sec (2650ft/sec)
Calibre: 7.92mm (.312in) Mauser	Feed/Magazine: 50-round belt
Operation: Short recoil, air cooled	Cyclic Rate: 1200rpm
Weight: 11.5kg (25.35lb)	Range: 3000m (9842ft) +
Overall Length: 1220mm (48in)	

▲ **Maschinengewehr 42 (MG 42)**

German Fourth Army / 331st Infantry Division, Army Group Centre, May 1942

The MG 42 was renowned for its high rate of fire and ease of transport. It was simpler to manufacture in large quantities than its predecessor, the MG 34, which also remained in production until the end of the war.

Stalingrad
AUGUST 1942 – JANUARY 1943

Hitler's dream of conquest in the East came to ruin as the German Sixth Army was surrounded and utterly destroyed by the Soviets at Stalingrad, signalling the beginning of the end for Nazi Germany.

STALINGRAD, THE INDUSTRIAL CITY on the Volga that bore the name of the Soviet leader himself, was not necessarily a primary objective of the German advance into Russia – except in the mind of Adolf Hitler (1889–1945). Although Stalingrad was an important centre of manufacturing, its capture did not spell the difference between victory and defeat for Germany; however, Hitler was determined to capture the city.

As German offensive operations commenced in the spring of 1942, Hitler directed a powerful thrust towards the Caucasus and detailed a portion of that force, primarily the Sixth Army under General Friedrich Paulus (1890–1957), to capture Stalingrad. Fighting raged for months as the Germans took most of the city but then found themselves surrounded. Paulus requested permission to break out of the trap, but Hitler refused.

Luftwaffe chief Hermann Göring (1893–1946) asserted that he could keep the beleaguered Sixth Army supplied by air, but German planes were able to deliver only a fraction of the supplies needed to maintain the Germans in Stalingrad in fighting condition. An effort to relieve the city on the ground

was turned back, and the fate of the Sixth Army was sealed. Expecting Paulus to fight to the last man, Hitler promoted him to field marshal, aware that no German commander of such high rank had ever been taken alive. Instead, Paulus surrendered to the Red Army and went into captivity with more than 90,000 of his soldiers. The disaster at Stalingrad cost the Germans a total of more than 700,000 casualties.

The privation, death and destruction at Stalingrad reduced the city to a shambles, and German soldiers who experienced the fighting in the shattered streets or from house to house called the horrific experience *Rattenkrieg*, the war of the rats. While the threat of the sniper was constant, another hidden peril lay around the corner or through the next door. Along with the Tokarev, Mosin-Nagant or Karabiner 98k sniper rifle, the submachine gun reigned in the rubble of Stalingrad.

The Soviet PPSh-41 and the German Maschinenpistole 40, or MP 40, were commonly in use during the battle for Stalingrad. The PPSh-41 had been designed for mass production with a minimum of components, stamped from steel and

Specifications

Country of Origin: USSR	Barrel Length: 266mm (10.5in)
Date: 1941	Muzzle Velocity: 490m/sec (1600ft/sec)
Calibre: 7.62mm (.3in) Soviet	Feed/Magazine: 35-round box magazine or
Operation: Blowback	71-round drum magazine
Weight: 3.64kg (8lb)	Cyclic Rate: 900rpm
Overall Length: 838mm (33in)	Range: 120m (394ft)

▲ **PPSh-41**
Soviet Sixty-Second Army / 284th Rifle Division, Stalingrad Front, September 1942
The mass-produced PPSh-41 submachine gun included a barrel lined with chrome to reduce wear. Its drum magazines could hold up to 71 rounds of ammunition.

assembled within a matter of hours to equip formations of the Red Army as large as divisions.

Like the PPSh-41, the open-bolt, blowback-operated MP 40 was mass produced, and during World War II more than a million of the MP 40 family were built. The weapon fired the 9mm (.35in) Parabellum cartridge and was capable of a cyclic rate of fire of 500 rounds per minute. Automatic-fire mode was the single option with the MP 40, although the rate of fire, which might be considered low, allowed an accomplished user to squeeze off single shots with careful manipulation of the trigger. The weapon was fed by a 32-round detachable box magazine or a 64-round dual-magazine configuration.

The MP 40 was one of a long line of submachine guns that stretched back more than 20 years. It followed the MP 38 and came about primarily due to the need for more rapid production, taking advantage of stamped parts. It combined the elements of guns from several design concerns, but its principal proponent was Heinrich Vollmer (1885–1961), who had also been instrumental in the development of the ubiquitous MG 34 infantry machine gun.

The MP 40 was intended for issue to squad or platoon leaders of the German Army, while the lion's share of the weapons was to go to airborne troops and those who operated in confined spaces such as armoured vehicle crews. However, during the Battle of Stalingrad the Germans encountered entire squads or platoons of Red Army troops equipped with the PPSh-41 and were overmatched in terms of firepower. As the war on the Eastern Front

▲ **Tokarev SVT-40**

Soviet Sixty-Second Army / 35th Guards Rifle Division, Stalingrad Front, September 1942

Based on a design by Fedor Tokarev (1871–1968), the SVT-40 assault rifle entered production in the spring of 1940 following the termination of its predecessor, the SVT-38. The weapon was fed by a 10-round box magazine, and more than 1.5 million were manufactured during World War II.

Specifications

Country of Origin: USSR	Barrel Length: 610mm (25in)
Date: 1940	Muzzle Velocity: 840m/sec (2755ft/sec)
Calibre: 7.62mm (.3in)	Feed/Magazine: 10-round detachable box
Operation: Gas operated	magazine
Weight: 3.9kg (8.6lb)	Range: 500m (1640ft) +
Overall Length: 1226mm (48.27in)	

Specifications

Country of Origin: USSR	Barrel Length: 605mm (23.8in)
Date: 1927	Muzzle Velocity: 840m/sec (2756ft/sec)
Calibre: 7.62mm (.3in) Soviet	Feed/Magazine: 47-round pan magazine
Operation: Gas operated, air cooled	Cyclic Rate: 500–600rpm
Weight: 9.12kg (20.1lb)	Range: 2000m (6560ft)
Overall Length: 1290mm (50.8in)	

▲ **Degtyaryov DP-28**

Soviet Sixty-Second Army / 244th Rifle Division, Stalingrad Front, November 1942

The primary Soviet infantry light machine gun of World War II, the DP-28 was fed by a 47-round pan magazine mounted on the top of the weapon. It was capable of firing up to 600 rounds per minute.

progressed, it became common for the *Wehrmacht* to equip larger units in the same fashion as the Soviets, with the full firepower of multiple submachine guns.

The MP 40 was generally considered a reliable weapon, and US and British soldiers who captured MP 40s in the West often pressed them into service. Still, there were problems at times with the 32-round magazine. Soldiers often grasped the magazine with one hand to stabilize the weapon and caused the feed to malfunction, particularly when debris had got into the chamber. The forward-folding stock allowed the

weapon to be carried more easily but did not hold up well in prolonged use.

German troops used the *Flammenwerfer* (flamethrower) to eliminate pockets of resistance within Stalingrad, spraying flames into houses and sewers. The Flammenwerfer 35 equipped the German forces early in the war, and this was followed by the Flammenwerfer 41 with side-by-side fuel tanks and a range of 25–30m (82–98ft). The Flammenwerfer 41 was modified so that the trigger and muzzle sections were similar to the infantry rifle in an effort to avoid drawing concentrated enemy fire to the operator.

Specifications

Country of Origin: Germany	630mm (24.75in) stock folded
Date: 1940	Barrel Length: 248mm (9.75in)
Calibre: 9mm (.35in) Parabellum	Muzzle Velocity: 395m/sec (1300ft/sec)
Operation: Blowback	Feed/Magazine: 32-round box magazine
Weight: 3.97kg (8.75lb)	Cyclic Rate: 500rpm
Overall Length: 832mm (32.75in) stock extended;	Range: 70m (230ft)

▲ Maschinenpistole 40 (MP 40)

Army Group B / German Sixth Army / 44th Infantry Division, September 1942

The MP 40 was simple to manufacture and remarkably robust, even in the harsh winter weather of the Eastern Front. Its long service life extended into the 1990s.

Specifications

Country of Origin: Germany	Fuel Capacity: 11.8 litres (2.6 gallons)
Date: 1941	Duration of Fire: 10 seconds
Weight: 35.8kg (79lb)	Range: 25–30m (82–98ft)

▶ Flammenwerfer 41

Army Group B / German Sixth Army / 389th Pioneer Battalion, September 1942

The deadly flamethrower was employed at Stalingrad by the Germans to clear houses, strongpoints and even sewers of tenacious Red Army soldiers. Spewing fuel mixed with propellant, the weapon not only burned victims but consumed available oxygen in confined spaces.

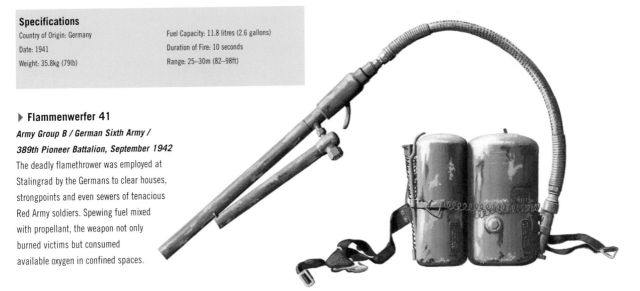

Eastern Front
1943–45

With the disastrous defeat at Stalingrad, German fortunes in the East were irretrievably reversed. The Red Army gained strength with renewed industrial capacity and fresh divisions of infantry transferred from beyond the Urals to fight the Nazis.

WORLD WAR II on the Eastern Front was a prolonged and brutal affair. Hitler had told the German people that land in the East would provide *Lebensraum*, or living space. However, by 1943 it was apparent that the *Wehrmacht* was destined to defend the borders of the Reich itself as overwhelming numbers of Red Army troops led by capable commanders such as Marshals Georgi Zhukov (1896–1974), Konstantin Rokossovsky (1896–1968) and Ivan Konev (1897–1973) drove the Germans from Russian soil and liberated most of Eastern Europe, which remained under Soviet domination for the next half-century.

As the Red Army advanced on all fronts, Stalin promoted mistrust and competition among his top commanders in order to prevent their gaining too much regard among the Soviet people or threatening his own iron grip on the Red Army and the nation. Two long years after the turning point at Stalingrad, the Red Army had raised the siege of Leningrad in the north, liberated the Ukrainian capital of Kiev and killed or captured hundreds of thousands of German troops. The battle for Berlin itself lasted from mid-April 1945 to early May, and when the end came Hitler had already committed suicide in his bunker beneath the shattered city.

▲ **Soviet sniper**
Armed with a Mosin-Nagant 1891/31 rifle equipped with a x4 PE telescopic sight, a Red Army sniper poses in full winter camouflage during the winter of 1942–43.

From Kursk to Berlin: Red Army
1943–45

The Red Army rose like the proverbial phoenix from the ashes of defeat of 1941, becoming the largest and arguably the most powerful land army in the world by the end of World War II.

B Y THE SUMMER OF 1943, the Soviets had seized the initiative on the Eastern Front, driving the *Wehrmacht* westwards across hundreds of kilometres of territory. Near the city of Kursk, 450km (280 miles) south of Moscow, the Red Army had advanced in force, creating a large salient, or bulge. The Germans recognized an opportunity to trap thousands of Soviet troops and tanks inside the salient and to shorten their defensive lines by eliminating it.

In July, the Germans attacked. The largest armoured battle in history followed. In the south, the Germans pushed towards the town of Prokhorovka where a wild melee of armour and panzergrenadiers and Red Army troops firing automatic weapons erupted. When the Soviets committed their armoured reserves to the fight, Hitler acknowledged that the offensive was a failure and halted further operations.

As mentioned earlier, the Soviets remember 1944 as 'The Year of 10 Victories', commemorating the

◀ **Tula-Tokarev TT33**

Soviet Thirty-Third Army / 144th Rifle Division, Eastern Front, July 1943

A reliable and sturdy weapon, the 7.62mm (.3in) TT33 pistol was patterned after the earlier TT30, of which more than two million were manufactured. The TT33 was the result of an altered frame, barrel and trigger.

Specifications

Country of Origin: USSR	Barrel Length: 116mm (4.57in)
Date: 1933	Muzzle Velocity: 415m/sec (1362ft/sec)
Calibre: 7.62mm (.3in) Soviet	Feed/Magazine: 8-round detachable box
Operation: Short recoil	magazine
Weight: .83kg (1.83lb)	Range: 30m (98ft)
Overall Length: 194mm (7.6in)	

▲ **Mosin-Nagant M1938 carbine**

Soviet Tenth Army / 330th Rifle Division, Eastern Front, July 1943

The short-barrelled carbine version of the Mosin-Nagant M91/30 rifle, the M1938 was developed and tested in 1938, but did not enter production until 1939. It was not designed to take a bayonet.

Specifications

Country of Origin: USSR	Overall Length: 1020mm (40in)
Date: 1938	Barrel Length: 510mm (20in)
Calibre: 7.62mm (.3in)	Muzzle Velocity: 800m/sec (2625ft/sec)
Operation: Bolt action	Feed/Magazine: 5-round box magazine
Weight: 3.45kg (7.62lb)	Range: 500m (1640ft)

SOVIET RIFLE BRIGADE PERSONNEL & EQUIPMENT, 1943	
Personnel type/Equipment item	Strength
Officers	58
NCOs	193
Other ranks	677
Submachine guns	126
Bolt-action rifles	220
Semiautomatic rifles	403
Light machine guns	36
Medium machine guns	12
Heavy machine guns	0
Anti-tank rifles	8
Anti-tank mortars	7
50mm (2in) mortars	12
82mm (3.2in) mortars	0
120mm (4.7in) mortars	0
45mm (1.8in) anti-tank guns	0
76mm (3in) guns	0
Horses	89

against German Panzerfaust and Panzerschreck teams and mopping up pockets of resistance. In the hands of a number of these Red Army soldiers was the Tokarev SVT-40 assault rifle. A gas-operated, short-stroke piston rifle with a tilting bolt, the SVT-40 was based on a design undertaken by Fedor Tokarev (1871–1968) in about 1930. Tokarev had previously worked on a recoil-operated semiautomatic rifle and abandoned that effort.

The SVT-40 was the successor to an earlier model, the SVT-38, and fired the Soviet 7.62mm (.3in) cartridge. Fed by a 10-round detachable box magazine, it entered production at the Tula Arsenal in the summer of 1939. More than 1.5 million were manufactured during the course of the war. About 150,000 examples of the SVT-38 had been manufactured and issued to troops during the Winter War with Finland in 1939–40. Contrary to most Soviet small-arms designs, the SVT-38 was well built with precision machining.

By the summer of 1941, however, the SVT-40 had been authorized for distribution to Red Army troops and incorporated some improvements to the previous

succession of offensive operations that carried the Red Army to the gates of Berlin by the spring of 1945. Two of these actions stand out among the others. Early in the year, an offensive finally lifted the siege of Leningrad, which had dragged on for 900 days and cost the lives of more than a million civilians. At mid-year, Operation Bagration utterly destroyed German Army Group Centre and drove the last German troops from Russian soil before the Red Army advanced into Germany.

In January 1945, the Soviet offensive along the rivers Vistula and Oder opened the drive to Berlin through East Prussia and Silesia. By mid-April, Zhukov's 1st Belorussian Front and Konev's 1st Ukrainian Front were pressing into the suburbs of the city. On 2 May, Red Army troops captured the Reich Chancellery and raised their flag above the defeated city. Victory had come at a tremendous price with estimates of Soviet military and civilian deaths at 20 million.

As Soviet armour rumbled through the streets of Berlin, infantry supported the tanks, protecting

▶ **Guards soldier**

Armed with a PPS-43 submachine gun, a corporal from the 1st Ukrainian Front pauses during the advance through suburban Berlin, April 1945.

▲ Tokarev AVT-40

Soviet Eleventh Guards Army / 5th Guards Motor Rifle Division, Kursk Front, July 1943

The Tokarev AVT-40 was a fully automatic version of the SVT-40 semiautomatic rifle. Its 10-round magazine limited the supply of ammunition available to the weapon, and it proved unstable in combat.

Specifications

Country of Origin: USSR
Date: 1940
Calibre: 7.62mm (.3in)
Operation: Gas-operated short-stroke piston
Weight: 3.9kg (8.6lb)
Overall Length: 1226mm (48.27in)

Barrel Length: 610mm (25in)
Muzzle Velocity: 840m/sec (2756ft/sec)
Feed/Magazine: 10-round detachable box magazine
Range: 500m (1640ft)

Specifications

Country of Origin: USSR
Date: 1943
Calibre: 7.62mm (.3in) Soviet
Operation: Blowback
Weight: 3.36kg (7.4lb)
Overall Length: 820mm (32.3in)

Barrel Length: 254mm (10in)
Muzzle Velocity: 500m/sec (1640ft/sec)
Feed/Magazine: 35-round detachable box magazine
Cyclic Rate: 650rpm
Range: 100m (328ft) +

▲ PPS-43

Soviet Eleventh Guards Army / 31st Guards Rifle Division, Orel Offensive, August 1943

The PPS-43 submachine gun was a modified version of the earlier PPS-42; it was designed and produced in the city of Leningrad while under siege. Remarkably, the weapon was a success and served with Soviet forces for years.

▲ SKS carbine

Soviet First Guards Tank Army / 12th Motor Rifle Brigade, 1st Belorussian Front, March 1945

The SKS carbine did not appear in combat until 1945 as a shorter rifle for troops who operated in vehicles and other close-quarters situations. A semiautomatic weapon, its ammunition supply was limited by a 10-round box magazine.

Specifications

Country of Origin: USSR
Date: 1945
Calibre: 7.62mm (.3in)
Operation: Gas-operated short-stroke piston
Weight: 3.85kg (8.49lb)

Overall Length: 1021mm (40.2in)
Barrel Length: 521mm (20.5in)
Muzzle Velocity: 735m/sec (2411ft/sec)
Feed/Magazine: 10-round integral box magazine
Range: 400m (1312ft)

weapon, particularly a modified magazine release and a hand guard made of a single piece. It was also easier to manufacture and lighter than the SVT-38. When German forces invaded the Soviet Union, substantial numbers of the SVT-40 were already in service and helped eventually to turn the tide of the war on the Eastern Front.

In 1943, the Soviets introduced the Goryunov SG-43 medium machine gun, finally intending to replace the old Model 1910 Maxim Guns still in service. Like other Soviet machine guns, the SG-43 was often mounted on a wheeled carriage, although a tripod option was available. This gas-operated weapon fired the 7.62mm (.3in) cartridge at a rate of up to 700 rounds per minute, and it was fed by ammunition belts of 200 or 250 rounds. It had a range of 1000m (3280ft). After World War II, the SG-43 was exported to several nations of the Communist Bloc. The SG-43 was difficult to load, and its barrel was cumbersome to change in the field.

Specifications

Country of Origin: USSR

Date: 1943

Calibre: 7.62mm (.3in) Soviet

Operation: Gas operated, air cooled

Weight: 13.6kg (29.98lb)

Overall Length: 1120mm (44.1in)

Barrel Length: 719mm (28.3in)

Muzzle Velocity: 850m/sec (2788ft/sec)

Feed/Magazine: 200- or 250-round belt

Cyclic Rate: 500–700rpm

Range: 1000m (3280ft)

▲ **Goryunov SG-43**

Soviet Fifteenth Army / 238th Rifle Division, 2nd Belorussian Front, June 1944

The SG-43 medium machine gun entered service with the Red Army in 1943 as a replacement for the venerable Model 1910 Maxim Gun. The SG-43 was often placed on a two-wheeled carriage or mounted on a tripod.

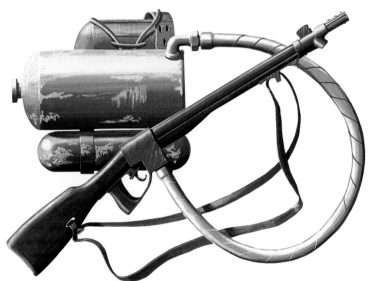

Specifications

Country of Origin: USSR

Date: 1943

Weight: 22.7kg (50lb)

Fuel Capacity: 9 litres (5 gallons)

Duration of Fire: 8–10 seconds

Range: 23–27m (75–89ft)

◀ **ROKS-3**

Soviet Fifteenth Army / 64th Engineer Brigade, June 1944

The ROKS-3 flamethrower was a wartime expedient version of the ROKS-2. It was designed for mass production, and performance was improved with the introduction of thicker fuel, increasing its range.

Retreat and Defeat: German Army 1943–45

Götterdämmerung for the Third Reich began on the Eastern Front in 1943. Defeats at Stalingrad and Kursk were followed by relentless Red Army offensive action, and despite temporary setbacks the Soviets crushed German resistance.

THE GERMANS COMMITTED tremendous numbers of *Wehrmacht* and SS troops and enormous amounts of weapons large and small to the maelstrom of World War II on the Eastern Front. Among these were legions of their finest tanks, the Mark V Panther and Mark VI Tiger; their most fanatical armoured and infantry formations in the SS divisions; thousands of their reliable 88mm (3.5in) anti-aircraft guns that had proved deadly in the anti-tank role; and the first assault rifles to see action. None of these had stabilized, let alone reversed, the situation in the East by the end of 1943.

German defeats at Stalingrad and in the great tank battle of Kursk placed momentum solidly on the side of the Red Army, although from time to time the Germans did mount successful counterattacks. These, however, were only temporary, pyrrhic victories. None were sustainable due to a lack of troops and materiel to exploit any progress. The German armed forces were being bled white by the Red Army.

During 1944, the Soviets advanced steadily towards the German frontier. By the spring of 1945, they had marched into Warsaw, Prague and Vienna, liberating the capitals and major cities of Eastern Europe and forcing the Germans to press old men of the *Volkssturm* and boys of the Hitler Youth into the defence of the Fatherland.

As the Red Army moved inexorably westwards, Hitler became delusional, ordering phantom armies or formations that had long been decimated in the crucible of combat to counterattack. His generals often petitioned the *Führer* to withdraw from exposed positions in order to prevent further needless loss of life and resources; however, Hitler ordered his troops invariably to stand fast. These orders were sometimes ignored and troops pulled out despite the *Führer*'s decrees.

In the south, thousands of German and Romanian troops were trapped in the Crimea and rendered useless for months. Hitler ordered the garrison of Sevastopol to fight to the last shell; however, such an effort was unrealistic due to the rapid movement of Soviet forces. The Axis troops who could be evacuated were taken by sea to the Romanian city of Constanta on the Black Sea coast. Approximately 100,000 German and Romanian soldiers were lost in the fighting.

With deficiencies in manpower and equipment at critical levels, German forces in the East were sometimes organized into 'fire brigades' whose purpose was to rapidly move to areas of Soviet breakthroughs

▶ **Walther PPK**

Army Group B / German Fifteenth Army / 84th Infantry Division, June 1944

The double-action PPK was smaller than other Walther pistols of the PP series and originally intended for police work. It was easily concealed and could be drawn and fired rapidly.

Specifications

Country of Origin: Germany	Barrel Length: 80mm (3.15in)
Date: 1931	Muzzle Velocity: 290m/sec (950ft/sec)
Calibre: 7.65mm (.301in)	Feed/Magazine: 7-round detachable box
Operation: Blowback	magazine
Weight: .59kg (1.3lb)	Range: 30m (98ft)
Overall Length: 148mm (5.8in)	

▲ **Squad action**
A German squad armed primarily with with Kar 98 rifles advances warily somewhere in northern Germany, early 1945.

and attempt to contain breaches in German lines. Such a strategy was born of necessity but wore the Germans down through painful attrition.

The Battle of Berlin began in earnest in mid-April 1945 and was concluded during the first week of May as Red Army troops took control of the German capital following weeks of artillery bombardment and fighting that was characterized by bloody, close-quarters shoot-outs from street to street and house to house. The Germans made the Soviets pay dearly for their conquest of Berlin. In the two weeks of fighting that preceded the city's capture the Soviets suffered more than 360,000 killed, wounded and missing. The Germans lost at least 125,000 dead during the period, and more than 20,000 of these were civilians. By the time Berlin fell, most high-ranking Nazis had committed suicide or attempted to flee towards the Western Allies in fear of Soviet reprisals against them.

Wartime weapons evolution

The war on the Eastern Front had become a proving ground for advancing small-arms technology. The rifle, assault rifle, submachine gun, infantry support machine gun and anti-tank weapons were evaluated, modified, discarded or simplified for mass production. The firepower of the individual soldier was substantially augmented, and German innovation was largely responsible for the evolution of infantry weapons.

The majority of the 425,000 Sturmgewehr 44 assault rifles manufactured during the war were sent to the Eastern Front. Many firearms experts consider the Sturmgewehr 44 to be the first assault rifle to enter combat, but its development was slowed by interference from Hitler, and its continuation was in doubt for a time. As alluded to above, earlier incarnations of the assault rifle – first designated the Maschinenkarabiner 42 (Mkb 42), then the Maschinenpistole 43 (MP 43) – were quietly continued, eventually becoming the Sturmgewehr 44, literally translated as Storm Rifle 44.

Actually, it was reported that Hitler named the Sturmgewehr 44 after test-firing the weapon he had opposed. During a conference, Hitler had questioned several commanders from the Eastern Front as to their most pressing needs. One of them replied that more of the new automatic rifles they had received would be beneficial. The *Führer* was shocked to learn of its covert development but later acquiesced. The Sturmgewehr 44 went on to revolutionize individual small arms around the world, inspiring a generation of new weapons.

German forays into the development of semiautomatic rifles were less successful. The highly accurate, gas-operated Gewehr 43 rifle was designed by the Walther firm and showed some promise although it was slow and costly to produce. German soldiers were impressed with the Soviet Tokarev SVT-40 semiautomatic rifle, another gas-operated weapon, which they encountered during Operation Barbarossa. Walther studied captured examples of the SVT-40 and developed a gas operating system similar to that of the Soviet weapon.

The high manufacturing cost of the Gewehr 43, particularly when it entered production in the autumn of 1943 and Germany was experiencing serious shortages of raw materials, limited the availability of the weapon. It was issued to a relative few German troops in the final two years of the war.

Production of the Gewehr 43 and its predecessor, the Gewehr 41, totalled slightly more than 400,000 including over 50,000 units of a sniper version that was fitted with a telescopic sight.

While both automatic and semiautomatic rifles were effective combat weapons, German industrial capacity failed to produce enough of them to stave off defeat in World War II. The same may be said of other German weaponry that appeared during the war. Small arms, armoured vehicles and tanks, jet aircraft and rockets were products of the German industrial base. However, the mismanagement of these projects, their general lack of support from high-ranking Nazis, or their sheer expense prevented a tipping of the balance of power towards the Axis.

Specifications

Country of Origin: Germany	Barrel Length: 418mm (16.5in)
Date: 1943	Muzzle Velocity: 700m/sec (2300ft/sec)
Calibre: 7.92mm (.312in) Kurz	Feed/Magazine: 30-round detachable box
Operation: Gas operated	magazine
Weight: 5.1kg (11.24lb)	Cyclic Rate: 550–600rpm
Overall Length: 940mm (37in)	Range: c.300m (984ft)

▲ Maschinenpistole 43 (MP 43)

Army Group Centre / First Panzer Army / 20th SS (Estonian) Grenadier Division, March 1945

The MP 43 was essentially the same weapon as the famed Sturmgewehr 44, the *Maschinenpistole* designation being given to the project that produced the StG 44 to avoid Hitler's disapproval of the weapon's development.

▲ Sturmgewehr 44 (StG 44)

Army Group Centre / German Seventeenth Army / 6th Volksgrenadier Division, March 1945

The Sturmgewehr 44 may be considered the first true assault rifle to enter combat. It served as the basis for a generation of future infantry automatic weapons around the world.

Specifications

Country of Origin: Germany	Barrel Length: 418mm (16.5in)
Date: 1944	Muzzle Velocity: 700m/sec (2300ft/sec)
Calibre: 7.92mm (.312in) Kurz	Feed/Magazine: 30-round detachable box
Operation: Gas operated	magazine
Weight: 5.1kg (11.24lb)	Cyclic Rate: 550–600rpm
Overall Length: 940mm (37in)	Range: c.400m (1312ft)

Chapter 6

World War II: Pacific Theatre

**Japanese expansion throughout Asia and the
Pacific was driven by the rise of militarism in Japan as well
as by shortages of land and raw materials that could sustain
a growing population. Since the early twentieth century,
Japan had gained preeminent status in Asia, its military
steadily increasing in strength along the model of Western
powers. By the 1930s, the Japanese Army had conquered
vast territories in northern China, and conflict with the only
nation strong enough to oppose continuing expansion in the
region, the United States, loomed. By the time the US
declared war on Japan following the 7 December 1941
attack on Pearl Harbor, the Japanese soldier was well
trained and equipped with modern weapons, many of
which had been made to high standards of
precision in Japan.**

◀ **Tommy Gun**

A US Marine of the 1st Marine Division draws a bead on a Japanese sniper with his Thompson submachine
gun, Wana Ridge, Okinawa, 1945. His companion is armed with a Browning Automatic Rifle (BAR) squad
support weapon.

Introduction

World War II in the Pacific spanned the jungles of Southeast Asia, the vastness of China, the Arctic reaches of the Aleutians, and remote tropical islands. While fighting men endured tremendous hardships, their small arms were subjected to the harshest of conditions.

On Sunday 7 December 1941, Japanese attacks against the US Pacific Fleet anchorage at Pearl Harbor and other installations on the island of Oahu and across Asia were launched within hours of one another. The aim was to seize the initiative in the Pacific with the intent of expanding the empire and maintaining control over significant territory occupied through mandate, treaty or military action during the previous half-century. Japanese propagandists had mounted a continuing effort to promote 'Asia for Asians'. Their creation of the Greater East Asia Co-Prosperity Sphere was political posturing that advocated the removal of Western influence from Asia and the Pacific. In truth, 'Asia for Asians' meant Asia for exploitation and domination by Japan.

Onslaught of the Rising Sun

The Japanese Army had been active in China since 1931, and following the outbreak of hostilities the well-disciplined force reeled off an unbroken string of victories. Hong Kong fell on Christmas Day 1941, and the Japanese tide rolled into the spring of 1942. In the Philippines, US and Filipino forces under the command of General Douglas MacArthur (1880–1964) were pushed into a defensive perimeter on the Bataan peninsula and then to the island fortress of Corregidor. In May 1942, Corregidor capitulated, and more than 100,000 were taken prisoner.

On the Malay peninsula, the Japanese drove relentlessly towards the British bastion of Singapore, swiftly outflanking and defeating British and Commonwealth troops. On 15 February 1942, Singapore fell, and 120,000 soldiers under the command of Lieutenant-General Arthur Percival (1887–1966) were captured. The Japanese occupied Burma and threatened India, the jewel in the crown of the British Empire, with invasion.

In the Pacific and Indian Oceans, the Imperial Japanese Navy appeared invincible. Three days after Pearl Harbor, naval aircraft sank the British battleship *Prince of Wales* and the battlecruiser *Repulse*, sent to the Orient to bolster the defences of Singapore and the Malay peninsula. Admiral Isoroku Yamamoto (1884–1943), architect of the attack on Pearl Harbor, had warned the Japanese military establishment, 'For six months, I will run wild in the Pacific. After that, I make no guarantees.'

Yamamoto was correct almost to the day in his prediction. By June 1942, scarcely a month after the debacle in the Philippines, the US Navy denied the Japanese bid to capture Midway Atoll, a scant 1770km (1100 miles) from Hawaii. The victory at Midway was the turning point of the war in the Pacific and virtually erased Japanese superiority in aircraft carriers, planes and trained pilots. However, the island road to Tokyo would be long and costly. Victory at sea would necessarily be accompanied by victory on land.

Jungle fighting and island hopping

In August 1942, US forces landed on the island of Guadalcanal in the Solomons chain. Six months of bitter fighting followed before the Japanese withdrew from the island. Commonwealth troops held the line in the China–Burma–India Theatre and in New Guinea. The Allies assumed the offensive to the south in 1943, and General MacArthur triumphantly returned to the Philippines in the autumn of 1944. US Marines and Army troops stormed ashore and fought horrific battles on small, previously obscure islands such as Tarawa, Saipan, Peleliu, Iwo Jima and Okinawa during an island-hopping campaign that carried the war across the expanse of the Pacific to the doorstep of the Japanese home islands.

Invasion of the home islands

In early 1945, Allied war planners contemplated the costliest operation of the war, an invasion of Japan itself. Estimates of Allied casualties ran into the hundreds of thousands. However, the invasion proved unnecessary with the dropping of atomic bombs on the cities of Hiroshima and Nagasaki. Ironically, a war that had been fought on land with a plethora of small arms was ultimately ended with the most destructive weapon yet seen in human history.

▲ **Jungle fighters**
US Marines pose for a photo in the jungle of Bougainville, Solomon Islands, 1943. Most are armed with M1 Garand rifles, although a few are carrying the M1903
Springfield and M1 carbine, both popular with troops involved in jungle warfare.

The Japanese troops that fought the Allies across the Pacific and on the Asian continent were equipped with an assortment of small arms including the Type 38 and Type 99 Arisaka rifles, the Type 11 and Type 96 light machine guns, the Type 1, Type 3 and Type 92 heavy machine guns, and the Type 100 submachine gun. Generally these weapons were of quality manufacture until late in the war when concentrated US bombing had taken its toll on Japan's industrial capacity and submarines of the US Navy had choked the lifeline of supplies and raw materials for Japanese factories, crippling the war effort and finally helping to bring the Empire of the Rising Sun to its knees.

Imperial Japanese Army
1941–45

The Japanese Empire began to modernize its military and look to expand throughout Asia as resources were scarce for its growing population. The primary tool of that expansion was a military machine that rivalled the great powers of the West.

THE JAPANESE SOLDIER who conquered vast areas of the Asian continent and the Pacific stood approximately 1.6m (5ft 3in) tall. He was imbued with the belief that the Japanese were a superior people and that service to the emperor, particularly service resulting in his death in battle, was glorious. He was trained to follow the Code of Bushido, stressing that it was his duty to fight to the death. Surrender was not an option.

In 1943, the US military published a report titled *Some Basic Tactics of the Japanese*. Its content reveals the perception of the American commanders who faced the Japanese enemy. 'From almost every fighting front in the Pacific there have come reports that it has been necessary to completely wipe out all Japanese opposition before the objective could be attained. The following…taken from a British source [is] illustrative of some basic Japanese tactics. "When I received my mobilization orders, I had already sacrificed my life for my country…you must not expect me to return alive…." The last blood smeared page of a diary captured in Burma has "Three cheers for the Emperor" scrawled across it.'

Fanatical fighters

In keeping with Bushido, the Japanese soldier sacrificed himself without hesitation, fighting to the death rather than bringing dishonour upon himself and his family. At Tarawa in the Gilbert Islands, only 17 of the 3000-man garrison were taken alive following the bloody 76-hour fight with US Marines for control of the atoll. At Saipan in the Marianas, only 900 of an estimated 31,000 Japanese defenders surrendered during the fighting in mid-1944.

For some historians, the impetus behind the wave of atrocities that were perpetrated by Japanese troops against Allied prisoners of war is rooted in strict adherence to the Bushido code. Since the Japanese were unwilling to surrender themselves, it seemed plausible to them that Allied prisoners should be held to the same standard and treated harshly for their dishonourable conduct. Incidents of summary executions and forced labour as well as the infamous Bataan Death March are indicative of such behaviour.

The Japanese soldier displayed great courage and endurance during World War II, covering extreme

▶ **94 Shiki Kenju (Type 94)**

Imperial Guards Division / 4th Konoye Regiment, Muar, Malaya, January 1942

Firing a weak 8mm (.314in) round, the Type 94 pistol was intended for use by vehicle crews and officers. It was designed for mass production and as a more compact pistol than the earlier Type 14.

Specifications

Country of Origin: Japan	Barrel Length: 96mm (3.78in)
Date: 1934	Muzzle Velocity: 305m/sec (1000ft/sec)
Calibre: 8mm (.314in)	Feed/Magazine: 6-round box magazine
Operation: Not known	Range: Not known
Weight: .688kg (1.52lb)	
Overall Length: 183mm (7.2in)	

distances on foot while carrying a pack of weapons, ammunition, food and personal items that often weighed in excess of 27kg (60lb). Rapid manoeuvre, concealment and ambush were identified as Japanese strengths by the American authors of the *Tactics* report; however, when it seemed that the situation called for desperate measures, the Banzai charge characterized the defence of a Pacific island. Hundreds of Japanese soldiers, sometimes fortified with sake, Japanese rice wine, hurled themselves at entrenched US Marines with utter disregard for personal safety. The results were predictable, but the soldier of Nippon had remained true to his creed.

When war broke out between Japan and the United States, the Imperial Japanese Army numbered 1.7 million men in 51 divisions. As the war progressed, the number of men under arms swelled to 5.5 million.

As fortunes were reversed, great numbers of these troops were isolated on Pacific islands, bypassed in the Allied island-hopping offensive or cut off from resupply on the Asian mainland. In fact, the Japanese lifeline of essential war materiel was choked by interdiction from American submarines, resulting in an erosion of the combat efficiency of the Japanese soldier on all fronts.

Specifications*

Country of Origin: Japan	Barrel Length: 657mm (25.87in)
Date: 1939	Muzzle Velocity: 730m/sec (2394ft/sec)
Calibre: 7.7mm (.303in) Arisaka	Feed/Magazine: N/A
Operation: Bolt action	Range (Grenade): 100m (328ft)
Weight: 3.7kg (8.16lb)	* Of rifle without grenade
Overall Length: 1120mm (44.1in)	

▲ **Type 99 rifle with Type 2 grenade launcher**

1st Independent Anti-Tank Battalion, Bukit Timah, Singapore, February 1942

A grenade launcher was available for both the Type 99 and Type 38 bolt-action rifles. The effective range of the grenade was about 100m (328ft).

▲ **Type 99 rifle**

9th Infantry Brigade, Batu Pahat, Johore, Malaya, January 1942

The Type 99 rifle was developed as a heavier-calibre shoulder arm to replace the Type 38. However, war with the United States prevented full implementation and the two rifles were common during World War II.

Specifications

Country of Origin: Japan	Barrel Length: 657mm (25.87in)
Date: 1939	Muzzle Velocity: 730m/sec (2394ft/sec)
Calibre: 7.7mm (.303in) Arisaka	Feed/Magazine: 5-round internal box magazine,
Operation: Bolt action	stripper-clip-loaded
Weight: 3.7kg (8.16lb)	Range: 500m (1640ft)
Overall Length: 1120mm (44.1in)	

By 1945, Japan had succumbed to the weight of US and Commonwealth arms. However, a handful of individual soldiers, refusing to believe that their country would surrender, held out in the jungles of the Philippines and other locations across the Pacific, abandoning their posts only when former comrades or commanding officers coaxed them into the open in the 1970s.

Japanese small arms

The Imperial Japanese Army fielded two prominent bolt-action rifles during World War II, the Arisaka Type 38 and Type 99. These were identified according to the 38th year of the Meiji period and the year 2099 of the Japanese calendar respectively. Colonel Nariakira Arisaka (1852–1915) headed the commission established to develop modern shoulder

Specifications

Country of Origin: Japan	Overall Length: 966mm (38.03in)
Date: 1911	Barrel Length: 487mm (19.17in)
Calibre: 6.5mm (.256in) Arisaka	Muzzle Velocity: 685m/sec (2246.8ft/sec)
Operation: Bolt action	Feed/Magazine: 5-round internal magazine
Weight: 3.3kg (7.28lb)	Range: 400m (1312ft)

▲ Type 44

38th Infantry Division / 38th Engineer Battalion, Guadalcanal, November 1942

A compact version of the Type 38 rifle, this carbine is also referred to as the Type 44 cavalry rifle. It fired an identical cartridge but was equipped with a needle-style bayonet.

Specifications

Country of Origin: Japan	Barrel Length: 589mm (23.2in)
Date: 1941	Muzzle Velocity: 770m/sec (2500ft/sec)
Calibre: 7.7mm (.303in) Arisaka	Feed/Magazine: 30-round metallic feed trays
Operation: Gas operated	Cyclic Rate: 450rpm
Weight: 31.8kg (70.1lb)	Range: 1400m (4593ft)
Overall Length: 1077mm (42.4in)	

▲ Type 1

16th Infantry Division, Luzon, Philippines, April 1942

The Type 1 heavy machine gun, a scaled-down version of the Type 92, was introduced in 1941 and became a primary weapon of Japanese infantry units during World War II.

arms for the Japanese military, and both rifles are commonly known as Arisakas. Both were also heavily influenced by the German Mauser design.

The Type 38 fired a 6.5mm (.256in) cartridge, and practical experience in the Sino-Japanese wars of the 1930s indicated the need for a higher-calibre weapon. The Type 99 was intended to replace the Type 38; however, this was never accomplished and both served throughout World War II. More than 3.5 million examples of the Type 99 were built from 1939 to 1945 at nine arsenals, seven of which were located in Japan with one in Mukden, China, and another at Jinsen in Korea.

Fed by a five-round internal box magazine that was loaded from stripper clips, the Type 99 fired a heavier 7.7mm (.303in) cartridge and was notable for its monopod, which was intended to steady the weapon for firing, and an anti-aircraft sight. The

▲ Type 96

Sixteenth Army, Java, March 1942

Intended to replace the Type 11 light machine gun, the Type 96 was also based on the French Hotchkiss design. The hopper feed of the Type 11 was replaced with a 30-round box magazine.

Specifications

Country of Origin: Japan	Barrel Length: 555mm (21.75in)
Date: 1936	Muzzle Velocity: 730m/sec (2300ft/sec)
Calibre: 6.5mm (.256in) Arisaka	Feed/Magazine: 30-round box magazine
Operation: Gas operated, air cooled	Cyclic Rate: 450–500rpm
Weight: 9kg (20lb)	Range: 1000m (3280ft)
Overall Length: 1055mm (41.5in)	

▲ Type 97 sniper rifle

39th Brigade, New Britain, New Guinea, April 1944

An adaptation of the Type 38 infantry rifle, the Type 97 sniper rifle fired the same weak 6.5mm (.256in) round. Its low muzzle flash made detection of concealed snipers difficult.

Specifications

Country of Origin: Japan	Barrel Length: 797mm (31.4in)
Date: 1937	Muzzle Velocity: 762.1m/sec (2500ft/sec)
Calibre: 6.5mm (.256in) Arisaka	Feed/Magazine: 5-round internal magazine,
Operation: Bolt action	stripper-clip-loaded
Weight: 3.95kg (8.7lb)	Range: 800m (2620ft)
Overall Length: 1280mm (50.7in)	

Type 99 was also the first rifle to be equipped with a chrome-lined barrel for easier cleaning. Each weapon was marked on the barrel with the chrysanthemum, identifying the rifle as the property of Emperor Hirohito (1901–89), and many of those that were surrendered by the end of World War II had their emblems defaced in order to preserve the emperor's honour. Contrary to some reports of the poor quality of the Type 99, those built prior to and during the early years of the war were of good quality and performance. Similar to the experience with German rifles, as shortages of materials and the exigencies of war pressed Japanese industrial capacity, quality declined substantially.

▲ **Type 100**

62nd Infantry Division, Okinawa, April 1945

The only Japanese submachine gun of World War II, the Type 100 was inferior to Western counterparts with a weak 8mm (.314in) round and low rate of fire.

Specifications

Country of Origin: Japan	Barrel Length: 228mm (9in)
Date: 1942	Muzzle Velocity: 335m/sec (1100ft/sec)
Calibre: 8mm (.314in) Nambu	Feed/Magazine: 30-round box magazine
Operation: Blowback	Cyclic Rate: 450rpm (1942); 800rpm (1944)
Weight: 3.83kg (8.44lb)	Range: 70m (230ft)
Overall Length: 890mm (35in)	

▲ **Type 92**

Thirty-Second Army / 44th Independent Mixed Brigade, Okinawa, April 1945

Differing mainly in its heavier 7.7mm (.303in) cartridge from its predecessor, the Type 3, the Type 92 was nicknamed the Woodpecker by Allied troops.

Specifications

Country of Origin: Japan	Barrel Length: 700mm (27.5in)
Date: 1932	Muzzle Velocity: 715m/sec (2350ft/sec)
Calibre: 7.7mm (.303in)	Feed/Magazine: 30-round metal strip
Operation: Gas operated, air cooled	Cyclic Rate: 450rpm
Weight: 55kg (122lb)	Range: 2000m (6560ft)
Overall Length: 1160mm (45in)	

Therefore, late-war rifles have been noted for inferior performance.

Japanese machine guns

French design heavily influenced the development of Japanese machine guns during the 1920s and 1930s. The air-cooled, gas-operated Type 11 fired a 6.5mm (.256in) cartridge identical to that of the Type 38 rifle from an open hopper magazine that was loaded with five-round clips. Although this arrangement enhanced the rate of fire, the open magazine allowed debris to accumulate in the hopper and receiver, causing frequent jamming.

By 1936, prolific designer Kijiro Nambu (1869–1949) had introduced the Type 96, firing the same cartridge from a 30-round detachable box magazine with a rate of fire of up to 500 rounds per minute. When the jamming problem persisted,

▼ Japanese Machine-Gun Company, 1942

The standard Japanese machine-gun platoon included four Type 92 heavy machine guns firing the 7.7mm (.303in) round, each with a crew of three men. However, in the field it was noted that many of these platoons included only two weapons. Japanese machine-gun companies consisted of three platoons of four guns, totalling 12 weapons, or four platoons of two guns each, totalling eight. The Type 92 machine gun was often transported affixed to its tripod for rapid deployment in combat.

Platoon 1 (2 x Type 92)

Platoon 3 (2 x Type 92)

Platoon 2 (2 x Type 92)

Platoon 4 (2 x Type 92)

▲ Type 97 anti-tank rifle

2nd Mixed Brigade, Iwo Jima, March 1945

Packing a tremendous recoil, the Type 97 anti-tank rifle was inaccurate. It was lightweight and easily transportable, firing a 20mm (.79in) round from a seven-round magazine.

Specifications

Country of Origin: Japan	Barrel Length: 1200mm (47.2in)
Date: 1937	Muzzle Velocity: 750m/sec (2460ft/sec)
Calibre: 20mm (.79in)	Feed/Magazine: 7-round detachable box
Operation: Gas operated	magazine
Weight: 59kg (130lb)	Range: 350m (1148ft) against 30mm (1.18in)
Overall Length: 2060mm (81.1in)	armour; 700m (2296ft) against 20mm (.79in)
	armour

Nambu offered the solution of oiling the rounds; however, this only compounded the issue.

Both the Type 11 and the Type 96, which served throughout World War II, were based on the French air-cooled Hotchkiss of pre-World War I vintage, while the Type 96 incorporated some elements of the Czech ZB vz.26. The top-mounted box magazine of the Type 96 reduced the weight of the weapon, while finned gun barrels eased changing in combat conditions. The Type 96 was also fitted with a bipod and a mounting for a bayonet.

The Type 99 light machine gun was introduced in 1939 and closely resembled the Type 96. The oiling mechanism was removed, and the Type 99 also fired the heavier 7.7mm (.303in) cartridge. It was capable of firing up to 700 rounds per minute, and an airborne version was produced with a detachable stock. Like the Type 96, the Type 99 could take a telescopic sight.

Heavy machine gun

The primary heavy machine gun of the Imperial Japanese Army was the Type 92, again based on a French Hotchkiss modified by Kijiro Nambu. It was recognized by its unique tripod that included extended legs for ease of carry and quick combat deployment. An updated version of the earlier Type 3 that was produced under licence as a copy of the Hotchkiss Model 1914, the Type 92 heavy machine gun was introduced in 1932 and fired the 7.7mm (.303in) cartridge from a 30-round metal strip at up to 450 rounds per minute. The low number of rounds per strip reduced the rate of fire substantially.

Allied soldiers who encountered the Type 92 nicknamed it the Woodpecker due to the distinctive clicking sound of its report. Oiled cartridges created jamming issues for this weapon as well. A smaller and lighter version of the Type 92, the Type 1, was introduced in 1941 and often used as an anti-aircraft weapon. It was tripod-mounted and, like the Type 3, readily identifiable with its prominent cooling rings.

The compact, semiautomatic Type 94 Shiki Kenju pistol was designed by Nambu as a mass production replacement for the larger Type 14. Intended for use by air crews, armoured troops and officers, it fired an 8mm (.314in) cartridge and was fed by a six-round detachable box magazine. More than 70,000 of these pistols were manufactured between 1934 and 1945.

▶ Model 93

Fourteenth Army, Luzon, Philippines, February 1945

The Model 93 flamethrower was used by the Kwantung Army in China but failed to operate efficiently in cold weather. The improved Model 100 entered service in 1940.

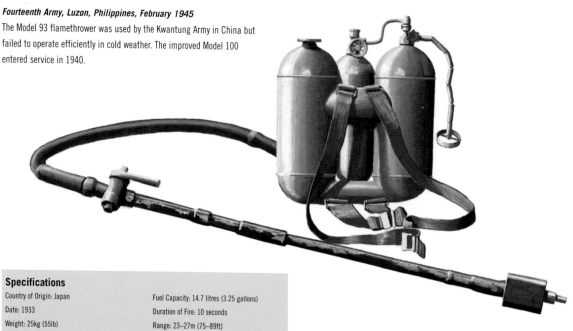

Specifications

Country of Origin: Japan	Fuel Capacity: 14.7 litres (3.25 gallons)
Date: 1933	Duration of Fire: 10 seconds
Weight: 25kg (55lb)	Range: 23–27m (75–89ft)

Allied Forces: Burma and New Guinea
1942–44

Months of difficult jungle fighting taxed the endurance of the Japanese and Allied soldiers in New Guinea and in Burma on the Asian mainland. Along with fighting one another, the soldiers were plagued by disease and torrential rains.

THE FIRST JAPANESE REVERSAL of World War II on land at Guadalcanal was accomplished while Allied troops, primarily Australian and American under the command of General Douglas MacArthur (1880–1964), were fighting the enemy in the jungles and along the unforgiving Kokoda Track on the island of New Guinea. Initially defending Port Moresby at the southeastern tip of the island, the Allies assumed the offensive and executed a series of amphibious landings and overland campaigns that eventually killed thousands of Japanese troops in combat while strangling enemy resupply efforts and leaving survivors to subsist on starvation rations.

Meanwhile, the British Fourteenth Army under Lieutenant-General William Slim (1891–1970) and American and Chinese forces under Lieutenant-General Joseph Stilwell (1883–1946) mounted a resurgent campaign in Burma, denying the Japanese follow-up territorial gains beyond their high-water mark of 1942 and winning victories at Myitkyina, Imphal and Kohima. In the China–Burma–India

Theatre, the British Chindits of Brigadier Orde Wingate (1903–44) and the American 5307th Composite Unit, better known as Merrill's Marauders and commanded by Brigadier-General Frank Merrill (1903–55), conducted long-range penetration operations behind Japanese lines, disrupting communications and keeping enemy forces off balance during prolonged jungle fighting across great distances.

Jungle weapons

The rigours of combat in the unforgiving jungles of Burma and New Guinea took their toll on both men and equipment. Heavy rain, searing heat and prolonged periods in the field caused weapons to fail or to be abandoned altogether.

In response to the need for a lighter, shortened version of the Lee-Enfield rifles in widespread use, the No. 5 Jungle Carbine was deployed in 1944 to elements of the British Army. The No. 5 was an adaptation of the shortened Lee-Enfield No. 4 that was originally intended for airborne troops. The No. 5 was 100mm

Specifications

Country of Origin: United States	Barrel Length: 665mm (26.25in)
Date: 1914	Muzzle Velocity: 600m/sec (1970ft/sec)
Calibre: 7.7mm (.303in)	Feed/Magazine: Magazine feed
Operation: Gas operated, air cooled	Cyclic Rate: 550rpm
Weight: 11.8kg (26lb)	Range: 1000m (3280ft)
Overall Length: 965mm (38in)	

▲ **Lewis Gun**

9th Australian Division / 15th Australian Infantry Battalion (Queensland), New Guinea campaign, March 1943

The Lewis Gun was pressed into prolonged service during World War II to supplement low Allied inventories of the Bren and other light machine guns. The Lewis was innovative during World War I, employing a gas-operated system.

ANZAC INFANTRY BATTALION, 1944 (TROPICAL)	
Unit	Strength
Battalion HQ	
Regimental Aid Post	1
Headquarters Company	1
Signals Platoon	1
Machine-Gun Platoon	1
Mortar Platoon	1
Pioneer Platoon	1
Administration Platoon	1
Tank-attack Platoon	1
Rifle Companies	4
Rifle Company HQ	
Rifle Platoons	3
Rifle Platoon HQ	
Rifle Sections	3
PIAT (projector, infantry, anti-tank)	1
50mm (2in) mortar	1
Rifle Section	
Bren light machine gun	1
Owen/Austen submachine gun	2
Sniper rifle	1

Although it was capable of a rate of fire of up to 30 rounds per minute, the No. 5 had problems with accuracy. It was plagued by what soldiers termed a 'wandering zero', meaning that the weapon could not be sighted and counted on to fire accurately to the same point at a later time. The No. 5 was fed by a 10-round magazine loaded from five-round charger clips, and more than 300,000 examples of this model were produced between 1944 and 1947.

The venerable Lewis

A relic of World War I, the air-cooled Lewis Gun was gas-operated and fired the 7.7mm (.303in) British cartridge from a top-mounted drum magazine of 47 or 97 rounds at a rate of up to 600 rounds per minute. Although the original design was American, it was perfected by the British and produced from 1913 to 1953. While the British Army had begun replacing the Lewis Gun with the updated Bren, many examples of the older model were still in service during the early months of the Pacific War. Early shortages of machine guns resulted in the reissuing of nearly 60,000 surplus Lewis Guns to regular army units and the British Home Guard, while a large number were also supplied to Britain by the United States through the Lend-Lease programme.

Individual automatic weapons were relatively scarce during the jungle war, and the innovative Charlton Automatic Rifle designed by New Zealand

(3.9in) shorter and a kilogram (2.2lb) lighter than the No. 4, and this was accomplished by drilling out the bolt knob, reducing woodwork and reworking the barrel and receiver. A rubber buttplate and a flash suppressor helped to absorb the substantial recoil from the 7.7mm (.303in) round and to conceal the firer from detection by the enemy.

Specifications

Country of Origin: New Zealand	Overall Length: 1150mm (44.5in)
Date: 1941	Barrel Length: Not known
Calibre: 7.7mm (.303in)	Muzzle Velocity: 744m/sec (2440ft/sec)
Operation: Gas operated	Feed/Magazine: 10- or 30-round magazine
Weight: 7.3kg (16lb)	Range: 910m (2985ft)

▲ **Charlton Automatic Rifle**

3rd New Zealand Division / Vella Lavella, Solomon Islands, September 1943

The Charlton Automatic Rifle was intended to supplement the Allied light machine guns in service in the Pacific War. The weapon was an adapted version of older Lee-Enfield and Lee-Metford rifles.

▲ **ANZAC invasion**
Operating with USMC support, infantry from the 3rd New Zealand Division land on the island of Vella Lavella in the Solomon Islands, September 1943. Most are armed with SMLE rifles, while their landing craft are fitted with Lewis machine guns.

inventor Philip Charlton (1902–78) was a semiautomatic version of the Lee-Enfield and Lee-Metford rifles to supplement the meagre supply of Bren and Lewis light machine guns. Most of the rifles converted by Charlton were early models that dated from the turn of the twentieth century. Firing the 7.7mm (.303in) cartridge, the Charlton was fed by a 10-round magazine or larger 30-round magazine that also worked with the Bren Gun. Two versions of the Charlton were manufactured. The New Zealand version included a bipod and forward pistol grip. The Australian version was lighter and did not incorporate either of these features.

The Austen submachine gun was an Australian adaptation of the British Sten. Firing the 9mm (.35in) cartridge, the Austen entered service with Australian forces in 1942, and slightly fewer than 20,000 were produced by the end of World War II. The blowback-operated weapon was capable of firing up to 500 rounds per minute from a 28-round side-mounted box magazine that was compatible with the Sten Gun. The Austen, however, never achieved the popularity among Australian soldiers of another model, the 9mm (.35in) Owen, which was fed by a 33-round top-mounted box magazine. The Owen was considered a more reliable weapon, and more than 50,000 were manufactured from 1941 to 1945. Designed by inventor Evelyn Ernest Owen (1915–49), the blowback-operated Owen was the only weapon of its type developed in Australia and used in World War II. It reached service with the Australian Army in 1943 and fired the 9mm (.35in) Parabellum cartridge fed by a 32-round detachable magazine. About 50,000 Owen submachine guns were produced during World War II, and while a few reached Australian troops in the desert, the majority of were supplied to troops fighting the Japanese in the jungles of the Southwest Pacific.

▲ Austen

Australian First Army / 4th Division, Lae, New Guinea, 1944

The Austen was an Australian adaptation of the British Sten Gun with a foregrip. An improved model, the M2, and a suppressed variant were introduced later. Its manufacturing process included several diecasting steps.

Specifications

Country of Origin: Australia	Barrel Length: 196mm (7.75in)
Date: 1942	Muzzle Velocity: 380m/sec (1246ft/sec)
Calibre: 9mm (.35in) Parabellum	Feed/Magazine: 28-round detachable box
Operation: Blowback	magazine
Weight: 3.98kg (8.75lb)	Cyclic Rate: 500rpm
Overall Length: 845mm (33.25in)	Range: 50m (164ft)

Specifications

Country of Origin: Australia	Barrel Length: 247mm (9.75in)
Date: 1941	Muzzle Velocity: 380m/sec (1247ft/sec)
Calibre: 9mm (.35in) Parabellum	Feed/Magazine: 33-round detachable box
Operation: Blowback	magazine
Weight: 4.21kg (9.28lb)	Cyclic Rate: 700rpm
Overall Length: 813mm (32in)	Range: 70m (230ft)

▲ Owen Machine Carbine

5th Australian Division, New Britain, April 1945

The Owen Machine Carbine, commonly called the Owen Gun, was developed and manufactured in Australia, reaching frontline troops by early 1943. The majority of the 50,000 Owen Guns manufactured were deployed in the Pacific.

Specifications

Country of Origin: United Kingdom

Date: 1942

Calibre: 9mm (.35in) Parabellum

Operation: Blowback

Weight: 2.95kg (6.5lb)

Overall Length: 762mm (30in)

Barrel Length: 196mm (7.7in)

Muzzle Velocity: 380m/sec (1247ft/sec)

Feed/Magazine: 32-round detachable box
    magazine

Cyclic Rate: 500rpm

Range: 70m (230ft)

▲ Sten Mk II

Australian 7th Division, Battle of Buna-Gona, New Guinea, January 1943

Unsuited to rough conditions, the Sten had a poor reputation among Australian soldiers, due to its tendency to either jam when used in jungle conditions or to fire off uncontrollably.

Specifications

Country of Origin: United Kingdom

Date: 1907

Calibre: 7.7mm (.303in)

Operation: Bolt action

Weight: 3.93kg (8.625lb)

Overall Length: 1133mm (44.6in)

Barrel Length: 640mm (25.2in)

Muzzle Velocity: 634m/sec (2080ft/sec)

Feed/Magazine: 10-round box, loaded with
    5-round charger clips

Range: 500m (1640ft)

▲ Lee-Enfield Rifle No. 1 Mk III SMLE

British Fourteenth Army / 7th Indian Infantry Division, Battle of the Admin Box, Arakan, Burma, February 1944

The Lee-Enfield Mk III became the primary infantry weapon of Commonwealth forces during World War II. The bolt-action rifle was one of a long-serving series of weapons, with specialized variants still active today.

▲ Rifle No. 5 Mk I (Jungle Carbine)

British Fourteenth Army / 2nd Battalion Royal Norfolk Regiment, Mandalay, Burma, December 1944

Known unofficially as the Jungle Carbine, the No. 5 was abandoned in 1947. The 7.7mm (.303in) round gave it a fearsome recoil.

Specifications

Country of Origin: United Kingdom

Date: 1944

Calibre: 7.7mm (.303in) British Service

Operation: Bolt action

Weight: 3.24kg (7.14lb)

Overall Length: 1000mm (39.37in)

Barrel Length: 478mm (18.7in)

Muzzle Velocity: 610m/sec (2000ft/sec)

Feed/Magazine: 10-round detachable box
    magazine

Range: 1000m (3280ft)

US Forces: Island Hopping
1942–45

The US Marine Corps bore the brunt of the brutal fighting that characterized the war in the Central Pacific. Amphibious landings on hotly contested beaches resulted in heavy casualties.

A S DOZENS OF LANDING CRAFT carrying troops of the US 2nd Marine Division churned towards the beaches of Tarawa Atoll in the Gilbert Islands on 20 November 1943, many of them encountered an unforeseen obstacle – a lengthy coral reef that only the few tracked landing craft available could traverse. The Marines in flat-bottom landing craft were forced to disembark and wade up to 500m (546 yards) to the beaches, all the while enduring heavy Japanese machine-gun and rifle fire.

Despite the early difficulties and the prospect that a Japanese counterattack might push the Marines into the sea, Tarawa was declared secure after 76 hours of heavy fighting. The Marines and elements of the US Army's 27th Division blasted the Japanese out of concrete bunkers, reinforced pillboxes and other strongpoints, taking only a handful of prisoners.

Tarawa was the first of a series of amphibious landings across the Central Pacific that were undertaken simultaneously with the Allied thrust northwards from Australia to New Guinea and the Philippines. Marine planners learned significant lessons from the Tarawa operation, in which more than 1000 Marines were killed and 2100 wounded.

▲ **Jungle firepower**

Surrounded by thick jungle foliage, US Marines man a Browning M1917A1 heavy machine gun as the Japanese mount a counterattack against the American advance on Cape Gloucester on the island of New Britain, January 1944.

More accurate reconnaissance of invasion beaches could avoid problems such as those encountered at the reef, while more tracked landing craft would be needed for future operations. Aerial and naval bombardment that had been counted on to soften up the Japanese defences had been proved largely ineffective, and adjustments were made to achieve plunging fire against enemy concrete emplacements.

The island road

Despite the tactical adjustments made following the capture of Tarawa, the Marines' trek towards Tokyo was fiercely contested island by island. When Marines of the 3rd, 4th and 5th Divisions landed on Iwo Jima in February 1945, they encountered a labyrinth of Japanese bunkers and reinforced gun emplacements, each of which was either reduced with direct fire or satchel explosives or sealed with its occupants inside. The interlocking fields of fire of Japanese machine guns and continuing artillery and mortar fire caused heavy casualties among the Marines, eventually killing more than 6800 and wounding over 19,000.

On 23 February 1945, four days into the assault on Iwo Jima, a Marine patrol reached the summit of 170m (556ft) Mount Suribachi and planted the US

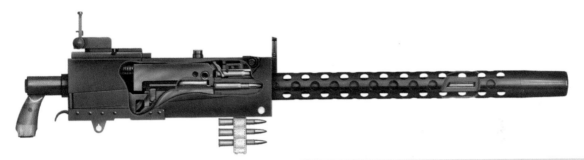

▲ Browning M1919A4

USMC / 1st Tank Battalion, Guadalcanal, September 1942

The Browning M1919A4 machine gun provided effective infantry fire support and was light enough for rapid displacement under combat conditions. It was an adaptation of the Browning Model 1917.

Specifications

Country of Origin: United States	Barrel Length: 610mm (24in)
Date: 1936	Muzzle Velocity: 853m/sec (2800ft/sec)
Calibre: 7.62mm (.3in) Browning	Feed/Magazine: 250-round belt
Operation: Recoil, air cooled	Cyclic Rate: 400–600rpm
Weight: 14kg (31lb)	Range: 2000m (6560ft) +
Overall Length: 1041mm (41in)	

Specifications

Country of Origin: United States	Barrel Length: 266mm (10.5in)
Date: 1941	Muzzle Velocity: 280m/sec (920ft/sec)
Calibre: 11.4mm (.45in) M1911	Feed/Magazine: 12- or 25-round box magazine
Operation: Delayed blowback	Cyclic Rate: 500rpm
Weight: 2.89kg (6.37lb)	Range: 120m (394ft)
Overall Length: 787mm (31in)	

▲ Reising Model 55

USMC / 1st Marine Division / 1st Parachute Battalion, Battle of Edson's Ridge, Guadalcanal, September 1942

.A compact, lightweight semiautomatic carbine that has sometimes been described as a submachine gun, the Reising Model 55 was developed in 1940 and produced until the end of World War II. It entered service to supplement the supply of Thompson submachine guns and was manufactured with a folding stock.

flag atop the extinct volcano, creating the most famous photographic image of the Pacific War. Still, more than a month of bitter combat lay ahead. One area of strong resistance came to be known as the Meat Grinder. Individual Japanese soldiers dug spider holes and popped up to fire on advancing Marines. Fanatical groups of enemy soldiers flung themselves at American lines and died by the score.

The heavy losses sustained at Iwo Jima and the prolonged, costly invasion of Okinawa, a scant 547km (340 miles) from the mainland of Japan, during which more than 12,000 Americans died and 39,000 were wounded, influenced the decision by President Harry Truman (1884–1972) to drop atomic bombs on the Japanese cities of Hiroshima

and Nagasaki. The end of the war came quickly, with Japan formally surrendering in early September 1945, and an invasion of the Japanese home islands that would have cost both sides horrendous casualties was avoided. The decisive factor in the Allied victory in the Pacific, however, was not the atomic bomb. It was the perseverance of Allied fighting men and the capabilities of the small arms they carried.

Forward firepower

A major contributing factor to the inexorable advance of the US Marines across the Central Pacific was the quality of their small arms. The M1 Garand was arguably the finest standard issue rifle of the war for a simple reason. While its contemporaries in other

▲ M1 Garand

USMC / 1st Marine Regiment, Guadalcanal, October 1942

The semiautomatic M1 Garand rifle gave US Marines a combat advantage with sustained-fire capability. Often Japanese formations were unable to hold their positions with bolt-action rifles that laid down a much slower rate of fire.

Specifications

Country of Origin: United States	Overall Length: 1103mm (43.5in)
Date: 1936	Barrel Length: 610mm (24in)
Calibre: 7.62mm (.3in) US .30-06	Muzzle Velocity: 853m/sec (2800ft/sec)
Operation: Gas operated	Feed/Magazine: 8-round internal box magazine
Weight: 4.37kg (9.5lb)	Range: 500m (1640ft) +

▲ M1 carbine

USMC / 3rd Division, Guam, August 1944

The M1 carbine proved to be a handy, compact weapon for operations in the jungle, although some soldiers complained of its lack of stopping power in protracted operations where heavy fire needed to be brought to bear on fixed or defended positions.

Specifications

Country of Origin: United States	Barrel Length: 457mm (18in)
Date: 1942	Muzzle Velocity: 595m/sec (1950ft/sec)
Calibre: 7.62mm (.3in) Carbine	Feed/Magazine: 15- or 30-round detachable box
Operation: Gas operated	magazine
Weight: 2.5kg (5.47lb)	Range: c.300m (984ft)
Overall Length: 905mm (35.7in)	

Allied and Axis armies were bolt-action weapons, the gas-operated, rotating-bolt M1 was semiautomatic, feeding 7.62mm (.3in) cartridges to the firing chamber from an eight-round en-bloc clip and allowing the American soldier and Marine to produce a rate of fire of up to 50 accurate shots per minute at a range of some 300m (984ft).

The sustained fire of the M1 at the squad level proved potent in close-quarter fighting, sometimes overwhelming Japanese troops armed with the bolt-action Type 38 or Type 99 Arisaka rifles. The penetration of the .30-06 Springfield rifle round also provided plenty of stopping power. In contrast to the success of their massed Banzai charges while fighting against the Chinese in the 1930s, the Japanese encountered a much more formidable wall of fire from the US Marine shouldering the M1 Garand. The rifle was actually in production from 1936 to 1963, and approximately 6.5 million were manufactured during the period. The M1 was the first semiautomatic rifle to become standard issue in any army.

THE 'E' SERIES MARINE BATTALION, *CIRCA* 1943–44		
Unit	Officers	Men
Headquarters Company	12	125
Battalion Headquarters Section	9	22
US Navy Medical Detachment	2	32
Intelligence Section		12
Supply Section		6
Communications Platoon	1	39
Company Headquarters		14
Weapons Company	8	220
Company Headquarters	3	38
Mortar Platoon	2	56
Three Machine-Gun Platoons, each	1	42
Three Rifle Companies, each	6	190
Company HQ	2	26
Weapons Platoon		
Platoon HQ	1	3
Mortar Section		16
Machine-Gun Section		19
Three Rifle Platoons, each		
Platoon HQ	1	6
Three Rifle Squads, each		12
Total Strength of 953 all ranks	38	915

▾ US Marine Rifle Squad, May 1944

The standard rifle squad of the US Marine Corps in 1944 was a potent self-contained unit with 13 riflemen. Organized in three fire teams, the sub-units included one man armed with the semiautomatic Browning Automatic Rifle (BAR), while three carried the semiautomatic M1 Garand rifle. The squad leader was often issued the M1 carbine, while at times he might be equipped with a Thompson or M3A1 submachine gun. Infantry support machine guns were regularly deployed from the battalion level for additional fire support.

Squad Leader (1 x M1 carbine)

Fire Team 1 (3 x M1 Garand, 1 x BAR) Fire Team 2   **Fire Team 3**

The M1 carbine was a versatile semiautomatic rifle issued to lighter troops such as airborne units and the crews of vehicles and tanks, and some officers. Firing a 7.62mm (.3in) carbine round, it actually shared only one common part, a buttplate screw, with the M1 Garand rifle. The M1 carbine was also intended to give rear-echelon troops a heavier weapon than the standard issue pistols of the World War II period.

Designed by a trio of US Army engineers, the M1 carbine entered service in the summer of 1942 and was in common circulation until the 1970s. It was fed by a 15- or 30-round box magazine, and the selective fire, fully automatic M2 variant was capable of firing up to 900 rounds per minute. While the weapon was praised for its light weight and handy size, its firepower came into question when in the hands of frontline troops who reported that it sometimes failed to knock down an approaching enemy soldier. In fairness, the M1 carbine was not originally intended as a frontline weapon, although it found its way to the front on many occasions and was extensively utilized throughout the Korean and Vietnam conflicts.

Semiautomatic firepower at the Marine fire-team level was regularly supplied by the World War I-vintage Browning Automatic Rifle (BAR) and the Thompson submachine gun. Later in the war, the M3 and M3A1 submachine guns – light, mass-produced 11.4mm (.45in) weapons – began to appear. Nicknamed the Grease Gun, the M3 and M3A1 entered service in 1944 and never fully replaced the earlier weapons.

Browning MGs

Two strongly performing machine guns that helped turn the tide of the Pacific War were the Browning Model 1919A4 and the Browning M2HB. These weapons and similar contemporary models were responsible in large part for holding the line against Japanese pressure at Gaudalcanal and then decimating furious Banzai charges to break the back of enemy resistance during later operations on islands such as Saipan and Iwo Jima.

The M1919A4 was in widespread use with US (and NATO) military organizations for more than half a century. During World War II, its versatility as an infantry, anti-aircraft and aircraft-mounted machine gun was noted. The weapon was an improvement to the earlier Model 1917 design by John Browning and was produced until the end of World War II in 1945. This short-recoil machine gun was capable of firing up to 600 rounds of 7.62mm (.3in) ammunition per minute and was fed by a 250-round belt.

Although it could be operated by as few as two men, an optimal M1919A4 crew comprised four: a gunner, an assistant gunner and a pair of ammunition carriers. Present at the platoon level, the machine gun gave company commanders the option to deploy heavier firepower at a lower tactical level more

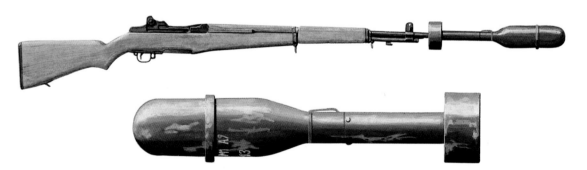

▲ **M1 Garand with M11A2 rifle grenade**

US Army / 40th Infantry Division, New Britain, June 1944

A potent rifle-grenade-launcher model of the M1 Garand was available during World War II. While few variants of the standard infantry rifle other than the sniper version saw action, this was an exception.

Specifications*

Country of Origin: United States	Barrel Length: 610mm (24in)
Date: 1936	Muzzle Velocity: 853m/sec (2800ft/sec)
Calibre: 7.62mm (.3in) US .30-06	Feed/Magazine: N/A
Operation: Gas operated	Range (Grenade): 100m (328ft)
Weight: 4.37kg (9.5lb)	* Of rifle without grenade
Overall Length: 1103mm (43.5in)	

rapidly. The M1919A4 was air-cooled. It was mounted on a tripod and weighed a relatively light 14kg (31lb), allowing the gun to fulfil its combat mission of heavier sustained fire support combined with light weight and ease of movement.

The M2HB machine gun was a heavy 12.7mm (.5in) weapon, and since it entered production in 1921 more than three million have been produced. The weapon has undergone a series of modifications through the years and remains a standard heavy machine gun of NATO armed forces today. The original M2 design included a water-cooling jacket; however, a subsequent variant eliminated the water-cooling system for an air-cooled configuration. This caused the barrel to overheat rapidly during prolonged firing and generated the need for a thicker barrel. This resulted in the HB, or heavy barrel, designation, introduced in 1933.

▲ **Thompson 1928**

USMC / 1st Marine Regiment / 2nd Battalion, Okinawa, May 1945

The first Thompson submachine gun widely adopted for military service, the 1928 differed little from the earlier 1921, although it employed a simplified delayed-blowback operation.

Specifications

Country of Origin: United States
Date: 1928
Calibre: 11.4mm (.45in) M1911
Operation: Delayed blowback
Weight: 4.88kg (10.75lb)
Overall Length: 857mm (33.75in)

Barrel Length: 266mm (10.5in)
Muzzle Velocity: 280m/sec (920ft/sec)
Feed/Magazine: 18-, 20-, 30-round detachable
   box magazine
Cyclic Rate: 700rpm
Range: 120m (394ft)

▲ **M3A1 'Grease Gun'**

US Army / 37th Infantry Division, Battle for Manila, February 1945

The M3A1 'Grease Gun', an improved version of the M3, did not enter service in large numbers before the end of World War II. The M3A1's removable stock was equipped with a built-in magazine-loading tool.

Specifications

Country of Origin: United States
Date: 1944
Calibre: 11.4mm (.45in) .45 ACP
Operation: Blowback
Weight: 3.61kg (7.95lb)
Overall Length: 745mm (29.33in)

Barrel Length: 203mm (8in)
Muzzle Velocity: 280m/sec (920ft/sec)
Feed/Magazine: 30-round detachable box
   magazine
Cyclic Rate: 450rpm
Range: 90m (295ft)

During World War II the belt-fed M2HB was capable of a cyclic rate of fire of up to 575 rounds per minute and could fire a range of ammunition types. As an infantry support weapon, it was either fired from a tripod or mounted on trucks, halftracks and tanks. It proved extremely effective against enemy troop concentrations, and its heavy round was capable of penetrating light armoured vehicles as well as shooting down low-flying enemy aircraft.

Many heavy weapons battalions of the US Army and formations of the US Marine Corps were issued at least one Browning M2HB. While the weapon was superior to any machine gun fielded by the Japanese, it was not in widespread use in the Pacific due to the difficulties inherent in jungle fighting and the weight of the weapon at roughly 58kg (128lb) including the tripod. Even so, it was sometimes deployed in a static, defensive role.

Fire breather

Island fighting was a nasty business, and often the only method of clearing Japanese soldiers from honeycombed caverns and bunkers was with the flamethrower. It was a fearsome weapon, and the US Marines became particularly adept with it on Iwo Jima. The M2-2 portable flamethrower was introduced by the United States military in 1943 as an improvement to the M1 and M1A1 designs of earlier in the war. It was recognized by its three tanks (two of gasoline fuel and one of nitrogen propellant),

▲ **Semiautomatic**
Armed with an M1 carbine, a US Marine awaits the signal to move out in the battle to recapture Guam from the Japanese, July 1944.

prominent nozzle, and dual handgrips. The M2-2 could spout roughly 2.27 litres (4 pints) of flame per second to an effective distance of 20m (65.5ft) with a burn time of about 47 seconds.

▲ **M1918A2 Browning Automatic Rifle (BAR)**
USMC / 3rd Division / 24th Regiment, Iwo Jima, March 1945
The Browning Automatic Rifle provided semiautomatic fire support to the lowest operational unit of the Marine infantry, the fire team. Although it was a heavy item and its bipod was of questionable value, the BAR was a primary infantry weapon throughout World War II.

Specifications

Country of Origin: United States	Barrel Length: 610mm (24in)
Date: 1938	Muzzle Velocity: 860m/sec (2822ft/sec)
Calibre: 7.62mm (.3in)	Feed/Magazine: 20-round straight box magazine
Operation: Gas operated, tilting breech block	Cyclic Rate: 500–650rpm
Weight: 8.8kg (19lb)	Range: 1000-1500m (3280–4921ft)
Overall Length: 1215mm (47.8in)	

Although it was an effective weapon, particularly at close range, and could kill by burning and by consuming available oxygen in an enclosed space, it was hazardous for a single soldier to operate since enemy troops targeted those with the packs visible.

The advent of the flamethrowing tank rendered the portable flamethrower functionally obsolescent, although some of these devices were deployed during the Korean and Vietnam Wars.

▲ Browning M2HB

US Army / 11th Airborne Division 'Angels' / 152nd Airborne Antiaircraft Battalion, Leyte, December 1944

The Browning M2HB heavy machine gun was devastating against Japanese personnel and light vehicles. Due to its weight, the weapon was often deployed in a defensive role in the Pacific.

Specifications

Country of Origin: United States

Date: 1933

Calibre: 12.7mm (.5in)

Operation: Short recoil, air cooled

Weight: 38.5kg (84lb)

Overall Length: 1655mm (65in)

Barrel Length: 1143mm (45in)

Muzzle Velocity: 898m/sec (2950ft/sec)

Feed/Magazine: 110-round belt

Cyclic Rate: 450–575rpm

Range: 1800m (5905ft) effective

◀ M2-2

USMC / 3rd Division / 21st Regiment, Iwo Jima, March 1945

The flamethrower was a feared weapon that was quite effective against Japanese strongpoints and soldiers sequestered in caves. However, its range was limited and Marines that operated it accepted especially hazardous duty.

Specifications

Country of Origin: United States

Date: 1943

Weight: 30.8kg (68lb) filled

Fuel Capacity: 18.2 litres (4 gallons)

Duration of Fire: 8–9 seconds

Range: 20–40m (65.5–132ft)

Glossary

Bolt
The part of a firearm which usually contains the firing pin or striker and which closes the breech ready for firing.

Blowback
Operating system in which the bolt is not locked to the breech, thus it is consequently pushed back by breech pressure on firing and cycles the gun.

Breech
The rear of the gun barrel.

Breech-block
Another method of closing the breech which generally involves a substantial rectangular block rather than a cylindrical bolt.

Carbine
A shortened rifle for specific assault roles.

Chamber
The section at the end of the barrel which receives and seats the cartridge ready for firing.

Closed bolt
A mechanical system in which the bolt is closed up to the cartridge before the trigger is pulled. This allows greater stability through reducing the forward motion of parts on firing.

Delayed blowback
A delay mechanically imposed on a blowback system to allow pressures in the breech to drop to safe levels before breech opening.

Double action
Relates to pistols which can be fired both by cocking the hammer and then pulling the trigger, and by a single long pull on the trigger which performs both cocking and firing actions.

Gas operation
Operating system in which a gun is cycled by gas being bled off from the barrel and used against a piston or the bolt to drive the bolt backwards and cycle the gun for the next round.

GPMG
Abbreviation for General Purpose Machine Gun. A versatile light machine gun intended to perform a range of different roles.

HMG
Abbreviation for heavy machine gun.

LMG
Abbreviation for light machine gun.

Locking
Describes the various methods by which the bolt or breech block is locked behind the chamber ready for firing.

Long recoil
A method of recoil operation in which the barrel and bolt recoil for a length greater than that of the entire cartridge, during which extraction and loading are performed.

Muzzle brake
A muzzle attachment which diverts muzzle blast sideways and thus reduces overall recoil.

Open bolt
A mechanical system in which the bolt is kept at a distance from the cartridge before the trigger is pulled. This allows for better cooling of the weapon between shots.

Receiver
The body of the weapon which contains the gun's main operating parts.

Recoil
The rearward force generated by the explosive power of a projectile being fired.

Recoil operated
Operating system in which the gun is cycled by the recoil-propelled force of both barrel and bolt when the weapon is fired. Both components recoil together for a certain distance before the barrel stops and the bolt continues backwards to perform reloading and rechambering.

Self-loading
Operating system in which one pull of the trigger allows the gun to fires and reload in a single action.

Shaped charge
An anti-armour charge designed to concentrate the effect of an explosive warhead by focusing a cone of superheated gas on a critical point on the target.

Short recoil
A compressed version of recoil operation in which the barrel and bolt move back less than the length of the cartridge before the bolt detaches and continues backwards to perform reloading and rechambering.

SMG
Abbreviation for submachine gun.

Further Reading

Books:

Chant, Chris. *Small Arms.* Silverdale Books, 2003.

Dougherty, Martin J. *Small Arms: From the Civil War to the Present.* Barnes & Noble, 2005.

Dougherty, Martin J. *Small Arms Visual Encyclopedia.* Amber Books Ltd, 2011.

Philip, Craig. *The World's Great Small Arms.* Barnes & Noble, 2002.

Stronge, Charles. *Sniper in Action.* Amber Books Ltd, 2010.

Zaloga, Stephen J. and Leland S. Ness. *Red Army Handbook, 1939–1945.* Sutton Publishing Ltd, 1998.

Useful web sites:

http://www.bayonetstrength.150m.com/
Offers a detailed breakdown of unit organisation from battalion level and below for every major combatant nation in World War II. Also includes a section on small arms of the period.

http://www.historyofwar.org/index.html
A detailed, wide-ranging general guide to warfare, weapons and battles, with a comprehensive section on World War I and World War II.

Index

Page numbers in *italics* refer to illustrations and tables.